Internet Server Construction Kit for Windows®

Greg Bean

John Wiley & Sons, Inc.

New York • Chichester • Brisbane • Toronto • Singapore

Publisher: Katherine Schowalter
Editor: Tim Ryan
Managing Editor: Angela Murphy
Text Design & Composition: Benchmark Productions, Inc.

This text is printed on acid-free paper.

This publication is designed to provide accurate and authoritative information in regard to the subject matter covered. It is sold with the understanding that the publisher is not engaged in rendering legal, accounting, or other professional service. If legal advice or other expert assistance is required, the services of a competent professional person should be sought.

Library of Congress Cataloging-in-Publication Data:

Bean, Greg.
    Internet server construction kit for Windows / Greg Bean.
        p.   cm.
    Includes index.
    ISBN 0-471-12696-9 (pbk.: alk.paper)
    1. Internet (Computer network) 2. Client/server computing.
3. Microcomputers–Access control. I. Title.
TK5105.875.I57B42 1995
005.7 1365–dc20   95-15112

Printed in the United States of America

10 9 8 7 6 5 4 3 2 1

Contents

Acknowledgements

My thanks to the many software authors who crafted the fine products described in this book. Whether their products were a result of a labor of love or pure commercial interest (or both) is inconsequential. The result is of great benefit to us. And for that, we thank them.

Many thanks to Ryan Dobb and Tom Rabenhorst for their technical assistance and guidance throughout the project, and to John Beverungen for his keen "reader perspective." Thanks to my sons, Brian and Matt, and to my sister, Mary Stuthmann, for their help with the "little" things that freed me for the bigger task. Thanks to Sandy Cooksey for her help in preparing the manuscript.

Thanks to all the true professionals at John Wiley & Sons, including Angela Murphy, Kerri-Alexis Werner, Mike Green, and copyeditor Jill Bond, and especially to Tim Ryan, who provided valuable suggestions and insights, and managed the project to successful completion.

Finally, thanks to my wife and friend, Mary Ellen, who provided the patience, support, and inspiration to make this book possible.

Introduction

Who Is This Book For?

This book is designed for people who know at least a little about the Internet, have some familiarity with personal computers and Internet client software, and want to set up an Internet server, such as a World Wide Web (WWW), Gopher, or File Transfer Protocol (FTP) Server. It matters little whether you fall into the category of power user, aspiring power user, or into the technical support personnel camp. University libraries, departments that provide their own computing support, small businesses, and distributed entities of large corporations are prime candidates for utilizing a microcomputer for building an information server. In other words, this book is recommended for all who would like to make their information available to others on the Internet with a minimum investment in hardware, software, personnel, and that most precious of resources, time.

If you doubt the growth of Internet servers in large corporations, government, and international organizations, you need only peruse the World Wide Web. There, you willl find the likes of IBM, Digital, NASA, Pizza Hut, the White House, the Library of Congress, and many smaller organizations with a large presence on the Internet. Some of these organizations have extensive support staffs well steeped in UNIX and TCP/IP, while others have increasingly taken an easier, more effective and efficient route to setting up servers, via an Intel 386/486 or Pentium running Microsoft Windows 3.1, Microsoft Windows for Workgroups, Microsoft Windows 95, or Microsoft Windows NT.

What Will I Learn?

There is a wealth of server software available on the Internet and more arriving every day. However, many people are still asking questions such as: "Where can I find a mail server for Windows NT?" And, more importantly, "How do I learn about server concepts and get practical information about getting started in server construction?" This book will answer many of your questions about setting up servers and help you get off to a quick start as an information provider.

This book provides the following information:

- The practical information and software tools necessary to quickly, efficiently, and effectively set up your own Internet server in a Windows or Windows NT environment.

- A discussion of the underlying concepts, protocols, and principles you'll need to know to understand how your server operates.

- Detailed coverage of many of the popular Windows World Wide Web, Gopher, FTP, WAIS, Finger, and Mail servers, so that you can compare and contrast the features of each, and select the ones that are best suited to your requirements.

What Do You Need to Use This Book?

There are several essential ingredients that you'll need to get started on your server project. This book will discuss the necessary hardware, software, and telecommunications components for Internet server construction.

To get the most out of this book, you will need the following:

- A Windows 3.1, Windows for Workgroups, Windows 95, or Windows NT computer, at least minimally configured by Microsoft's stated standards or specifications.

- A network connection, dialup, or direct connect, to test and eventually launch your Internet server project.

- An Internet account, either provided by your organization or by an Internet service provider, that will allow you to test your mail server, "finger" your finger server, and perform other routine tasks in your role as server administrator.

- A World Wide Web browser to access and test your Gopher, WWW, or FTP server from the "client" side.

What's in This Book on the CD?

This book is divided into chapters that deal with specific software products that you can readily acquire and install. Some of the products are freeware, some shareware, and some are commercial offerings. Regardless of product type, all offer a significant number of features and opportunities to the information provider.

The CD provides a complete and readily accessible toolkit that includes the following:

- A complete set of Windows server products, so that you can begin immediately to install and run your own Internet server.

- Supporting files for the examples illustrated in subsequent chapters, so that you don't have to spend your time creating test databases, sample home pages, image maps, and so on.

- Some sample program code so that, if you are so inclined, you can begin to create utility programs (Common Gateway InterfaceCGI) to add a high level of functionality to your WWW server.

- Relevant supporting documentation for those who are eager to learn even more about the technologies introduced and explored in this book.

Overview

Following is a brief overview of the chapters and what they include:

Chapter 1 *Building Servers* You may still be asking yourself whether running your own server is the right alternative given your project requirements, time, money, and motivations. This chapter explores some of the other alternatives that you can consider, as well as the housekeeping matters and other considerations you should weigh prior to embarking on this adventure.

Chapter 2 *Internet Standards and Protocols* If you're going to travel in Internet server circles, you'll need to know the technical details and jargon that accompany the network connection. Additionally, if you're going to be like most Windows Internet server administrators, and have to personally grapple with the likes of protocols such as SLIP and PPP, you'll need the information in this chapter to ensure a firm communications foundation for your server.

Chapter 3 *Server Application Background and Concepts* You probably have used the Internet before by sending mail, using a Gopher client, or "surfing the Net" with a Web browser. But, you probably haven't given much thought to what goes on beneath it all. This chapter covers application server (such as WWW and Gopher) protocol definition, operation, and concepts so that you cannot only run the software, but understand what you're running.

Chapter 4 *FTP Servers* The previous chapters set the stage—now the practical "meat." Chapter 4 is the first of a series of chapters that deals with the software available in the marketplace, and how you acquire, install, and configure it. This chapter covers a number of File Transfer Protocol (FTP) offerings, and illustrates how to install and configure them in a Windows or Windows NT environment.

Chapter 5 *Gopher Servers* This chapter discusses Gopher, which has met with widespread acceptance and success as an effective information delivery tool. And, of course, there are a number of alternatives from which you can choose, if Gopher is your server application of choice.

Chapter 6 *World Wide Web Servers* Without a doubt, most of the interest and activity surrounding Internet servers is in the area of the World Wide Web. That same interest and activity is well evidenced in the number of servers from which you can choose, and more are appearing every day. In this chapter, nine different Web servers are described in detail, with the necessary information to install and prototype your server of choice. For those commercial products for which you may not have access to the software, extensive details and screen shots are provided to give you a good idea of product features before you by.

Chapter 7 *HTML Authoring and Editing* A Web server is only as good as the information content it provides. And to become a good information provider, you need some essential Web authoring tools. This chapter covers a few of the many Hypertext Markup Language (HTML) editors and also gives examples of a program called Mapedit, which enables you to create clickable maps for your Web pages.

Chapter 8 *Web Utilities* The single most important aspect of the Web server is its capability to run programs that add significant utility to your server. You'll, of course, want fill out forms, gateways to back-end databases, and statistics on who is accessing your server and which pages are popular. Not only are there "off-the-shelf" programs available, but you can code your own if you want. A sample Visual Basic program is described and the source code for the sample is included on the CD.

Chapter 9 *Finger Servers* Windows and Windows NT servers can just about do it all. How about a Finger server? Yes, we can do Finger servers, and the installation and configuration of these products are covered in this chapter.

Chapter 10 *Mail Servers* The missing link on the desktop Internet server has, to date, been in the area of electronic mail. Now you can, whether with Windows 3.1 or Windows NT, provide mail services for others within your organization. Two excellent mail packages are covered in this chapter. These products are, in fact, fully functioning SMTP and POP mail servers, and have robust features that enable you to offer such advanced capabilities as mailing lists (like "listservs"), normally found only in the UNIX environment.

Chapter 11 *Wide Area Information Servers* (WAIS) Last, but not least, is Wide Area Information Server (WAIS) software. If one of your requirements is to provide full text documents that are searchable by keyword, study WAIS as an alternative for your information delivery needs. Examples are provided that explain how to tightly integrate WAIS with the Web and Gopher, so that these other applications can serve as a front-end to your WAIS databases.

Building Internet Servers

Why Build an Internet Server?

Given your interest in this book, you are obviously entertaining the idea of setting up an Internet server to provide information to others or at least to find out what all the fuss is about. You might have many reasons for wanting to operate a server on the Internet. A significant audience awaits your published information, whether you present it via Gopher, the World Wide Web, File Transfer Protocol, or a Wide Area Information Server (WAIS). Millions of Internet users are eager to explore the information you wish to make available. Whether your needs for information publishing are personal or professional, the current Windows desktops offer you a unique communications opportunity. Unix is still the predominant server platform on the Internet because the two have grown up together over the past quarter century.

Today, however, with the power and simplicity inherent in the Windows desktop, most of the numbers growth in server platforms undoubtedly is in the Windows and Windows NT environments.

Fax machines, having been around as long as the Internet, suddenly one day took hold as an essential business tool and then quickly moved into the personal market. Now many homes are equipped with this business technology. Internet servers are following the same track. Around as long as the Internet, servers are evolving from the expensive, esoteric Unix realm to the business desktop, and gradually into our homes. Desktop business and personal servers are upon us. Much as fax machines and cellular phones have become affordable and essential business and personal tools, servers are finding a way into the workplace and even into our personal lives. Commercial vendors of Internet server software are now directing their marketing to personal publishing initiatives, and rightly so. Individuals can publish information from their desktops at work, making departmental information available to both internal and external clients. Small businesses can establish an Internet presence equal in appearance and quality to the IBMs and GMs of the world, and at a small-business price.

On the personal side, we are seeing entertaining contributions where servers display individuals' personalities and humor on a range of topics, or provide on-line résumés for potential employers through multimedia Web pages. Regardless of purpose, individuals implementing personal servers are gaining state-of-the-art technical skills, having a good time, and developing a new communications medium.

The publishing opportunity on a Windows and Windows NT system allows the information provider to achieve many organizational and personal strategic advantages. In your business you have a somewhat limited network of collaborative opportunities as well as a limited marketing reach. With an Internet server, for example using the World Wide Web (WWW), you can easily and cost-effectively assemble and disseminate information valuable to your current and future clients.

Before operating a server, your marketing reach may have extended geographically only as far as your mailed brochure would go (with the wastebasket as the possible ultimate destination), or your investment in getting the word out amounted to an annual payment for the Yellow Pages ad. Now your message, if presented tastefully, can reach a much wider, even global market, can enhance your business and personal reputation, and can attract others for collaborative projects. And, if your information provides valuable content to the Internet, you and your organization will be recognized very quickly as the experts in your field.

True opportunities for commerce are on the near horizon for information providers as well. Implementing encryption and enhanced security on Windows and Windows NT servers will create further business opportunities that will include transactions supporting our core businesses. Individuals and businesses will be able to browse in your catalogs and price books, check on availability, and submit an order, assured of substantial security and confidentiality. And with demographically converging forces in the form of more computers in the home, less time to shop at the mall, and increasing reliance on mail-order purchasing, offering your products through an Internet server may well be a business necessity.

Within the Windows and Windows NT environment, Internet users until now have approached the Network of networks from the client side. You make a connection to the Internet, either through work or home, via a modem or direct connection, and read mail, browse Gopher sites, and enjoy the graphical interface to the World Wide Web. If you currently use the Internet from the client side, you're well prepared to move into the role of information provider, or server administrator. Just as you have a client software application running, you will have a server application running under Windows, perhaps on the same machine, or perhaps on a dedicated machine.

In this book I explain the essential technical concepts of Internet server installation and configuration. With this information you will better understand the software currently in the marketplace, compare the features of each package, gain a fundamental understanding of the underlying technologies, and install and configure your server for productive operation.

If you move beyond the experimental or prototype stage, server installation, support, and enhancement will require you to commit many of your resources (time, people, and money, to name a few). Thus it is probably appropriate to take a few moments to review some of the issues you will face as an information provider.

What Lies Ahead

You may be wondering what is involved in this server construction endeavor. By way of summary, you'll need to:

- Acquire the necessary hardware. Depending on the software you choose and the popularity of your server, the configuration can range from an old IBM PC XT to a fully loaded Digital Alpha PC.

- Select an Internet Service Provider and choose your connection method (e.g., ISDN, 14.4kbps modem) or negotiate with your network administrator for assistance in networking your server.

- Acquire, configure, and implement the software (e.g., a Web server). Products range from public domain to commercial, and from minimally to fully featured.

- Attend to system administration and information provider issues including:

  - security

  - performance

  - information content

Are These the Only Alternatives?

If we examine how information is implemented on the World Wide Web (WWW), for example, you have at least two other alternatives to setting up your own server:

- Let someone, usually an Internet service provider, author your Web pages and house them on their server. We'll call this the *Provider* alternative.

- Or, you can create HTML documents, or pages, on that same server. We'll call this the *Public HTML* alternative.

Let's briefly examine the pros and cons for each option.

The Provider Alternative

Having someone else become the provider of your information relieves you of responsibility for administering a server, authoring pages, and such things as seeding newsgroups with announcements of your pages. Prices for this kind of service are becoming more and more competitive, but the fee is still fairly sizable. Let's summarize one model from a provider in the Washington, D.C., area that is probably among the lower-priced provider alternatives:

Setup charge for up to 10 Web pages	$ 500
Scanned images for your pages, each	$ 10
Monthly provider fee to house your pages (plus your connection fee)	$ 100
Fee for changes to your pages, each	$ 20

Thus your costs would be $100 a month and (assuming four images) $540 up front. Your first-year costs would be about $1740. Not terribly distressing, I suppose, but here are a few additional considerations to weigh in deciding whether you should handle the work in-house on your own server:

- One very important issue to remember is that your information probably is highly dynamic. Your company changes, your literature changes, your products change, and on and on. Therefore your pages will or should change. One beauty of Gopher or the Web compared to the printed page is that the information on the server is dynamic, changing as your organization changes, whereas the printed page becomes stale and obsolete. Notice the $20-per-page cost for changes in your pages. If your information is especially dynamic, you can incur sizable charges, and more important, you will also have to deal with lead times to have your provider publish the information.

- Another shortcoming, varying from vendor to vendor, is the ability to incorporate utilities into your documents. Among these are fill-out order forms, back-end databases, guestbooks, and maps, which are often desirable additions to your pages. For a number of reasons, among them the security of server utility programs, the maintenance involved in these documents, and other system-administration issues, providers often want to stick to providing simple text and graphics. Thus, if you had hoped to realize the real power of a server, you'll instead have to settle for text and a few graphics to define your Internet presence, or pay significantly more than the prices above to accomplish sophisticated server capabilities.

The Public HTML Alternative

Authoring your own pages and placing them in a UNIX directory in your account with your Internet service provider is a good entry-level alternative. The model generally works something like this:

Your provider has a directory structure established such that if you deposit your HTML files and graphics in a designated subdirectory of your account, the provider's Web server will seek out these documents when someone points their browser (e.g., Netscape or Mosaic) to:

```
http://your.provider.net/~youraccountname
```

This is sometimes referred to as **public_html space**. What are the downsides here? Not many. In fact, it's a good crawl-before-you-walk alternative and often friendly providers will offer this option within the cost of your monthly account fee, or, at worst, cut the price of the provider alternative above by about half because you did all the document-authoring work. The catch is that, on this alternative and the provider alternative, the provider will charge additional fees if the traffic to your server exceeds a specified volume. We'll call this the price of fame, and it certainly is reasonable, since the provider allocates more computing resources to your pages, you should bear some of the additional cost. Another downside is that once you see some of the exciting and rewarding things you can do with your own server you will probably want to move to more sophisticated features such as the utilities described above.

Costing Your Server

As with any other investment, you should evaluate the costs associated with the apparent benefit. If you are trying to justify, to yourself or others, the investment in an in-house server, you may want to create a comparison sheet. Of course, we offer this comparison only as a model because every situation is different. If you're in a large organization with a T1 connection already established, perhaps connection costs won't be factored into the equation (or they may be factored in, but only on a pro rata basis). Let's suppose, in the example below, that yours is a home-based business, or a new business startup, and you want to set up a server. Your costs might look something like this:

Intel 486—$2,500

The speed of the processor, quantity of disk space, and other hardware considerations will depend on such things as the amount of information you intend to provide, the projected popularity of your information, the software you intend to run, and the number of services you expect to offer (e.g., FTP, WWW). Another factor will be the hardware requirements of the operating environment you choose. For example, if you choose Windows NT, you'll need at least 16 megabytes of memory, and a few hundred MB of disk, whereas the requirements for Windows 3.1 will be less. Where there are specific requirements or recommendations for software detailed in subsequent chapters, minimum configurations are identified in the chapters or in the documentation accompanying the software distribution.

28.8-K Modem—$250

Quite a number of reviews in the current trade press compare the performance and merits of high-speed modems. And of course you get what you pay for. Such a modem may cost as much as $900 if you want to get a product superior in quality. The lower-end modem products, generally touted for personal use, can be purchased for less than $200. If your server is likely to have low traffic volume and is more for pleasure than business, you may also want to consider a 14.4-Kbps modem, which is even less expensive. Correspondingly, at the high end you may want to examine other connection alternatives like ISDN, or possibly a 56-Kbps line. In some areas the cost of ISDN can be as low as $40 to $50 per month (plus connect time), with an initial hardware investment of about $1,000.

Dedicated Analog Telephone Line—$25/month

If you decide to take the dialup modem route, you'll need a separate telephone line in addition to your current voice line. This is the local telephone-company charge to bring another line into your home or office.

Twenty-Four-Hour/Seven-Day Dedicated Dialup Internet Connection—$150/month

Yes, you can pay a provider $25 to $35 per month for a SLIP or PPP connection (to be explained later), but normally you will have a usage limit of four to six hours a day. Additional usage over the limit usually comes in at about $1.00 an hour. If you plan to go live with your server, you'll want to at least move to this full-time 28.8-K dialup connection.

Personnel

Someone will have to take care of and feed this server beast. How much time this chore will take depends on how much you want to get out of the server. If you intend to make the server a critical piece of your organization's business strategy, don't take this cost and commitment lightly. Allow yourself or someone else ample time to build, maintain, and support the server. Of course, if this is your personal server, built as a shrine to your favorite rock group, the time and resources commitment probably will be significantly less.

Why a Microcomputer Server?

Because the predominant Internet operating environment is UNIX, it will come as no surprise that most Gopher, FTP, and World Wide Web servers have been built with the UNIX operating system. Today, however, a number of factors make microcomputer platforms equally or more attractive alternatives on which to build your server:

- Robust implementations of Gopher, FTP, World Wide Web (WWW), and other servers are available for microcomputers.

- The cost of a microcomputer capable of adequate performance as a server has dropped significantly. The hardware configurations necessary to support many of the servers described in this book are priced in the $2,000 to $3,000 range.

- At the high end of the microcomputer continuum, machines such as the Intel Pentium and Digital Equipment's Alpha PC offer tremendous performance and scalability, formerly found only in the UNIX workstation environment.

- A paradigm shift is under way as user departments develop Internet information resources (e.g., through HTML authoring) that previously were developed in the glass house (the MIS department). This shift is similar to the transition of low-end mainframe database applications to departmental databases (e.g., dBase) in the 1980s. Power users are discovering that HTML authoring is within their talents and can be done through a variety of desktop software tools. They are discovering too that fully featured Internet servers can be installed in that same desktop environment.

- Support costs for microcomputer server implementations are significantly lower than those found in the UNIX environment. Certainly the cost of hardware, and more importantly, the cost of support personnel is significantly lower with a microcomputer.

- Many organizations want to establish internal information distribution systems that are not connected to the Internet. The challenges they face are identical in many respects to those faced by organizations that wish to connect to the Net. The main challenges are security, performance, and hardware and software support and can be met with microcomputer-based enterprise-wide networks.

- In application development, such issues as a common user interface, fast and efficient servers, and rapid development tools have been addressed with various industry tools with varying degrees of success. Many organizations are discovering that Gopher, the Web, and their respective browsers provide an excellent common graphical user interface (GUI) for many information-distribution applications.

The Trend in Selecting Server Platforms

Machines running Windows 3.1, Windows for Workgroups, and Windows NT have evolved into viable Internet servers mainly because of Microsoft's commitment to TCP/IP as its strategic networking protocol. With lower-cost

Internet connections widely available, and TCP/IP software maturing on all the Microsoft platforms, the number of Internet servers based on Windows and Windows NT will greatly increase. The Internet currently has more than four million connected systems and approximately seventy million copies of Windows 3.1 are in the marketplace, growing by more than a million a month. Just how many of the millions of Windows and Windows NT systems will be connected as servers remains to be seen. You can be sure that with Windows 3.1 and Windows NT server software available and being enhanced, and Windows95 soon to be delivered, much of the future growth of servers will be on Windows 3.1, Windows95, and Windows NT platforms.

Types of Servers

The many types of servers and various implementations are covered in this book. The following chart lists the type of server (e.g., Gopher), the name of the product (e.g., Go4ham), and the operating system it runs on (e.g., Windows 3.1). The servers' features, structure, and varied approaches to information presentation and retrieval are explained in subsequent chapters. To introduce and summarize them, however, we list them in Table 1.1.

Table 1.1 Server Types and Software Covered in This Book			
Server Type	Product Name	Windows 3.1	Windows NT
File transfer protocol (FTP)	WinQVT	X	X
	WFTPD	X	X
	Serv-U	X	
	Microsoft NT FTP		X
	Beame & Whiteside FTP	X	X
Gopher	Hamburg Gopher	X	
	Beame & Whiteside Gopher	X	
	ZBServer	X	
	EMWAC Gopher		X

Table **1.1** *Continued*			
Server Type	Product Name	Windows 3.1	Windows NT
World Wide Web (WWW)	SerWeb	X	
	Web4HAM	X	
	Windows httpd—	X	
	Beame & Whiteside—httpd	X	
	ZBServer	X	
	EMWAC HTTPS		X
	Processer Software Purveyor		X
	CSMHTTPD Computer Software Manufacture		X
	O'Reilly WebSite		X
Finger	Fingerd	X	
	Beame & Whiteside Finger	X	
	EMWAC Fingers		X
Mail	Ipswitch Imail	X	X
	Internet Shopper NT Mail		X
Wide Area Information Server (WAIS)	EMWAC WAIS		X

Assumptions and Considerations

There are a number of prerequisites or assumptions that will allow you to move more easily through the concepts, terms, and instructions in this book. By addressing these details now you can assure yourself of a smoother running installation both in the near and long term.

Operating Environment

Most of the software described assumes you are running the latest version of the operating environment in question. For example, if you are running the NT operating system, I assume you are using the NT 3.5 release. If you aren't, now is a good time to upgrade. I assume too that you have a basic working knowledge of the operating environment. In other words, you can point and click your mouse, have an idea of directory structures, and understand basic operating-system commands. You should also have an elementary understanding of the Internet from the client side. In other words, it will be helpful if you have used a product such as NetScape or Mosaic, and have read a book or two on Internet tools, resources, and concepts. If you haven't had the opportunity to use these tools, the information in this book and the works recommended in the Appendix will give you a quick introduction.

Freeware and Shareware

Most of the software described in this book is in the public domain or is shareware, and often therefore is mistakenly considered free. When you utilize software from the accompanying CD, or download any of the programs described in this book, carefully review any restrictions and guidelines on use and distribution. Pay all registration or shareware fees. A lot of work went into the software described in this book and the programs are worth much more than you'll pay. When some day you have a question for the software's author, you'll be glad you paid.

Changing Server Software

How much work has gone into each of these software products shows in the frequency of new-version releases. Realize that newer versions of some of the software products may have been released since this book went to press. The concepts usually remain the same, but you may have to deal with retrieving new versions via FTP, learning new features, and understanding modified operating methods.

An older version of NCSA Mosaic displayed this legend on startup: Changing as rapidly as time. That describes just about all the software in this book and on the enclosed CD. As quickly as you get acquainted with the server software, the software author goes and enhances it. That's a good habit, but it does make keeping up with the changes difficult. To find the latest versions of the software in this book, and to learn about new software, you can access this URL (Uniform Resource Locator, defined in greater detail later) with your favorite WWW browser:

```
http://www.charm.net/~cyber
```

This web page, titled *Building Internet Servers*, will serve as a supplement to this book, offering information on the latest server software, changes in the location of existing software, and other valuable information for server builders. Add this page to your browser hotlist at your first opportunity.

Your Internet Connection

One major assumption about server networking is that you have a full-time, twenty-four-hour, high-speed connection to the Internet. This hookup can range from a dialup SLIP (Serial Line Internet Protocol) connection to a direct high-speed connection (e.g., T1 at 1.5 megabits/sec). You don't have to have a full-time connection to test the software, but if you want to offer to the public your server and the information it houses, it may be difficult to do part time. Prices are continually dropping, and in the not-too-distant future, a full-time SLIP or ISDN (Integrated Services Digital Network) connection may be within reach of many small businesses and households. Until then, shop wisely for your SLIP connection (that is, if you aren't directly connected). Find out if there are time limitations on SLIP access (e.g., four hours a day) and see if you can find reasonably priced unlimited access. Although pricing varies widely from geographic region to region and from provider to provider, currently a twenty-four-hour, seven-day dialup 14.4 Kbps connection can cost as little as $100 a month in the Baltimore-Washington, D.C., area. And, in some areas of the United States, you can get a single B channel ISDN connection for $40 to $50 per month plus connect time and installation costs.

If you are directly connected to the Internet within your organization or business, you'll probably need only an ethernet board and TCP/IP installed on your machine. This book is particularly addressed, though, to the small to medium-sized organization positioned at the low end of the high-speed-connection continuum. In other words, you will be using a dialup modem (perhaps at 14.4 or 28.8 Kbps) running SLIP or PPP (Point to Point Protocol) to establish your PC as a *node* (or server) on the Internet. Contact your Internet service provider or computer center if you'll be using this type of connection (for more information on choosing a service provider, refer to the Appendix). The provider or computer-center personnel usually are happy to help by recommending a version of SLIP or PPP, providing supporting documentation, and, of course, giving you an Internet Protocol (IP) address. Just bear in mind as you read that references to your TCP or SLIP or PPP connection apply to your chosen method of connection.

Uniform Resource Locators (URLs)

The acronym URL, I've often said, is the catchword for the 1990s. For that reason, and some more important technical ones, familiarize yourself with the URL concept. We'll define and discuss URLs in Chapter 3, but for now, consider the URL to be a PATH statement that can point to files not only on your server, but on remote machines. We'll use the URL format throughout the book to point to Web pages, and, most important, FTP servers, which house valuable server software. Referring to files that you'll need to retrieve, we'll tell you, for example, to use Netscape and Open Location **ftp://ftp.cs.dal.ca/htmlasst/** and retrieve the file **htmlasst.zip**. This procedure effectively makes an anonymous ftp connection to the designated server and puts you in the proper directory to retrieve the file in question. You can then click on your choice of files and they will be transferred. You can also retrieve software by using Anonymous FTP, through your FTP client, if you prefer this approach over Netscape or Gopher (see the Appendix for a sample session). With either method, Netscape or FTP client, you can connect to the sites listed in each chapter and retrieve the necessary software. The sites listed are just a sampling of the FTP sites that make the software available. You can also use Archie to locate other FTP sites that make the software in this book available.

Housekeeping Matters

You'll confront a number of important housekeeping issues in setting up each server software package including these.

Running the Programs

For each software program that you wish to install, you can create an icon (a *Program Item* see Figure 1.1) for the program in the Windows Program Manager Group (Figure 1.2) or just **Run** it from File Manager by displaying the executable file and double-clicking on it. Which approach you take is up to you and primarily a matter of convenience.

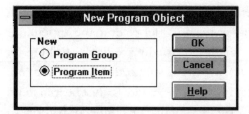

Figure 1.1 Windows Program Item.

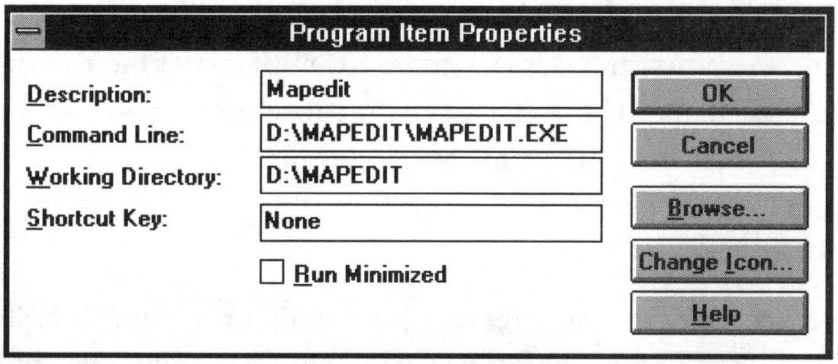

```
┌──────────────────────────────────────────────────────────┐
│ ▬            Program Item Properties                       │
├──────────────────────────────────────────────────────────┤
│ Description:        │ Mapedit                    │  ┌────────┐ │
│                     └────────────────────────────┘  │   OK   │ │
│ Command Line:       │ D:\MAPEDIT\MAPEDIT.EXE     │  └────────┘ │
│                     └────────────────────────────┘  ┌────────┐ │
│ Working Directory:  │ D:\MAPEDIT                 │  │ Cancel │ │
│                     └────────────────────────────┘  └────────┘ │
│ Shortcut Key:       │ None                       │  ┌────────┐ │
│                     └────────────────────────────┘  │ Browse…│ │
│                          ☐ Run Minimized            └────────┘ │
│                                                  ┌────────────┐ │
│                                                  │Change Icon…│ │
│                                                  └────────────┘ │
│                                                     ┌────────┐ │
│                                                     │  Help  │ │
│                                                     └────────┘ │
└──────────────────────────────────────────────────────────┘
```

Figure 1.2 Windows Program Item properties.

Your Server Name

Most servers in this book require some configuration, and often you will be asked to configure your server's address. This could be your TCP/IP address, something like **130.85.185.77**, or it may be your Fully Qualified Domain Name (FQDN), like **sunsite.unc.edu**. When you see the expression **your.server. here**, key in your IP address or fully qualified domain name to properly configure the software. Now is the time to register a domain name if you haven't already done so. If your organization is already connected to the Internet, you probably know one or more of the organizational hosts. Perhaps you have an account on the machine **fido.ajax.com**, which is an example of a fully qualified domain or host name. You now need to have your machine name defined. Think of a name (and the CD has an extensive treatise on machine naming in the document FYI-5) and ask your network administrator to configure your machine, with its new name, into the Domain Name Server or into a local hosts file. If you are connected through an Internet service provider, contact them for assistance. In all probability, if your shell (UNIX) account user name is **blotto** at the provider charm.net, your server name will be **blotto.charm.net**.

PKUNZIP

When you retrieve software from the Internet, it will very often arrive in a compressed archive called a .ZIP file. These files can be unarchived with the program PKUNZIP.EXE. Files are packaged or compressed with a program called PKZIP, which puts them into a nice tidy bundle, or software distribution with the .ZIP extension. Thus the software authors can fit more software in a compressed form on the distribution media, and if the distribution means is via the Internet, zipped files transfer quicker because they're smaller. But if you want to run the executable files or read the accompanying documentation, you'll need to unzip them first and this is where PKUNZIP comes in. You run the program with the name of the file you want to uncompress. If you retrieved a file called TWSKB20.ZIP from an FTP site and wanted to unzip it, the command (from the DOS prompt) would be:

```
PKUNZIP TWSK20B.ZIP
```

And then, in just a few seconds, the directory from which you ran PKUNZIP would be populated with the contents of the zipped file. One additional note: zipped files are the most prevalent means for distributing the software in this book. Some files, though, will be distributed as self-extracting archives and will have a .EXE extension. One example is the Chameleon Sampler (covered in Chapter 2), which is included in the self-extracting archive, SAMPLER.EXE. All you need to do, once you have retrieved the file to your local directory, is **Run** it from the DOS prompt or the Windows Program or File Manager.

Testing

The configuration settings used in each of the product installations are generally at the default, or close to the default. In other words, if a number of defaults are offered and you can bring up the software with the defaults for testing, for simplicity's sake, I'll leave them as is. For example, if a server's default data directory is C:\HTTP both the data files and program files may end up in the same directory. I would consider this acceptable practice for testing, but not for actual production work. You will have to examine your own configuration requirements and implementation objectives to arrive at production settings. More on this subject later.

Netscape

Netscape Navigator is a commercial Web browser distributed by Netscape Communications Corporation. We'll use this browser for testing the various servers covered in this book. If you're more familiar with another browser, such as NCSA Mosaic, then by all means use that browser.

Requirements   To use Netscape you must have direct access to the network. In other words, either your machine has a network card and it's connected to the network or you use your modem to call a server that allows SLIP or PPP connections. This direct access must support the Windows Socket networking specification.

The recommended hardware for Netscape includes a minimum of an 80386SX with 4 MB of RAM and Windows 3.1 running in Enhanced Mode.

The Netscape program requires a winsock.dll, which provides the TCP/IP networking under windows. Netscape for MS Windows is a Winsock1.1 compliant program that can use the Trumpet Winsock.

This installation procedure assumes that the system on which you are installing Netscape meets these criteria:

- Microsoft Windows is properly installed and configured.

- Utilities such as ftp, pkunzip, and an ASCII editor, such as Windows Notepad, are available.

- The system is connected to the Internet.

Netscape Installation The Netscape Navigator archive file, N16-100.EXE (or a later version), is available from:

`ftp://ftp.mcom.com/netscape/windows`

Once you've retrieved the file, follow these instructions to unpack and run the browser:

1. Move the self-extracting archive, NS16-100.EXE, to a temporary directory (e.g., C:\TEMP) and **Run** it to extract the necessary files.

2. Once the files are extracted, **Run** the SETUP.EXE program from the Windows File Manager to install the Netscape Navigator in a directory of your choice. The default directory is C:\NETSCAPE.

3. Click on the Netscape icon in the newly created program group and you can then view the release notes under the program's Help menu.

Internet
Standards
and Protocols

Protocols and Jargon—
What Do I Need to Know?

A number of concepts and principles apply to each of the protocols covered in this book (e.g., HTTP, FTP, Gopher). In this chapter we briefly summarize each of the protocols, offer ideas on server administration, and provide general information that should prove helpful as you install servers. Although the terminology varies greatly, I set out to give you some understanding of common concepts so that, for example, when you are asked to configure the *document root* for an HTTP server, you will remember the concept and realize that with some server implementations it may be called document root, but with others it may be called *data directory*. As you build your servers, you will encounter underlying or essential concepts. In this chapter we examine and explain the fundamental protocols and concepts of Internet servers.

It may be a relief to know that you don't necessarily have to immediately understand such concepts as how to construct an Internet address, address classes, or subnet masks. But for the eternally curious, I provide some detail here. If you are pragmatic, and, like the rest of the world, need to bring the server up quickly, you can return to this chapter later. You can hand your network administrator the TCP/IP Parameter Form (see Appendix) and she can give the completed form back to you so that you can move immediately into configuring your connection. You can do all this preparation without really understanding all the background behind the parameters. I do recommend, however, that you make at least one attempt to grapple with the jargon and concepts. Perhaps it would also be beneficial to ask your network administrator to explain some of the detail. Just remember, you don't have to compute any of these networking parameters; you'll be assigned them.

System Administration

One advantage that Windows 3.1 and Windows NT servers have over UNIX servers is ease of system administration. As commercial software implementations of Gopher and the World Wide Web server software arrive in the marketplace and mature, we will see system administration moving more and more toward the one-button installation nirvana. Despite this move toward simpler administration, you still have at least three reasons for understanding what lies beneath the graphical-system administration interfaces:

1. Although most of these servers are quite simple and straightforward in their installation, if you fail to understand essential concepts, such as server security, you may set yourself up for grave problems. Failure to understand how to maintain a secure anonymous ftp server, or inadequate attention to configuring access control on a World Wide Web server are two examples of how you could put some or all of the information on your server in jeopardy.

2. Many of the concepts are similar, and some are identical to their UNIX counterparts, and so you can now become conversant with your UNIX

coworkers, and, if need be, you can more easily make the transition to a UNIX platform should you ever need, want, or have to.

3. The one-button installation nirvana probably will never arrive, especially because servers will become much more fully featured, and therefore more complex. Although servers are becoming easier to install and administer, the sophistication of the technology is rapidly evolving. Access to back-end databases, sophisticated forms capabilities, image maps, and other novel applications are constantly adding complexity to the technology. Progressive simplification of system administration will continue to be impressive, albeit a game of catch up.

Requests for Comments (RFCs)

For more information on Internet standards and protocols, refer to the Request for Comments (RFCs). These documents are maintained by two entities of the Internet Society, the Internet Architecture Board (IAB) and the Internet Engineering Task Force (IETF). The Internet Society provides assistance and support to groups and organizations using, operating, and working to enhance the Internet.

Each of the protocols described in this book (and many, many more) are described in standards documents known as RFCs. I have included most of the RFCs referred to in this book on the accompanying CD. Often, these documents appear to be an exercise in esoterica, but their purpose of course is to define a protocol in the utmost detail. You will find that if you are trying to find out detailed information on a topic, either at the local bookstore or on the Internet, the RFCs may be the only place where you can find adequate descriptions and definitions.

An RFC is a description of a protocol, procedure, or service. Well over a thousand RFCs are available describing various standards and topics. RFCs are circulated among a community of interested parties before they become accepted Internet standards. The RFC process is itself described in an RFC, known as RFC 1310. Information on how to retrieve RFCs is detailed in the Appendix. I hope the RFC information will give those who thirst for detail plenty to consume.

Network Layers

One of the protocols defined in the RFCs is TCP/IP (Transmission Control Protocol / Internet Protocol), which includes a number of protocols spanning several network layers. If you are not familiar with the network-layer concept, a network model is illustrated in Figure 2.1.

Transmission Control Protocol (TCP) supplies a reliable, connection-based protocol over IP (Internet Protocol). TCP guarantees delivery of packets, ensures proper sequencing of the data, and includes a checksum that validates for accuracy both the packet header and its data. If during transmission the network either corrupts or loses a TCP/IP packet, TCP is responsible for retransmitting the packet. This reliability makes TCP/IP the preferred protocol for client-server applications and services such as electronic mail. Data in TCP headers ensures proper sequencing of information, and also provide a checksum to ensure reliability of both the TCP header and the packet data.

To travel to and from the physical network, packets must travel through each layer of the protocol stack. For Windows applications, though not technically a part of the TCP/IP suite of protocols, the Windows Sockets API (Application Programming Interface) talks to the application layer (e.g., WWW) and passes packets to and from the next layer, the Transport layer. Windows Sockets provides a common interface that is independent of

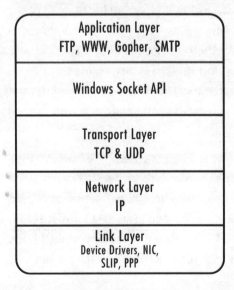

Figure 2.1 Network model.

different vendors' TCP/IP implementations. What do you see? If you run a program such as Netscape, it calls procedures from the WINSOCK.DLL dynamic link library. These procedures invoke procedures in the drivers supplied with the TCP/IP protocol stack. The TCP/IP drivers communicate with your machine's ethernet card through the packet driver. For serial connections, the TCP/IP drivers communicate with a SLIP or PPP driver to run network communications through a serial port.

Until the last few years, individuals who wanted a connection to the Internet but were not directly connected to it in a business or large organization, had to settle for a low-speed, nongraphically based connection via a dialup modem. Now, for a fairly reasonable monthly charge, anyone can connect to the Internet with a high-speed dialup connection running SLIP (Serial Line Internet Protocol) or PPP (Point to Point Protocol). And when I say high speed, I mean 14.4 Kbps or 28.8 Kbps. A SLIP or PPP connection essentially provides TCP/IP connectivity over dialup lines. By using SLIP or PPP, you accrue a number of benefits:

- You can run graphically based Internet client software tools such as Netscape, NCSA Mosaic, and HGopher, which not only afford great ease of use, but also shield you from the complexities of UNIX and the like.

- File transfers, as well as interactive sessions, can be run at very high speeds compared to the traditional 2400-bps asynchronous connections.

- And, most important, you can set up your PC to function as an Internet information server (i.e., run a Gopher or WWW Server).

SLIP and PPP are not the main subjects in this book, yet they are critical in successfully implementing an Internet Server if you'll be using a dialup rather than a direct connection. You may also want to test software at home via a SLIP connection even though you have a direct connection at work. Therefore, I cover installation and configuration of various SLIP and PPP products, like the Trumpet WINSOCK and NetManage's Chameleon. It really doesn't matter which you choose, SLIP or PPP. Essentially there's no difference in performance between the two that can be attributed to the differences in the two protocols.

From a technical perspective, the server's IO capabilities, the modems utilized, and the quality of a specific vendor's protocol implementation would be more significant than the differences between SLIP and PPP. If you are curious about tests and test methodology in comparing protocols, you can refer to Morning Star Technologies at:

```
http://www.morningstar.com/MorningStar/slip-ppp-compare.html
```

My advice is to choose the protocol that your service provider or computer center says they will support. Then when you have questions, you won't be left out in the cold. For detailed information about implementing and supporting SLIP and PPP, access this URL:

```
http://www.charm.net/ppp.html
```

Also, a FAQ (Frequently Asked Questions paper) describing SLIP and PPP applications and communications packages can be retrieved from:

```
ftp://ftp.cac.psu.edu/pub/dos/info/tcpip.packages
```

Link Layer

The lowest level of the network model, the Link Layer, is used in determining how to get packets out onto the physical network, and therefore is associated with the network interface card (NIC). We normally deal with this layer at the discussion level of an Ethernet card, for example, or a serial port connected to a modem. For the latter, we deal with two link-layer protocols, SLIP and PPP, which allow machines to communicate using TCP/IP, but over dialup lines. The Network layer deals with moving packets around the network. The Internet protocol, or IP, is responsible for routing your packets at this layer. Part of the protocol requires unique addresses called *IP addresses*.

Domain Names

We normally deal a lot more easily with English-language Internet addresses like **fido.ajax.com** than the numerical counterpart, which might be **130.85.185.4**. The machines responsible for routing packets on the Internet, however, have an easier time dealing with fido's numeric equivalent, when dealing with packet traffic. Therefore, each machine on the Internet must have a unique 32-bit address, also known as an IP address, which is structured into four numeric fields, each with a value of less than 256 and separated by periods. When these 32-bit numeric addresses must be translated into domain

Table 2.1 Various Abbreviations for Organizations	
DNS abbreviation	Type of organization
com	Commercial (e.g., **ibm.com**)
edu	Educational (e.g., **jhu.edu** Johns Hopkins University)
gov	Government (e.g., **whitehouse.gov**)
org	Noncommercial (e.g., **isoc.org** Internet Society)
net	Networking organizations (e.g., **clark.net** Clarknet)
mil	Military (e.g., **navy.mil**)

names, such as **fido.ajax.com**, the Internet uses the DNS (Domain Name System) to handle the conversion. DNS is a distributed database that maintains a mapping of domain names to numeric equivalents. The DNS maintains the names of hosts hierarchically, much as a file system does. The top-level names are designations you've probably seen, such as .COM, .EDU, and country codes, with which you are also probably somewhat familiar (e.g., UK, DE, CA). The various abbreviations you'll see for organizations are listed in Table 2.1.

The second level is a portion of the domain name maintained by the InterNIC (Internet Network Information Center) such as **ajax** (ajax being a fictitious commercial organization). The remaining portion of the domain name is administered by the organization's network administrator and represents the machine name, **fido** in our example. A further breakdown or subnetwork can be configured. An example might be **fido.acct.ajax.com** if the machine **fido** was located in a subnetwork in the accounting department (**acct**). The administrator will set up DNS services to handle requests for converting domain names to numeric addresses. Specifications for the DNS protocol are included in RFC 1034 and 1035.

If you wish to register your domain (e.g., **amway.com**), whether you do it through a service provider or through the InterNIC, you must answer a number of questions before receiving a domain name. Most service providers will take care of this formality for a very reasonable fee (like $75) and save you the time, trouble, and forms-processing learning curve. Much of the information on the form is self-explanatory and that which is not can easily be explained by people who have done it before, such as your service provider or your organization's network administrator.

Transport Layer

The transport layer controls the flow of data between machines on the network. Two protocols are used at the transport layer, TCP and UDP (User Datagram Protocol). TCP is a connection-based protocol designed to deal with unreliable links between machines. TCP takes a message, breaks it into packets, and passes them to the network layer for routing and delivery. TCP uses acknowledgment messages and checksums to guarantee delivery. UDP does not guarantee that data will make it to other machines on the network. Unlike TCP, applications that use UDP must include code to ensure reliable transmission.

This book deals primarily with the application level, or layer, describing implementations of various servers that are Winsock compatible.

At the network layer, Internet Protocol (IP) handles packet delivery for all other protocols within the TCP/IP suite. IP provides a connectionless delivery means for data packets. In other words, IP packets are not guaranteed to arrive at their destination, nor are they guaranteed to be received in the sequence in which they were transmitted. The checksum feature of the protocol ensures only the IP header's integrity. Therefore, responsibility for the data in the IP packet, and proper sequencing, is ensured only by using higher-level protocols.

IP Addressing

By definition, in Internet circles a *host* is any device that uses TCP/IP and is attached to the network. And, of course, that includes your PC as well as UNIX machines on the Net. To receive and deliver packets successfully between hosts, TCP/IP relies primarily on three pieces of information that the user provides: IP address, subnet mask, and default gateway.

The network administrator provides each of these pieces of information for configuring TCP/IP on your system.

Every *host*, or *node*, on a TCP/IP network is identified by a unique IP address. This address is used to identify a host on a network; it also specifies routing information on an *internetwork*, or internal network within an organization. The *IP address* identifies a computer with a 32-bit address that is unique on a

TCP/IP network. As we said in discussing domain naming, an address is stated in dotted decimal notation, which details each octet (eight bits, or one byte) of an IP address with its decimal value and separates each octet from its neighbors with a period. An IP address looks like this:

```
130.85.185.77
```

Notice that because IP addresses identify nodes on an interconnected network, each host on the internetwork must be assigned a unique IP address, valid for its network. This requirement explains why network administrators are entrusted with correctly assigning addresses from their blocks of available addresses.

Network ID and Host ID

The IP address comprises two pieces of information, the network ID and the host. The *network ID* identifies a group of computers and other devices all of which are located on the same logical network, and are separated or interconnected by routers. In internetworks, each network has a unique network ID. The *hosts ID* identifies your computer within a specific network ID. Again, a host is any device that is attached to the network and uses TCP/IP.

Networks that connect to the Internet must obtain an official network ID from the InterNIC to guarantee network ID uniqueness. Internet registration requests can be sent to **hostmaster@internic.net.** Normally, you won't receive your address(es) directly from the Internic. You will contact a service provider, such as those listed at the URL: **http://www.yahoo.com/Business-/Corporations/Internet_Access_Providers/**, or contact your organization's network administrator to get a TCP/IP address. They have previously contacted the Internic and received a block of associated IP addresses for distribution. For more information on this subject, you can use FTP to connect to **is.internic.net**, then log in as anonymous, and change to the **/infosource/faq** directory. Files there examine this topic in detail.

Host ID

After receiving a block of addresses, your network administrator must assign unique host IDs (IP addresses) to machines within the local network. Although organizational networks not connected to the Internet can choose to assign their own IP addresses, obtaining a valid block of addresses from the InterNIC allows a private network to connect to the Internet in the future without reassigning addresses.

Table 2.2 The Octets of the IP Address Defined as w.x.y.z			
Class	w value	Network ID	Host ID
A	1-126	w	x.y.z
B	128-191	w.x	y.z
C	192-223	w.x.y	z

Address Classes

You will oftens hear an address *class* referred to. For example, someone may say that your address is a Class C address. You may also be asked to configure the address class in some communications programs. Address classes are used to define networks of different sizes. The first octet in an IP address determines its class. Table 2.2 summarizes the relationship between the first octet in an address and its network ID and host ID fields. It also indicates the total number of network IDs and host IDs possible for each address class. Table 2.2 defines the octets in the IP address as w.x.y.z .

Subnet Masks

In the configuration of the TCP/IP implementations described in this book, you may be asked to provide a subnet mask. This and other parameters are, of course, provided by your network administrator or service provider. Subnet masks are 32-bit values that allow the recipient of IP packets to distinguish the network ID portion of the IP address from the host ID. Like an IP address, the value of a subnet mask is frequently represented in dotted decimal notation. Subnet masks are determined by assigning 1's to bits that belong to the network ID and 0's to the bits that belong to the host ID. Once the bits are placed, the 32-bit value is converted to dotted decimal notation, as shown in Table 2.3.

Table 2.3 Default Subnet Masks for Standard IP Address Classes		
Address class	Bits for subnet mask	Subnet mask
Class A	11111111 00000000 00000000 00000000	255.0.0.0
Class B	11111111 11111111 00000000 00000000	255.255.0.0
Class C	11111111 11111111 11111111 00000000	255.255.255.0

The result allows TCP/IP to determine the local computer's host and network IDs. For example, when the IP address is **198.69.33.74** and the subnet mask is **255.255.255.0**, the network ID is **198.69.33** and the host ID is **74**. Why are subnet masks necessary? One use for them is to further segment a network.

For example, suppose a network is assigned the Class B network address **130.85**. This is one of more than 16,000 Class B addresses capable of serving more than 65,000 nodes. The organization to which this ID is assigned, however, is composed of individual organizations with hundreds of nodes in multiple locales. Instead of applying for more network IDs, it is better to use subnetting to make more effective use of the assigned ID, **130.85**. The third octet in the IP address can be used as a subnet ID, to define the subnet mask **255.255.255.0**. This step splits the Class-B address into 254 subnets: **130.85.1** through **130.85.254**, each of which can have 254 nodes. Host IDs **0** and **255** should not be assigned to any machine because they are used as broadcast addresses, which are recognized by all computers. Any of these network addresses could be assigned to the individual entities in this example. Within each entity's local network, each computer is assigned a unique host ID, and they all have the subnet mask **255.255.255.0**.

The preceding example demonstrates a common subnetting method for Class B addresses. Sometimes only portions of an octet have to be segmented, using only a few bits to specify subnet IDs (as when subnets exceed 256 nodes). This information is provided to give you a basic understanding of subnet masks; you need only check with your network administrator to determine your correct subnet mask.

Internet Port Numbers

One basic ingredient of TCP is using *port numbers*. On your server, these numbers identify where the application or service listens for data. Common or known port numbers are used for specific services. For example, Table 2.4 shows the ports with which a few services are routinely associated.

If, when setting up your server, you have an opportunity to configure a port number, if possible use the default, the port which is generally stated in the documentation. Also, this default port number usually will be listed in the configuration file or configuration dialog box. If you choose to reassign a port number, use a number greater than 1024, for those below 1024 are usually assigned by default to a specific service, and are called *well-known* ports.

Table 2.4 Services and Their Associated Ports	
Service	Port
FTP	21
Telnet	23
Gopher	70
HTTP	80
Finger	79

TCP/IP on the Intel PC

If discussions of packet drivers, SLIP and PPP on a PC, and Winsocks are new to you, I recommend that you retrieve the FAQ on TCP/IP for a PC. The FAQ can be retrieved from:

```
ftp://ftp.netcom.com/pub/mailcom/IBMTCP
```

The file name is ibmtcp.zip. The whole issue of installing and configuring TCP/IP on a PC can be the most difficult hurdle in reaching the Internet with your PC. If you have a friendly network administrator who has dealt with TCP/IP on a PC, you may want to ask for his or her assistance when configuring your connection to the Internet. Getting help with this one step can save you a tremendous amount of time and gray hair.

To run TCP/IP on your PC you will need either an ethernet card (if you will be directly connected to the Internet) or a serial (COM) port (if you will use SLIP (Serial Line Internet Protocol) or PPP (Point to Point Protocol)), for a dialup modem connection. If you use an ethernet card (often referred to as a *network interface card* or *NIC*) it probably came with a driver that meets one of these specifications:

- Network Device Interface Specification (NDIS)
- Open Datalink Interface (ODI)
- Packet Drivers

Windows Sockets

The Windows Sockets standard ensures compatibility with Windows-based TCP/IP utilities that have been developed by more than thirty vendors. This standard includes the underlying TCP/IP stack and a full complement of client and server Internet application software. The Windows Sockets API is a networking API used by programmers creating applications for both the Microsoft Windows NT and Windows 3.1 operating systems. Windows Sockets is an open standard that is part of the Microsoft Windows Open System Architecture (WOSA) initiative. It is a public specification based on Berkeley UNIX sockets, which means that UNIX applications can be quickly ported to Microsoft Windows and Windows NT. Windows Sockets provides a standard programming interface supported by all the major vendors implementing TCP/IP for Windows systems.

Compliance with the Windows Sockets specification is critical to your server's efficient operation. Many of the problems associated with server operation on Windows 3.1 Web servers can be traced back to the Winsock implementation. Even though the Winsock is cited as compliant, this compliance in itself will not ensure flawless operation. Most Winsock implementations, if not all, were designed and tested primarily with client use in mind. At design time, the concept of server operation was still foreign to the Winsock authors. Therefore, you may find that your client browser operation is satisfactory, but reliable server operation will tend to be intermittent. Let's hope the Winsock implementations will improve with time and more reliable Windows 3.1 server operation will follow.

The Windows NT TCP/IP utilities use Windows Sockets, as do 32-bit TCP/IP applications developed by third parties. Under Windows NT, many of the 16-bit Windows-based applications created under the Windows Sockets standard will run without modification or recompilation. Most TCP/IP users will use programs that comply with that standard, such as ftp or telnet or third-party applications.

The Windows Sockets standard allows a developer to create an application with a single common interface and a single executable file that can run over many of the TCP/IP implementations provided by vendors. These are the goals for Windows Sockets:

- Provide a familiar networking API to programmers using Windows NT, Windows for Workgroups, or UNIX.

- Offer binary compatibility between vendors for heterogeneous Windows-based TCP/IP stacks and utilities.

- Support both connection-oriented and connectionless protocols.

Typical Windows Sockets applications include terminal emulation software, Simple Mail Transfer Protocol (SMTP) and electronic mail clients, various graphical client applications such as ftp and finger, and of course Internet servers.

If you are interested in understanding the details of Windows Sockets, specifications are available on the Internet from **ftp.microsoft.com** and can also be found in the Microsoft Win32 Software Developers Kit. Get a copy of the Windows Sockets specification via anonymous FTP at:

```
ftp://ftp.microsoft.com/advsys/winsock/spec11/
```

The filename is WINSOCK.ext, where .ext is the type of file format you want (e.g., TXT is ASCII, DOC is Microsoft Word).

Also available is an electronic mailing list designed for discussing Windows Sockets Programming. To subscribe to the list, send electronic mail to:

```
listserv@sunsite.unc.edu
```

and in the message body, type:

```
subscribe winsock firstname lastname
```

You can use the same procedure to subscribe to two mailing lists called winsock-hackers and winsock-users.

If you want to learn about Windows Sockets, including where and what a Winsock.dll is, and about standard APIs, retrieve the Winsock FAQ. You can retrieve it from **ftp://sunsite.unc.edu/pub/micro/pc-stuff/ms-windows/-winsock/FAQ**.

Trumpet Winsock

If you plan to use some of the public-domain software available on the Internet, such as Netscape or any of the server software packages detailed here, and you don't wish to buy a commercial TCP/IP package, you will need a public-domain Winsock. If you plan to use public-domain software, you'll acquire a public-domain Winsock and then collect client and server applications and build an Internet toolkit. Your alternative is to purchase a commercially available

Winsock (such as Chameleon, which we will cover shortly, or a number of others), and utilize some of the applications packaged with the Winsock. These generally include a number of client applications (e.g., Telnet, FTP, Gopher) and a few servers (e.g., FTP or even WWW). If you want to get a complete listing of vendors who offer TCP/IP for your Windows 3.1 and Windows NT systems, including a description of their offerings and prices, see:

`http://www.rtd.com/pcnfsfaq/SecA.html#A-3b`

The Trumpet Winsock is a Windows Sockets 1.1 compatible TCP/IP stack that provides a standard interface for many Windows networking applications to use. The Trumpet Winsock programs, written and distributed as shareware by Peter R. Tattam, are available from **ftp://ftp.utas. edu.au/pc/ trumpet/ winsock**. The filename is **twsk20b.zip**. Detailed documentation and sample configurations for the packet driver are available in the software distribution. We'll cover the essentials of the Trumpet Winsock product and then show you how to get a solid foundation for your server applications.

Installing Trumpet Winsock Ethernet Connection

If you have a direct connection via an ethernet card you must have a packet driver. Correspondingly, if you will be using SLIP or PPP, you must have a free serial port and a modem connected to your PC. The installation steps that follow are for a direct ethernet connection. If you will be using SLIP or PPP, you can skip this section and go to the section titled "Installing Trumpet Winsock-SLIP or PPP Connection."

To install the Trumpet Winsock:

1. The Trumpet Winsock zipped file, TWSK20B.ZIP, should be unzipped with PKUNZIP.EXE and the files copied to a directory you choose (e.g., C:\TRUMPET).

2. You should modify your AUTOEXEC.BAT to include the TRUMPET directory in the PATH. For example, PATH C:\DOS;C:\WINDOWS;C:\H-GOPHER;C:\TRUMPET.

Remember, to activate the new path, you will have to reboot.

3. Execute these commands to install the packet driver (3Com in this example) and the WINPKT virtual packet driver included in the distribution:

```
3c503 0x60 2 0x300
WINPKT 0x60
```

You can either just type these in at the DOS prompt to test the software, or you can add these lines to your AUTOEXEC.BAT file.

The first command installs the 3Com 3c503 model network card packet driver on vector **0x60** using IRQ 2 and I/O address **0x300**. The second line installs the WINPKT virtual packet driver using the same vector on which the 3c503 driver was installed. Many other detailed examples are included in the distribution documentation provided with the Trumpet Winsock software, including:

- Ne2000 packet driver using WINPKT

- Ne2000 packet driver with Netware using WINPKT

- Ne2000 packet driver with Netware using PKTMUX

- ODI setup with Netware access

- NDIS and Windows for Workgroups

- Cabletron using WINPKT

4. Start up Windows and run the TCPMAN.EXE program from the File Manager. Be sure to point to the proper directory (e.g., C:\TRUMPET) where you installed the software if you haven't changed your path in the AUTOEXEC.BAT file. From the TCPMAN menu bar, select **Setup**. A setup will appear where you should enter the necessary TCP/IP parameters that your network administrator or Internet service provider gave you (Figure 2.2). Table 2.5 shows sample values for each of the TCP/IP parameters. Substitute the values that you receive from your Internet Service provider or network administrator for each of those listed.

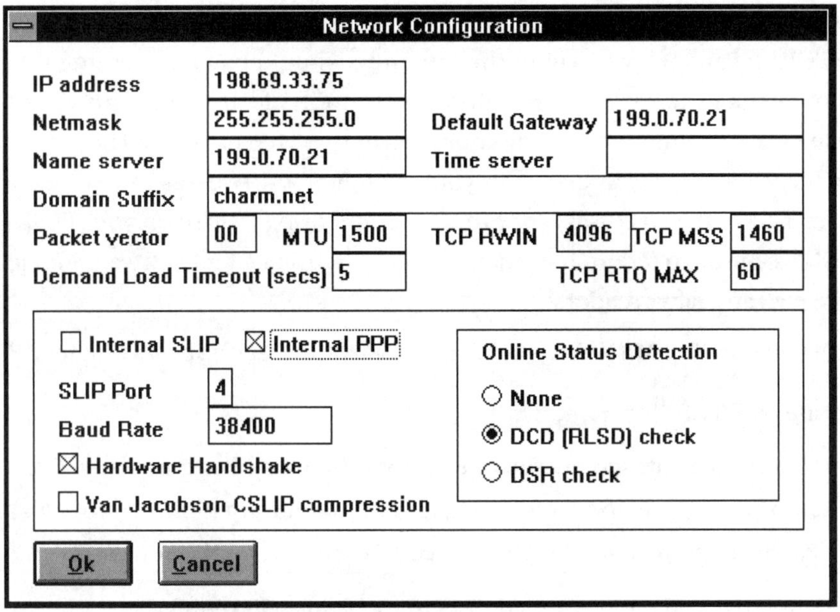

```
┌──────────────────────────────────────────────────────────────────┐
│ ▬                    Network Configuration                         │
├──────────────────────────────────────────────────────────────────┤
│                                                                    │
│  IP address      198.69.33.75                                      │
│  Netmask         255.255.255.0    Default Gateway  199.0.70.21     │
│  Name server     199.0.70.21      Time server                      │
│  Domain Suffix   charm.net                                         │
│  Packet vector   00   MTU 1500    TCP RWIN 4096  TCP MSS 1460      │
│  Demand Load Timeout (secs) 5              TCP RTO MAX    60        │
│                                                                    │
│  ┌──────────────────────────────────────────────────────────────┐ │
│  │ ☐ Internal SLIP   ☒ Internal PPP                              │ │
│  │                                  Online Status Detection       │ │
│  │ SLIP Port    4                   ○ None                        │ │
│  │ Baud Rate    38400               ◉ DCD (RLSD) check            │ │
│  │ ☒ Hardware Handshake             ○ DSR check                   │ │
│  │ ☐ Van Jacobson CSLIP compression                              │ │
│  └──────────────────────────────────────────────────────────────┘ │
│  ┌──────┐  ┌────────┐                                              │
│  │  Ok  │  │ Cancel │                                              │
│  └──────┘  └────────┘                                              │
└──────────────────────────────────────────────────────────────────┘
```

Figure 2.2 Trumpet TCPMAN setup screen.

Table 2.5 Parameters with Sample Values

Parameters	Sample values
IP Address	198.69.33.75
Subnet Mask	255.255.255.0
Gateway (Router)	199.0.70.21
Domain Name Server	199.0.70.21
Domain Name Suffix	charm.net
Host Name (name of your machine)	cyber.charm.net
POP3 Server	mailhost.charm.net
News Server	news.charm.net
Your Login	cyber

TCP/IP Parameters Form

The TCP/IP Parameters form in the Appendix should make collecting these parameters a little easier. You can use the form in discussions with your in-house network administrator or your Internet service provider. They should have the values readily available for your configuration. Use this form to record information that is necessary for properly configuring TCP/IP on your PC. This form is also used to record information for configuring client software for electronic mail and news readers.

When you start TCPMAN.EXE, the Trumpet startup screen appears (Figure 2.3).

Entering your TCP/IP parameters:

1. From the startup screen, select File from the menu bar and Setup. The setup screen will appear as in Figure 2.2. The information that follows describes the parameters you'll need to configure in the setup screen.

2. IP Address *. Enter your IP address in the form **198.69.33.75**.

3. If you use BOOTP, you must have a BOOTP service on the network or the Winsock will not load. BOOTP will automatically assign your IP address at connect time, but this is not a preferred approach. Be sure to ask your network administrator or service provider for a static (i.e., permanently assigned) IP address.

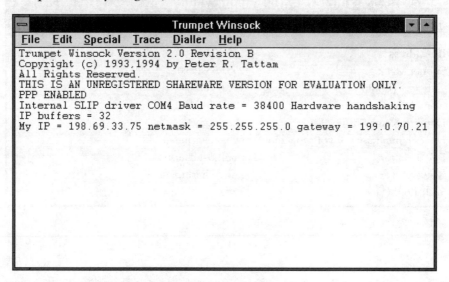

Figure 2.3 Trumpet TCPMAN startup screen.

4. **Netmask** *. This is your Internet subnet mask. For example, if your address is a class C address, it will be 255.255.255.0.

5. **Default Gateway** *. Enter the IP address of your default Internet gateway.

6. **Name Server** *. Enter the IP address of the machine that will function as your Domain Name Server (DNS). You may provide more than one by separating them with spaces.

7. **Time Server**. Currently unused, and so you can leave this field as is.

8. **Domain Suffix**. Enter domain suffixes (space separated) to be used when resolving names in the DNS.

9. **Packet Vector**. Leave this number at 00 to search for the packet driver, or enter the vector where you installed the packet driver. Enter the number in hexadecimal without the leading 0x . For example, you would enter 60.

10. **MTU. 1500** is the default and is the recommended setting.

11. **TCP RWIN. 4096** is the default for the TCP Receive Window.

12. **TCP MSS. 1460** is the default TCP Maximum Segment Size.

13. **Demand Load Timeout**. 5 seconds is the default.

    * These parameters will require your input. You can accept the default on the others.

Because we are configuring a direct connection rather than dialup, the Internal SLIP or Internal PPP box should not be checked and the boxes that are grayed out should be ignored. Once you have entered the necessary information, click on **OK**. Troubleshooting tips and so on are covered in the software distribution.

You can start the Winsock either by selecting Run from the Windows File menu and running TCPMAN.EXE, or adding the TCPMAN executable to a startup procedure (i.e., BATch file), or by setting up a program item and clicking on a Windows program icon.

Now you can select your favorite TCP/IP-based application through Windows (e.g., Netscape) and you should be able to establish a connection.

Installing Trumpet Winsock—SLIP or PPP Connection

As mentioned earlier, SLIP and PPP are protocols that allow an asynchronous dialup connection to handle the Internet Protocol (IP). The Trumpet Winsock handles these protocols and also has provision for dialup scripts to facilitate logons to your server.

The installation steps for SLIP or PPP are:

1. The Trumpet Winsock zipped file, TWSK20B.ZIP, should be unzipped with PKUNZIP and the files copied to a directory you choose (e.g., C:\TRUMPET).

2. You should modify your AUTOEXEC.BAT to include the TRUMPET directory in the PATH. For example, PATH C:\DOS;C:\WINDOWS;C:\ HGOPHER;C:\TRUMPET

3. Remember, to activate the new path you will have to reboot.

4. Start up Windows and **Run** the TCPMAN.EXE program from the File Manager. Be sure to point to the proper directory (e.g., C:\TRUMPET) where you installed the software. A startup screen will appear (Figure 2.3) from which you can select Setup from the File menu to view the configuration screen (Figure 2.2). Here, enter the necessary TCP/IP parameters that your network administrator or Internet service provider gave you. Each is described in the following steps.

5. **IP Address** *. Enter your IP address in the form **198.69.33.75** or enter **bootp** in lower case.

6. **Netmask** *. Your Internet subnet mask. For example, if your address is a class C address, it would be **255.255.255.0**.

7. **Default Gateway** *. Enter the IP address of your default Internet gateway.

8. **Name Server***. Enter the IP address of the machine that will function as your Domain Name Server (DNS). You may provide more than one by separating them with spaces.

9. **Time Server**. Currently unused.

10. **Domain Suffix***. Enter domain suffixes (space separated) to be used when resolving names in the DNS.

11. **Packet Vector**. Leave this number at 00 to search for the packet driver, or enter the vector where you installed the packet driver. Enter the number in hexadecimal without the leading 0x. For example, you would enter 60.

12. **Maximum Transmission Unit (MTU)**. Should be TCP MSS + 40.

13. **TCP RWIN**. The TCP Receive Window value should be set at 3 to 4 times the value of TCP MSS.

14. **TCP MSS**. The TCP Maximum Segment Size should be set to 512 bytes for SLIP and less than 255 when using CSLIP.

15. **Demand Load Timeout**. Five seconds is the default.

16. **Internal SLIP or Internal PPP**. Select the protocol you wish to use.

17. **SLIP or PPP Port**. Enter your comm port number (e.g., 1 = com1).

18. **Baud Rate**. The speed of your connection.

19. **Hardware Handshake**. Recommended if your connection supports it.

20. **Van Jacobson CSLIP Compression**. Select this if your server will support it. Usually esoteric information such as whether or not your provider will support CSLIP and other optional parameters will be detailed in the instructions mailed to you by the provider.

21. **OnLine Status Detection**. Select DCD or DSR status detection if your modem supports it.

22. When you are done, click on **OK**.

SLIP or PPP Dialing Scripts

You can use the manual login capability included with TCPMAN.EXE to make your connection to the SLIP or PPP server. Your Internet provider or network manager should supply you with information about the SLIP or PPP logon procedure. Logging on manually is best when you initially install the Trumpet Winsock. With the manual login procedure you will execute the necessary login steps to establish a connection; make note of them so that you can automate them by scripting.

About twenty commands are available to you in the scripting language and they are explained in the Trumpet Winsock documentation. Listed below is a sample script that will replicate the login steps necessary to login to Charm Net, an Internet service provider. This script was taken from the **login.cmd** file, included with the Trumpet software distribution and modified. The only changes that were necessary were replacing the **username** prompt with the **login:** prompt, which is the prompt provided at sign-on time at Charm Net, and some additional comments to give you a better idea of what the script is about. You might also want to check with your service provider or computer center to see if they have scripts already developed that you could copy. If you wish to change any of the files provided with the Trumpet distribution, you can edit the files using Windows Notepad or you can select **Edit Scripts** from the menu bar **Dialer** to modify the file.

You will provide the necessary variables for this script in the TCPMAN setup procedure. These include your provider's phone number, your account name at the provider, and your password. These will be stored in a file named TRUMPWSK.INI and retrieved each time you execute TCPMAN and the **login.cmd** script.

To initiate a SLIP or PPP connection through the Trumpet Winsock, **Run** TCPMAN.EXE and select **Login** from the **Dialer** menu item (Figure 2.4). Trumpet will then execute your login script and make your connection to the provider. Once you've made your connection, you can run Netscape to test it.

Sample Slip Dialing Script—Login.cmd

```
#trace on
#uncomment the trace line above to turn trace on for debugging the script
# in the following if statements, set up some strings for dialing up; use the load
#command to check for the variable values in the trumpwsk.ini file; if no value, prompt
#for it
```

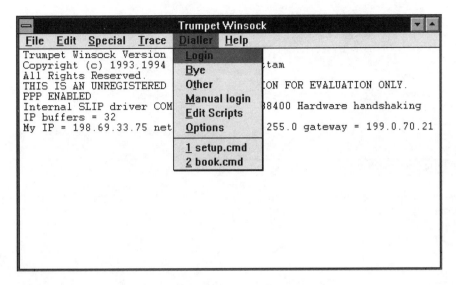

Figure 2.4 Trumpet TCPMAN Dialer menu.

```
if
![load $number]
 if [query $number "Enter your dialup phone number"]
 save $number
 end
end
if ![load $username]
 if [username "Enter your login username"]
 save $username
 end
end
if ![load $password]
 if [password "Enter your login password"]
 save $password
 end
end
$modemsetup = "&c1&k3"
$prompt = ">"
# userprompt and passprompt are the system prompts your server provides at login; if your
#system
# provides some other prompts, you'll want to change them here
$userprompt = "login:"
$passprompt = "password:"
#
$slipcmd = "slip"
$addrtarg = "Your address is"
$pppcmd = "ppp"
%attempts = 10
```

```
#
#————————————————————
# initialize modem and wait for an OK from the modem
#
output "atz"\13
if ! [input 10 OK\n]
 display "Modem is not responding"\n
 abort
end
#
# setup our modem commands
#
output "at"$modemsetup\13
input 10 OK\n
#
# send phone number
#
%n = 0
repeat
 if %n = %attempts
 display "Too many dial attempts"\n
 abort
 end
 output "atdt"$number\13
 %ok = [input 60 CONNECT]
 %n = %n + 1
until %ok
input 10 \n
#
# wait till it's safe to send because some modems hang up
# if you transmit during the connection phase
#
wait 30 dcd
#
# now prod the terminal server with a carriage return
#
output \13
#
# wait for the username prompt, then provide your username
#
input 30 $userprompt
output $username\13
#
# and the password
#
input 30 $passprompt
output $password\13
#
```

```
# we are now logged in
#
# Now wait for the >
input 30 $prompt
# Based on your choice of protocols, let the server know which you'll use by sending the
#string ppp or
# slip
#
if %ppp
 #
 # jump into ppp mode
 #
 output $pppcmd\13
 #
 input 30 \n
 #
 display "PPP mode selected. Will try to negotiate IP address."\n
 #
else
 #
 # jump into slip mode
 #
 output $slipcmd\13
 #
 # wait for the address string
 #
 input 30 $addrtarg
 #
 # parse address
 #
 address 30
 input 30 \n
 #
 # we are now connected, logged in, and in slip mode.
 #
 display \n
 display Connected. Your IP address is \i.\n
end
#
# now we are finished.
#
```

Trumpet Mailing List

To keep up to date on Trumpet Winsock you should join the Trumpet mailing list by sending a mail message to:

listproc@petros.psychol.utas.edu.au

and in the body of the message, type:

```
Subscribe trumpet-user Your Full Name
```

where Your Full Name should be replaced by your actual full name (e.g., John Smith).

Chameleon

The Chameleon Sampler Version 3.11 (Dialup serial line only; no direct connect capabilities) is available from NetManage, Inc. at:

```
ftp://ftp.manage.com/pub/demos/sampler/sampler.exe
```

Many individuals and organizations feel more secure with commercial-grade software than with public-domain software. An established TCP/IP vendor, with adequate support personnel and an installed customer base, adds significant stability to the fundamental component in your network. The $200 to $400 investment can be critical to success for your installation. If you have any doubts about supporting your server activities on shareware or freeware, make the investment in commercial-grade software.

Chameleon software, besides a Winsock, has several applications that normally you would have to assemble on your own from the various public-domain client applications readily available on the Net. The Chameleon sampler provides copies of FTP, Telnet, Mail, Ping, and Custom applications from an earlier version, rather than the current production version of NetManage's Chameleon TCP/IP for Windows product, and so one might consider its reliability and stability slightly behind those of the latest version. Nevertheless, it's a good alternative for testing your server. I recommend that, for best results, you use the latest version of your chosen Winsock. This software does not normally, of course, come in a sampler package; it is available at a commercial-product price.

The principal product in the Sampler is a native windows implementation of TCP/IP that is 100 percent DLL and fully compliant to the Winsock standard. Not only does it provide dialup access, the commercial version of Chameleon features connectivity to local area networks running Ethernet, Token Ring, or FDDI. NetManage's TCP/IP can run concurrently with NetWare, Banyan Vines,

LAN Manager, and PathWorks. The full Chameleon product has more than two dozen applications, including LAN support, MIME support for multimedia attachments to e-mail messages, a Gopher Client, an Internet News Reader, Scripting, Finger, Whois, an SNMP Agent, and optional support for both NFS client and server.

Beyond the Sampler, you can retrieve information about a thirty-day evaluation copy of the full Chameleon product at:

`ftp://ftp.netmanage.com/pub/demos/chameleon/readme.txt`

The Sampler Custom utility allows you to properly configure TCP/IP on your PC. It comes with configuration files (.CFG) that have many of the parameters for connecting to some popular Internet service providers. A file named PROVIDER.TXT in the Sampler distribution lists the provider configuration files included.

As with the Trumpet Winsock, before you start Custom you will need the information in Table 2.6 to configure your PC for TCP/IP (substitute your values for each parameter listed in the table).

Table 2.6 Information for Custom to Configure Your PC for TCP/IP	
Configuration parameters	**Sample values**
Your IP Address	**198.69.33.75**
Your Host Name (Your PC)	**cyber**
Your Domain Name	**charm.net**
Port	**COM4, 19200**
Modem	**Hayes**
Dialup number	**5583300**
Login Name	**cyber**
Login Password	********
Startup Command	**PPP**
Domain Name Server Address	**199.0.70.21**
MailBox Name	**cyber**
MailBox Password	********
Mail Gateway Name	**sowebo.charm.net**
Mail Server Name	**mailhost.charm.net**

Some parameters will be unnecessary with a dialup connection, including
Default Gateway and **Subnet Mask**.You need supply these parameters only if
you have a direct rather than a dialup connection.

To Install the Sampler

To initially install the Sampler, **Run** the self-extracting archive SAMPLER.EXE
from a directory (e.g., C:\NETMANAG). From the Windows **File** menu, select
Run and run the SETUP.EXE program included in the distribution.

Setup copies the necessary files to your Netmanage directory and gives you
an **installation complete** message. Click on **OK**.The Custom program will
be started and the configuration screen will be displayed (Figure 2.5). Select
each item (e.g., IP address, modem, as shown in Figure 2.6) and input the parameters for your configuration. Once the configuration is complete, select
Options and click on **Log**. This logging facility will enable you to follow
the connection sequence. Move the log window so that you can initiate a
connection.

Select **Connect** from the menu and follow the connection sequence in the log
window. Once a connection is made, you can close the log. Once you're
connected, you can minimize the Custom program and use any of your Internet
client or server applications.You might first try to Ping a host, such as the
Domain Name Server listed on your TCP Parameters Form, or you might want
to use Telnet to connect to your UNIX shell account.

```
Custom - D:\NETMANAG\CHARM.CFG
File   Interface   Setup   Services   Connect   Help

Interface:      PPP0 - COM4, 19200 baud
Dial:           5583300
IP Address:     198.69.33.75
Subnet Mask:    255.255.255.0
Host Name:      cyber.charm.net
Domain Name:    charm.net

Name         Type        IP              Domain
*PPP0        PPP         198.69.33.75    charm.net
```

Figure 2.5 Chameleon SAMPLER CUSTOM configuration.

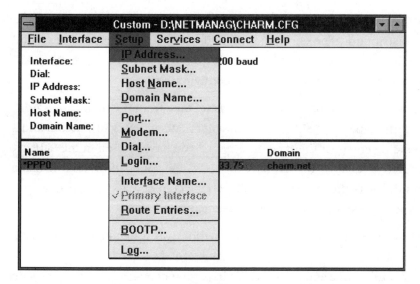

Figure 2.6 Chameleon SAMPLER CUSTOM configuration items.

If you wish to use one of the configuration files supplied rather than create a custom configuration, select **File**, then **Open**, and choose the .CFG file with the name corresponding to your Internet access provider (e.g., **cerfnet.cfg**). For specific information about the provider's configuration, help information is provided in .TXT files for each provider (e.g., **cerfnet.txt**).

Depending on the provider you select, a number of values are already correctly entered and do not need to be changed. Some providers will supply the IP address dynamically and will tell you to define your IP address as something such as **1.1.1.1**. This means of configuration may be fine for Internet client setup, but you should have a static, or permanent IP address if you're setting up a server. Discuss this address with your network administrator or your Internet Service provider; they should appreciate your need to have an assigned IP address.

Defining an Additional Interface

If your Internet provider is not included in one of the .CFG files, or if you'll be connecting to your organization's SLIP or PPP server, then you may want to configure additional .CFG files.

Start by **OPEN**ing the default configuration (TCPIP.CFG) included with the Sampler distribution. The configuration defined in TCPIP.CFG assumes a PPP interface. If you wish to use a SLIP connection, you will need to **ADD** a SLIP interface rather than change this default configuration.

To create your own configuration, select **Interface** from the menu, then **Add**, and select the type (e.g., SLIP). Custom will create an entry in Custom and a corresponding entry for the type of interface you have chosen in the SLIP.INI and name it (e.g., SLIP0). You may have to modify the connection script to make your connection to the server, depending on the connection dialogue that your server expects. A sample script is provided below.

In **Custom**, under **Setup**, enter the information you collected on the TCP/IP Parameters Form into the appropriate fields. Once you've loaded each parameter, select **File**, **Save** and then **Exit**. To have your changes take effect, be sure to exit and restart the program.

Developing a SLIP or PPP Script

The Chameleon script is used to replicate the logon connection sequence that normally is done manually.

The SLIP or PPP server might be a UNIX workstation, a dialup router, or a terminal server that is capable of supporting the appropriate protocol(s).

The scripts are stored in a file called SLIP.INI in the netmanage directory. For each configuration you create in Custom, an entry is added to the file with the name of the interface.

If you have to develop a custom script, the SLIP.INI file has plenty of examples. Also ask your provider (if they don't have a .CFG script already included with the distribution) or your computer center if they have a script developed for the Chameleon Sampler.

Sample Script

To modify the SLIP.INI file to add a connection dialogue for CHARM NET, first make a backup copy of SLIP.INI by copying it to SLIP.OLD. Then add these lines to SLIP.INI by using Windows Notepad or your favorite editor:

```
[Charmnet]
SCRIPT=login: $u$r word: $p$r
TYPE=PPP
```

To set up a script, you must first know the manual login sequence. Test the manual squence first, carefully noticing both the machine's prompts and your responses.

The example performs as follows:

1. Once a dialup connection is made, the server provides the prompt,
   login:

2. The u$ variable is provided back to the server with the username you configured in Custom.

3. The script next sends $r, a carriage return, to the server.

4. The script awaits the prompt **word:** (as in Password), and upon receiving it sends the stored password from Custom, followed by a carriage return (**$r**).

Slip Script Language Syntax

These commands are available for scripting:

$n	send a new line
$r	send a carriage return
$s	send a space
$b	cause a short break on the line
$t-	send a tab
$1–$9	pause the indicated number of seconds
$xXX	send the character with HEX code XX
$u	send the user id
$p	send the password
$c	send the SLIP COMMAND
$d	send the phone number
$$	send a $ character
$f	define a prompt

Within an <>expect> string you can include these escapes:

-          expect "-"

-n   skip an expect

-i   expect IP address (to replace your own)

$-   find the string following this symbol

TCP/IP for Windows NT

One beauty about Windows NT is that it's probably the first commercial operating system offering TCP/IP support right out of the box. To date, with other
operating systems you've had to purchase additional TCP/IP software for your
PC, or wrestle with public-domain solutions. NT comes with an excellent
TCP/IP implementation as well as related basic software such as FTP and
Telnet, and, very important, Windows Sockets support. Such tools have facili-
tated development of high-quality commercial and public-domain Internet
client and server software.

To make a connection to the Internet, you will need TCP/IP installed on your
NT Server. When I say NT Server I refer to an Intel or DEC Alpha PC running
either the Base NT operating system or NTAS, the NT Advanced Server.

The TCP/IP software is not installed as part of the NT operating system during
Express Setup. I assume that Windows NT has been successfully installed on
your machine.

Here are the network parameters that you will need to know before installing
TCP/IP. Refer to the TCP/IP Parameters Form listing these values in the
Appendix; they include:

- The IP address of your default gateway.

- Your machine's IP address.

- Your subnet mask.

- Whether you will be using a Domain Name Service (DNS) and, if so,
  the IP address of the DNS.

TCP/IP for Windows NT offers you several advantages:

The protocol is well integrated into the NT operating system, eliminating many configuration headaches and performance problems of DOS and Windows TCP/IP stacks.

Many standard Internet connectivity applications are available for accessing and transferring data between systems, including File Transfer Protocol (FTP) and Terminal Emulation Protocol (Telnet). Several of these standard utilities are included with Windows NT and many are available as freeware, shareware, and commercial applications.

Most important, TCP/IP is essential for connecting Windows NT to the Internet. TCP/IP and accompanying components such as Point to Point Protocol (PPP) and Serial Line Internet Protocol (SLIP) provide the foundation needed to connect your NT server to the Internet.

NT TCP/IP Components

NT TCP/IP includes:

- By definition, TCP/IP is a *suite* or collection of protocols rather than a protocol in itself. The suite of protocols includes Transmission Control Protocol (TCP), Internet Protocol (IP), User Datagram Protocol (UDP), Address Resolution Protocol (ARP), and Internet Control Message Protocol (ICMP). Support is also provided for PPP and SLIP, which are protocols used for dial-up access to the Internet.

- Essential TCP/IP utilities including finger, ftp, telnet, and others. These common Internet utilities provide a full complement of communications programs for interacting with other systems.

- TCP/IP diagnostic tools, including netstat, ping, route, tracert, and other tools that can be used to troubleshoot networking problems.

- *Services* such as an FTP Server, Dynamic Host Configuration Protocol (DHCP) service for automatically configuring TCP/IP on Windows NT computers, and TCP/IP printing for accessing printers connected to UNIX systems.

- With the 3.5 release of Windows NT, TCP/IP does not include a complete collection of TCP/IP utilities or some services (daemons) such as telneted and other server programs. Many of these products are available in the form of public-domain or commercial packages and are detailed in subsequent chapters.

NT TCP/IP and DHCP

Check with your network administrator to find this information before you install Microsoft TCP/IP on a Windows NT computer:

- Whether your installation uses Dynamic Host Configuration Protocol (DHCP) to configure TCP/IP. You can choose this option if a DHCP server is operating at your site. But if your system will be a DHCP server, you can't choose this option. See the *Microsoft TCP/IP Reference Manual* for information on installing, configuring, and using DHCP Servers.

- Whether this computer will be a Windows Internet Name Service (WINS) server and whether this computer will be a WINS proxy agent. Again, refer to the *Microsoft TCP/IP Manual* for additional information.

- If you are not using DHCP for automatic configuration, you need to obtain the values from the network administrator (listed below) so that you can configure TCP/IP manually. To collect the necessary data, refer to the TCP/IP Parameters Form in the Appendix, including:

  - The IP address and subnet mask.

  - The IP address for the default local gateway.

  - The IP addresses and the DNS domain name of the DNS servers on the network.

  - The IP addresses for WINS servers, if those are available on your network.

Installing NT TCP/IP

You must be logged on as a member of the Administrators group to install and configure TCP/IP.

To install Microsoft TCP/IP on your system:

1. Click on the Network option in Control Panel (Figure 2.7).

2. In the Network Settings dialog box (Figure 2.8), click on the **Add Software** button.

3. In the **Add Network Software** dialog box (Figure 2.9), select TCP/IP Protocol and Related Components from the Network Software list, and then click on the **Continue** button.

4. In the Windows NT TCP/IP Installation Options dialog box, check the components you want to install. For testing, click on **Connectivity Utilities**, **TCP/IP Network Printing Support**, **FTP Server Service** (if you want NT FTP), and **Simple TCP/IP Services**. Next, click on the **Continue** button. If any TCP/IP options have been installed previously, these are dimmed and not available in the Windows NT TCP/IP Installation Options dialog box. You can read the hints at the bottom of each TCP/IP dialog box for information about a selected item, or click on the **Help** button to get detailed on-line information while you are installing or configuring TCP/IP.

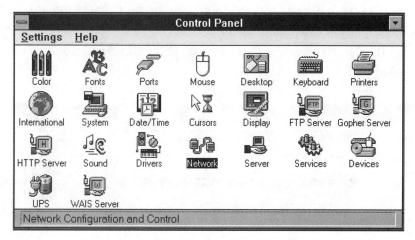

Figure 2.7 NT Control Panel Network option.

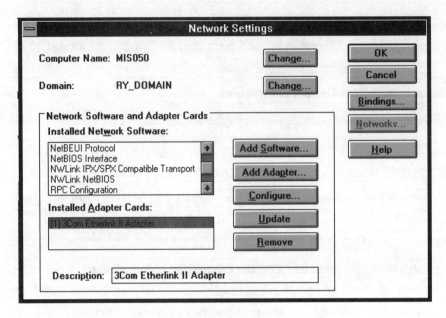

Figure 2.8 NT Network Settings dialog box.

5. Setup displays a message (Figure 2.10) asking for the full path to the distribution files. Key in the proper path and click on the **Continue** button. Files will now be copied to your hard disk. See the TCP/IP Installation Options below for a description of each component.

6. If you selected the option for installing the FTP Server service, you will be asked to configure this service. Directions are provided in the on-line Help for each dialog box. Detailed configuration information for configuring the FTP Server is listed under Using the NT FTP Server in Chapter 4.

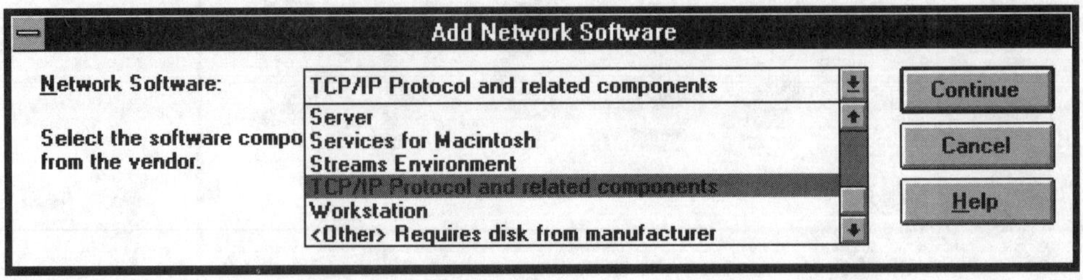

Figure 2.9 NT Add Network Software.

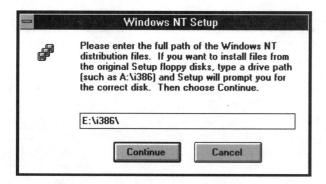

Figure 2.10 NT Path to software distribution.

7. In the Network Setting dialog box, click on **OK**. If you checked the Enable Automatic DHCP Configuration option and a DHCP server is available on your network, all settings are completed automatically. For your system to function properly on the Internet, TCP/IP must be configured with the IP addresses, subnet mask, and default gateway. TCP/IP can be configured by two methods. If your network has a DHCP server, it can automatically configure TCP/IP for your computer using DHCP. If it has no DHCP server, or if you are configuring a Windows NT Server computer to be a DHCP server, you must manually configure all TCP/IP settings. We assume that you will be configuring TCP/IP manually and therefore do not cover DHCP in this book. If you did not check the Enable Automatic DHCP Configuration, you must manually configure TCP/IP, as described in Configuring TCP/IP Manually below.

Configuring TCP/IP

Table 2.7 shows TCP/IP installation options.

Table 2.7 TCP/IP Installation Options	
TCP/IP Internetworking	Includes the TCP/IP protocol, Net BIOS over TCP/IP and Windows Sockets interfaces, and the TCP/IP diagnostic utilities.
Connectivity Utilities	Installs the TCP/IP client utilities. Select this option to install the connectivity utilities such as finger, ftp, and telnet.
TCP/IP Network Printing Support	Allows your system to print directly over the network using TCP/IP. Select this option if you want to print to UNIX print queues or TCP/IP printers.

Continued

Table 2.7 TCP/IP Installation Options *Continued*

FTP Server Service	Allows your system to function as an FTP Server that supports FTP clients.
Simple TCP/IP Services	Provides the software for the Character Generator, Daytime, Discard, Echo, and Quote of the Day services. Choose this option to allow your computer to respond to requests from other systems that support these protocols.
DHCP Server Service	Installs the server software to support automatic configuration and addressing for computers using TCP/IP on your network. This option is available only for Windows NT Server. Select it if this computer is to be a DHCP Server.
Enable Automatic DHCP Configuration	Allows automatic loading of TCP/IP parameters for your system. Select this option if a DHCP server is available on your network.

Configuring TCP/IP Manually

After you have installed TCP/IP, you must manually provide TCP/IP addressing information if you are installing TCP/IP on a DHCP server or if you cannot use automatic DHCP configuration (which we'll assume for testing). You must be logged on as a member of the Administrators group for the local computer to configure TCP/IP. To avoid duplicate addresses, be sure to use the values for IP addresses and subnet masks that are supplied by your network administrator. Duplicate addresses can cause some computers on the network to function unpredictably.

To manually configure the TCP/IP protocol:

1. When installing TCP/IP, the TCP/IP Configuration dialog box appears automatically when you click on the **OK** button in the Network Settings dialog box. This step is done after you have completed all the options in the TCP/IP Installation Options dialog box (Figure 2.11). If you are reconfiguring TCP/IP, start the Network option in Control Panel to display the Network Settings dialog box. In the Installed Network Software list box, select TCP/IP Protocol, and click on the **Configure** button. The screen in Figure 2.12 will be displayed.

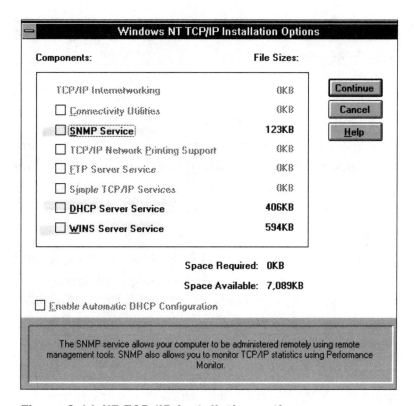

Figure 2.11 NT TCP/IP Installation options.

2. Select the network adapter for which you want to set an IP address in the Adapter list of the configuration dialog box. The Adapter list includes all network adapters installed on your system. You must set the IP addressing information for each adapter with the values provided by the network administrator.

3. For each network adapter, type in the values in the IP Address and Subnet Mask boxes. The value in the IP address box identifies the IP address for your computer. The value in the Subnet Mask box identifies the network membership for the selected network adapter and its host ID. This provision allows the computer to separate the IP address into host and network IDs. The subnet mask defaults to an appropriate value, as shown in Table 2.8.

Table 2.8 Subnet mask defaulting to an appropriate value.

Address class	Range of first octet in IP address	Subnet mask
Class A	1-126	255.0.0.0
Class B	128-191	255.255.0.0
Class C	192-223	255.255.255.0

4. For each adapter on the computer, type the correct IP address value in the Default Gateway box, as provided by the network administrator. This value specifies the IP address of the default gateway used to forward packets to other networks or subnets; it should be the IP address of your local gateway.

5. If WINS servers are installed on your network and you want to use WINS in combination with broadcast-name queries to resolve computer names, type IP addresses in the boxes for the primary and (optionally) the secondary WINS servers. The network administrator should provide the correct values for these parameters. These are global values for the computer, not just individual adapters.

   If an address for a WINS server is not specified, this computer uses name query broadcasts (the b-node mode for NetBIOS over TCP/IP) plus the local LMHOSTS file to resolve computer names to IP addresses. Broadcast resolution is limited to the local network. WINS name resolution is automatically enabled and configured for a computer that is configured with DHCP.

6. Later, we'll want to configure the advanced TCP/IP options for multiple gateways and other items, by clicking on the **Advanced** button, and continuing with the configuration procedure, as described in Configuring Advanced TCP/IP Options below.

7. If your site uses DNS for host name resolution, click on the **DNS** button and continue with the configuration procedure, as described in the next section.

8. If you do not want to configure DNS or advanced options, or if you have completed the other configuration procedures, click on the **OK** button. When the Network Settings dialog box reappears, click on the **OK** button.

Microsoft TCP/IP has been configured. If you are installing TCP/IP for the first time, you must restart the computer for the configuration to take effect. If you are changing your existing configuration, you do not have to restart your computer.

After TCP/IP is installed, the **\systemroot\SYSTEM32\DRIVERS\ETC** directory includes a default HOSTS file and a sample LMHOSTS.SAM file. The network administrator may require that you use replacement HOSTS and LMHOSTS files instead of these default files.

Configuring TCP/IP to Use DNS

Although TCP/IP uses IP addresses to identify and reach computers, users typically prefer computer names. Domain Name Service (DNS) is a naming service generally used in the UNIX networking community to provide standard naming conventions for IP workstations. Windows Sockets applications and TCP/IP utilities, such as ftp and telnet, can also use DNS to find systems when connecting to foreign hosts or systems on your network.

Contact the network administrator to find out whether you should configure your computer to use DNS. Usually you will use DNS if you are using TCP/IP to communicate over the Internet or if your private internetwork uses DNS to distribute host information. Microsoft's TCP/IP includes DNS client software for resolving Internet or UNIX system names. Microsoft Windows networking provides dynamic name resolution for NetBIOS computer names via WINS servers and NetBIOS over TCP/IP.

DNS configuration is global for all network adapters installed on a computer.

To configure TCP/IP DNS connectivity:

1. Start the Network Option in Control Panel to display the Network Settings dialog box (Figure 2.8). In the Installed Network Software list box, select TCP/IP Protocol, and then click on the **Configure** button.

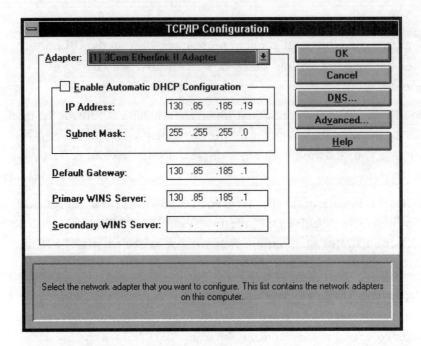

Figure 2.12 NT TCP/IP configuration.

2. In the TCP/IP Configuration dialog box (Figure 2.12), click on the **DNS** button.

3. In the DNS Configuration dialog box (Figure 2.13), you can (optionally) type a name in the Host Name box (usually your computer name).

The name can be any combination of A-Z letters, 0-9 numerals, and the hyphen (-) plus the period (.) character used as a separator. By default, this value is the Windows NT computer name, but the network administrator can assign another host name without affecting the computer name. Notice that some characters that can be used in Windows NT computer names, particularly the underscore, cannot be used in host names.

The host name is used to identify the local computer by name for authentication by some utilities. Other TCP/IP-based utilities, such as rexec, can use this value to learn the name of the local computer. Host names are stored on DNS servers in a table that maps names to IP addresses for use by DNS.

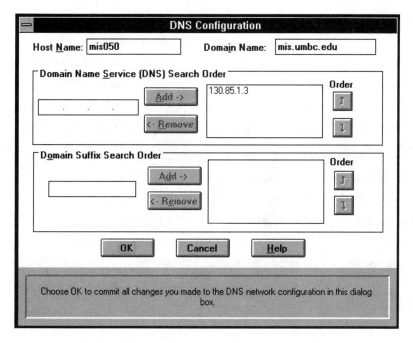

Figure 2.13 NT DNS configuration.

4. Optionally, type a name in the Domain Name box. This is usually an organization name followed by a period and an extension that indicates the type of organization, such as microsoft.com. The name can be any combination of A-Z letters, 0-9 numerals, and the hyphen (-) plus the period (.) character used as a separator. This DNS Domain Name is used with the host name to create a fully qualified domain name (FQDN) for the computer. The FQDN is the host name followed by a period (.) followed by the domain name. For example, this could be **mis050.mis.umbc.edu**, where mis050 is the host name and mis.umbc.edu is the domain name. During DNS queries, the local domain name is appended to short names. Notice that a DNS domain is not the same as a Windows NT or LAN Manager domain.

5. In the Domain Name System (DNS) Search Order box, type the IP address of the DNS server that will provide name resolution. Then click

on the **Add** button to move the IP address to the list on the right. The
network administrator should provide the correct values for this parameter. You can add up to three IP addresses for DNS servers. The servers
running DNS will be queried in the order listed. To change the order of
the IP addresses, select an IP address to move, and then use the up- and
down-arrow buttons. To remove an IP address, select it and click on the
Remove button.

6. In the Domain Suffix Search Order box, type the domain suffixes to add
   to your domain suffix search list, and then click on the **Add** button. This
   list specifies the DNS domain suffixes to be appended to host names
   during name resolution. You can add up to six domain suffixes. To
   change the search order of the domain suffixes, select a domain name to
   move, and use the up- and down-arrow buttons. To remove a domain
   name, select it and click on the **Remove** button.

7. When you are done setting DNS options, click on the **OK** button.

8. When the TCP/IP Configuration dialog box reappears, click on the **OK**
   button. When the Network Settings dialog box reappears, click on the
   OK button. The settings take effect after you restart the computer.

Configuring Advanced TCP/IP Options

If your computer has multiple network adapters connected to different
networks using TCP/IP, you can click on the **Advanced** button in the TCP/IP
Configuration dialog box to configure options for the adapters or to configure
alternate default gateways.

To configure or reconfigure advanced TCP/IP options:

1. Start the Network option in Control Panel to display the Network
   Settings dialog box (Figure 2.8). In the Installed Network Software list
   box, select TCP/IP Protocol and click on the **Configure** button.

2. In the TCP/IP Configuration dialog box (Figure 2.12), click on the
   Advanced button.

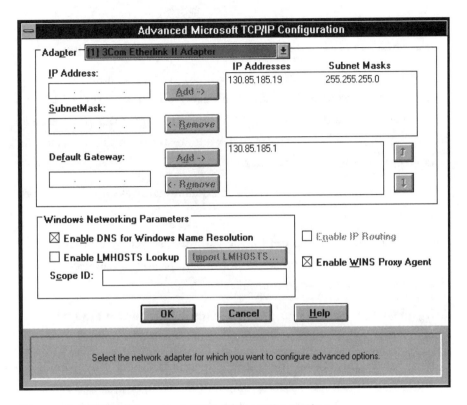

Figure 2.14 NT Advanced TCP/IP configuration.

3. In the Adapter box of the Advanced Microsoft TCP/IP Configuration dialog box (Figure 2.14), select the network adapter for which you want to specify advanced configuration values. The IP address and default gateway settings in this dialog box are defined only for the selected network adapter.

4. In the IP Address and SubnetMasks boxes, type an additional IP address and subnet mask for the selected adapter. Then click on the **Add** button to move the IP address to the list on the right. The network administrator should provide the correct values for this parameter.

Optimally, if your network card uses multiple IP addresses, repeat this procedure for each additional IP address. You can specify up to five additional IP addresses and subnet masks for identifying the selected network adapter. This facility can be useful for a computer connected to one physical network that includes multiple logical IP networks.

5. In the Default Gateway box, type the IP address for an additional gateway that the selected adapter can use. Then click on the **Add** button to move the IP address to the list on the right. Repeat this procedure for each additional gateway. The network administrator should provide the correct values for this parameter.

   This list specifies up to five additional default gateways for the network adapter selected.

   To change the priority order for the gateways, select an address to move and use the up- and down-arrow buttons. To remove a gateway, select it and click on the **Remove** button.

6. If you want to use DNS for DNS name resolution on Windows networks, check the Enable DNS for Windows Name Resolution option.

   If you check this option, the system finds the DNS server by using the IP address specified in the DNS Configuration dialog box, as described earlier in this chapter. Checking this option enables DNS name resolution for use by Windows networking applications.

7. If you want to use the LMHOSTS file for NetBIOS name resolution on Windows networks, check the Enable LMHOSTS Lookup option. If you already have a configured LMHOSTS file, click on the **Import LMHOSTS** button and specify the directory path for the LMHOSTS file you want to use. By default, Windows NT uses the LMHOSTS file found in **\systemroot\SYSTEM32\DRIVERS\ETC**.

   For any method of name resolution used in a Windows NT network, the LMHOSTS file is consulted last after querying WINS or using broadcasts, but before consulting DNS.

8. In the Scope ID box, type the computer's scope identifier, if required on an internetwork that uses NetBIOS over TCP/IP. Leave this box blank, unless told otherwise by your network administrator.

To communicate with each other, all computers on a TCP/IP internetwork must have the same scope ID. Usually this value is left blank. A
scope ID may be assigned to a group of computers that will communicate only with each other and no other systems. Such computers can
find each other if their scope Ids are identical. Scope Ids are used only
for communication based on NetBIOS over TCP/IP.

The network administrator should provide the correct value, if required.

9. To turn on static IP routing, check the Enable IP Routing option. This
   option allows this computer to participate with other static routers on a
   network. Check this option if you have two or more network cards and
   your network uses static routing, which also requires adding static
   routing tables.

10. If you want this computer to be used to resolve names based on the
    WINS database, check the Enable WINS Proxy Agent option.

    This option allows the computer to answer name queries for remote
    computers, so that other computers configured for broadcast name reso-
    lution can benefit from the name-resolution services provided by a
    WINS server.

    This option is available only if you entered a value for a primary WINS
    server in the TCP/IP Configuration dialog box, as described in
    Configuring TCP/IP earlier in this chapter. The proxy agent cannot,
    however, be run on a computer that is also a WINS server.

    Consult with the network administrator to determine whether your
    computer should be configured as a WINS proxy agent, because only a
    few computers on each subnetwork should be configured for this
    feature.

11. When you are done setting advanced options, click on the **OK**
    button. When the TCP/IP Configuration dialog box reappears, click
    on the **OK** button. When the Network Settings dialog box reappears,
    click on the **OK** button to complete advanced TCP/IP configuration

    You must restart the computer for the changes to take effect.

Server Application: Background and Concepts

Normally, when we think of protocols we envision such intricacies as how packets are assembled, moved around on the network, and reassembled, and how these activities are surrounded by myriad technical details and issues. Another level of protocols describe exchanges between application programs, which generally run under the client-server model. In this chapter I cover the essentials of the protocols (e.g., Gopher, HTTP) so that you will understand how clients and servers interact over the Internet. We'll also review the fundamental issues and concepts that you need to understand for the actual installation and configuration of servers, covered in subsequent chapters.

The Internet Gopher

Before we had the World Wide Web (WWW), perhaps the simplest and most widely accepted Internet tool for discovering information was the Internet Gopher, usually referred to merely as Gopher. Originally developed in 1991 as a CWIS (campus-wide information system) at the University of Minnesota, Gopher has evolved into a client-server system providing distributed information delivery with a worldwide reach. Gopher is based on the concept of a hierarchical menu system, as shown in Figure 3.1. When you first make a connection to a Gopher server you are presented a top-level menu. From there

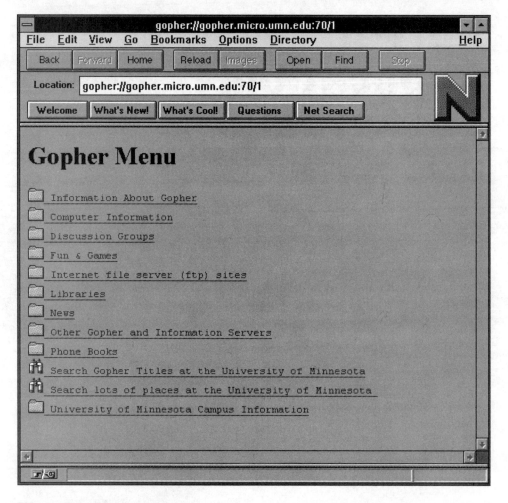

Figure 3.1 Gopher menu.

you can descend to submenus, down many levels into the gopher hole or burrow. With a sister product known as Veronica (Very Easy Rodent-Oriented Netwide Index to Computerized Archives), you can also locate information by keyword.

The Gopher Protocol

Although many of us have been frequent users of Gopher clients, when we venture into the world of building servers we quickly find that it helps to understand the underlying Gopher protocol. Internet RFC 1436 describes that basic protocol and reviews how to implement new client and server applications.

From our experience with Gopher we know that documents can reside on many servers all over the world. We also understand that Gopher clients, much like a file system, present users with a hierarchy of items and directories. When a client queries the server, the Gopher server returns either directory lists or documents. Each item in a directory is identified by a type (the kind of object the item is—see Gopher Item Type Characters, below), a user display string (a menu-item description used to browse and select from listings), a selector string (typically including a pathname with which the destination host locates the desired object), a host name (which host to contact to obtain this item), and an IP port number (the port at which the server process listens for connections). The user sees only the user display string. The client software can locate and retrieve any item by combining selector, host name, and port.

Gopher Item Type Characters

The client software decides what items are available by looking at the first character of each line in a directory listing. Here is a list of defined item type characters:

0   Item is a file.

1   Item is a directory.

2   Item is a CSO phone-book server.

3   Error.

4   BinHexed Macintosh file.

5   DOS binary archive.

6   UNIX uuencoded file.

7   Index-Search server.

8   Text-based Telnet session.

9   Binary file.

+   Redundant server.

s   Sound type.

M   MIME type.

h   HTML type.

T   Item points to a text-based tn3270 session.

g   GIF format graphics file.

I   Image file (sound, video). Client decides how to display.

i   Inline text type.

An example of how these file types are used is shown below.

Gopher Links

You can set up links on your server that allow you to point to and connect to
other servers. You can then not only give your clients access to information on
your server, but also provide seamless connections or *links* to other servers. To
make a link, create a file according to the information provided with each of
the Gopher Server implementations described in subsequent chapters. Here is
an example of a link:

```
Name=Gopher.FAQ
Type=0
Port=70
Path=0/Gopher.FAQ
Host=mudhoney.micro.umn.edu
```

Name is what the user will see at the menu, or Directory Title, level.

Type defines the kind of document the object is (e.g., 0 = text file,
     1 = directory).

Port specifies the server port used for Gopher (default 70).

Path includes the selector string that is used to retrieve the document.

Host specifies the fully qualified domain name where the information resides.

Numb (optional) specifies where in the menu this item will be listed on the menu (instead of being alphabetized).

Gopher: A Connectionless Protocol

The Gopher protocol is often described as *connectionless*. Many of us have cleverly used the world-tour analogy in Gopher demonstrations, visiting around the globe, knowing full well that we never really connected to a host (as in the traditional host terminal metaphor). In reality, the client sends a server a selector string and the server responds with a block of text terminated by a period on a line by itself, and closes the connection. No state is maintained by the server during communications with clients. One of the principles in the protocol design is that the protocol should be simple, quick, and efficient, because many of the servers and clients are small desktop machines.

The following information describes an elementary client server interaction and illustrates how the protocol functions (a tab is represented by the + symbol below):

Client: Opens a connection to **pokey.mis.umbc.edu** on port 70.

Server: Accepts the connection and waits.

Client: Sends an empty line followed by <CR><LF>, which, in effect, asks for the first menu.

Server: Sends a series of lines, each ending with <CR><LF>, which the client interprets and displays:

```
0About This Server Gopher:+About Server+pokey.mis.umbc.edu+70
0Campus Information+Campus/+umbc2.umbc.edu+70
0Registration Information+Registrar/+mis003.mis.umbc.edu+70
                   (Period on a line by itself)
                   (Server closes connection)
```

The first character on each line tells the type of object the line describes. It can be a document, directory, search service, or any of the other objects described above. Based on the Gopher type of object (first character), the Gopher client will give users some idea about the type of item this is (by displaying an icon, a folder icon on HGopher, a short text tag, or the like). The characters that follow up to the tab (represented above as a +), form a user display string to be shown to the user for use in selecting this document (or directory) for retrieval. The characters following the tab, up to the next tab, form a selector string that the client must send to the server to retrieve the document (or directory listing). The selector string is often a pathname or other file selector with which the server locates the item desired. The next two tab-delimited fields denote the domain name of the host that has this document (or directory), and the port at which to connect. If still other tab-delimited fields remain, the basic Gopher client should ignore them. A <CR><LF> denotes the end of the item.

In the example above, line one describes a document that the user will see displayed as About This Server. To retrieve this document the client will send the selector string: Gopher:About Server to **pokey.mis.umbc.edu** at port 70. The server will then respond with the content of the document, terminated by a period on a line by itself.

Now, suppose the user selects the line "Campus Information." This line is a directory reference, and so the user will see a listing of the directory she requested. These lines illustrate the client server interaction:

Client: (Connects to **umbc2.umbc.edu** at port 70).

Server: (Accepts connection but says nothing).

Client: Campus/ (Sends the selector string terminated by <CR><LF>).

Server: (Sends a series of lines, each ending with <CR><LF>).

```
0About the Campus Campus/AboutCampus umbc2.umbc.edu 70
0Campus Events Campus/Events umbc2.umbc.edu 70

  (more lines from the directory)
. (Period on a line by itself)
        (Server closes connection)
```

For each type code returned, a client will give the user some indication of the file type. In character-based displays a directory will be followed by a /, and on a Windows client such as Hgopher, a folder icon will be shown. Through helper applications, files may be processed further while arriving at the client, as in the transfer of a ZIPped file (type 9) being turned over to another application for unzipping.

Gopher+

The Gopher+ protocol is the basic Gopher protocol plus a set of enhancements to the syntax, semantics, and functionality of the original Gopher protocol. Servers and clients understanding the Gopher+ extensions will transmit extra information at the ends of list and request lines. Old, basic gopher clients ignore such information. New Gopher+ aware servers continue to work at their old level with unenhanced clients. With the extra information that can be communicated by Gopher+, clients may summon new capabilities augmenting some features of the original Gopher protocol.

Gopher+ enhancements rely on transmitting "extra" tab-delimited fields beyond those regular (old) Gopher servers and clients now use. If most existing (old) clients were to encounter extra information beyond the port field in a list (directory), most would ignore it. Enhancements to the basic protocol include:

Information about Item Attributes

A primary enhancement for the basic Gopher protocol is the ability to associate information about an item such as size, alternative views, the administrator, or abstract with the item.

ASK Blocks

Ask blocks allow you to create a form. When a user selects that document, the form is presented to the user. When the user completes the form, the responses are fed back to the Gopher server for processing.

Gopher+ Pictures, Sounds, and Movies

Gopher+ handles pictures, movies, and sounds by defining three item types: : for bitmap images, ; for movies, and < for sounds.

Administering the Gopher Server

Dress for Success

As an information provider on the Internet you will be judged not only by the quality of information that you present, but by its organization, presentation, readability, grammar, and punctuation. Pay particular attention to how your information appears to the thousands (okay, hundreds) of people who may visit your server. Their impressions of your server will, in fact, be impressions of your organization. Therefore:

- Ask your best proofreader, friendly neighborhood copy editor, or the like to review your text.

- Always test what you put into production. Go to your nearest client(s) and see what others will see, *before* others see. Be sure to view your information from several browsers (e.g., Macintosh, MS Windows, Xwindows, character-based). You can then catch problems or mistakes before they go live.

- Properly care for and feed the server beast. Make sure it has adequate power and anything else it needs. If the server is down or the connection is flaky, clients will be disenchanted with your service. Putting up a server requires that you properly attend to its administration, and that includes attending to such operational issues as environment, security, and performance.

About This Server

When you build your Gopher server, a document called something like "About the Ajax Corporation's Gopher Server" should be the first item in the server's top-level directory. This document should briefly describe what the server holds and list name, address, phone, and an e-mail address of the person who administers the server. The public needs this contact point for suggestions and comments. The best way to decide how and what you'll display is to visit many Gopher servers and see what the Best in Burrow have done. Then take some of these ideas and fashion your information in a style and format something like theirs.

Time-Sensitive Material

Gopher administrators should place the date of last update in files that are time-sensitive. Your organization's latest price list, schedule of events, and documents outlining employee policy are all time-sensitive materials.

User Display Strings

When you create a user display string in other words, a Gopher Directory Title fashion clear and concise titles. Your list will be displayed to your viewing public and will also be retrieved in Veronica searches. Make your title clear, concise, and descriptive and clients viewing your titles will get what they thought they'd find under the menu item.

All the Gopher Servers in the World

Once you have your Gopher server up and running you can have it listed as one of the world's Gopher servers. Send mail to **gopher@ebone.net** if your server is in Europe, and for all others to **gopher@boombox.micro.umn.edu.** In your mail message include this information:

- The name of your server (as you would like it to appear on Gopher menus).

- The fully qualified host name.

- The port number (by default, 70).

- An administrative contact person and his or her e-mail address.

- The location (country, state) of the server.

- Whether or not you are running a Gopher+ server.

- A selector string (optional) that will effectively serve as a path for people to access the server at some level other than its root.

The World Wide Web (WWW)

The World Wide Web project originated and is supported by CERN, the European Laboratory for Particle Physics. The Web is a distributed hypermedia system based on the client-server model. The end user runs a client program called a *browser*, such as Mosaic, which communicates with a server program (WWW) running on a host computer. And, like Gopher servers, the Web server's protocol, HTTP, is connectionless, meaning it does without an interactive logon when using the client software. The client program sends a user request to the server; the server handles the request, sends a response to the user, and closes the connection.

The Web appears to a user as a document with highlighted links to other documents and types of media (e.g., images, sound, and movies). Selecting with a mouse the highlighted words within a WWW document causes other documents to be opened, regardless of where on the Internet they reside. Figure 3.2 is a view of a Web server through the Netscape client browser.

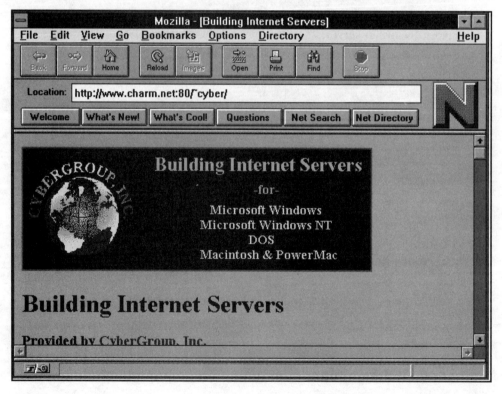

Figure 3.2 World Wide Web via Netscape.

Through the WWW interface you can reach and effectively act as a native client with:

- Gopher servers.

- WAIS servers.

- FTP servers.

- Usenet newsgroups.

- Telnet sites.

- Hytelnet resources.

- Various hypertext documents.

- . . . and more.

To access a Web server you need a browser, a Web client, in other words. The browsers can access Web servers and can also access files via FTP, NNTP (Network News Transport Protocol), Gopher, and various other methods. A number of browsers are available that span many operating environments, but those which especially interest us are the ones for Microsoft Windows. The browser that originally received most fanfare (and justifiably so) is NCSA Mosaic, which is available via FTP from the National Center for Supercomputing Applications (NCSA). Before you try Mosaic you may want to get some experience with the Web itself by accessing it via a Telnet connection. A number of character-mode browsers require no more than a VT100 connection. You can therefore connect to any or all sites below and use the basic Web without benefit of a graphically based product like Mosaic. Table 3.1 shows some WWW browsers that are available via Telnet.

Table 3.1 WWW Browsers Available via Telnet		
Site	Location	Login as:
ukanaix.cc.ukans.edu	U.S.	www
www.njit.edu	U.S.	www
vms.huji.ac.il	Israel	www

WWW Concepts and Terminology

As you work with the World Wide Web, you'll be introduced to several new names and acronyms. Here's a primer that will help you understand the essential WWW concepts. You will get much more familiar with these concepts as we work with the Microsoft Windows 3.1 and Windows NT World Wide Web Servers.

Hypertext Transfer Protocol (HTTP)

HTTP is a protocol with the lightness and speed necessary for a distributed collaborative hypermedia information system. It is a generic stateless object-oriented protocol, which may be used for many similar tasks such as name servers, and distributed object-oriented systems, by extending the commands, or methods used.

This definition is excerpted from the Internet Draft on HTTP. A lighter definition would explain HTTP as the client-server protocol used as the foundation for the World Wide Web. When dealing with Web clients, the HTTP server handles the client's request for information via the URL (see below) and negotiates the request. When it receives a request for a Home Page, the server will locate the HTML document and transfer the commands embedded in the document to display the file at the client.

Hypertext

Hypertext is textual material with pointers to other text. By activating the pointers (e.g., by clicking) you are presented with the supporting text.

Hypermedia

Hypermedia is an extension of hypertext. Hypermedia points not only to other text, but to other forms of information, including images, sound, and animation. The World Wide Web and many of its browsers support hypermedia.

Uniform Resource Locator (URL)

URLs are pointers to objects on the Internet. Examples are files, newsgroups, gopher servers, and Telnet sites. Consider a URL a worldwide extension of a file system on a local computer. Not only can this path or URL point to a local resource, but it can point to resources on distant machines. For more information on URLs, load this URL through a Netscape or Mosaic client:

```
http://www.ncsa.uiuc.edu/demoweb/url-primer.html
```

URLs have a prefix that indicates the retrieval method to use, such as FTP, Gopher, and of course HTTP. The rest of the URL is a pathname to your desired document.

Hypertext Markup Language (HTML)

Documents residing on World Wide Web servers are written in HTML, which is a simple SGML-like markup language (for more detail on SGML, see ISO 8879). HTML uses tags to indicate formatting commands. A tag, in HTML, is a left bracket (<) followed by a directive and zero or more parameters followed by a right bracket (>). An HTML document can include graphics, text, sound, video, and of course links to other HTML documents on other servers. A number of books on the market cover HTML programming in depth. Perhaps the most current and comprehensive information on HTML can be found on the World Wide Web. For a tutorial introduction to HTML, load this URL on your Netscape client:

```
http://www.ncsa.uiuc.edu/demoweb/html-primer.html
```

For reference information on HTML that includes HTML basic concepts and style pointers, see these sources:

```
http://info.cern.ch/hypertext/WWW/MarkUp/MarkUp.html
http://info.cern.ch/hypertext/WWW/MarkUp/HTML.html
http://www.ncsa.uiuc.edu/General/Internet/WWW/HTMLQuickRef.html
http://www.willamette.edu/html-composition/strict-html.html
http://www.pcweek.ziff.com/~eamonn/crash_course.html
http://oneworld.wa.com/htmldev/devpage/dev-page.html
http://www.vuw.ac.nz/who/Nathan.Torkington/ideas/www-html.html
```

Once you've had a chance to use and practice your HTML, you can move on to more advanced concepts like CGI programming, hypertext forms, and database access. The best source for advanced HTML programming is Cyberweb Software. The Cyberweb pages include plenty of tips and links to valuable Web-building resources. And if you get stuck, you can Ask Dr. Web your most puzzling HTML programming questions. Visit:

```
http://www.stars.com
```

Some Essential Web Concepts

Some fundamental concepts are found in most implementations of HTTP. These include security, MIME typing, directory indexing, error and access logs, supporting utilities, and the Common Gateway Interface (CGI), to name just a few. I explain these concepts here for a number of reasons, including:

- To appreciate the value of a given Web server you will need to measure it against various basic features. And to appreciate and understand these features, you will need to understand Web security, logging, and the like. Not all server implementations are fully featured. You will need to determine which features are important to your installation and how and if they are implemented in a server package. Then you will be able to determine which server implementation is best suited to your site.

- With graphically based server administration tools now at your service, you will have less of an opportunity to play with the low-level configuration files (if that should in fact be considered an opportunity). For example, many configuration parameters may be stored in an .INI file, but your configuration choices may be through a dialog box listing checkable options. Therefore, it is worth our while to take a moment and examine some of the underlying concepts (and files) found on most Web servers. The relationship between the Microsoft Windows 3.1 and NT interface with the underlying file system is depicted in Figure 3.3. The graphical interface is just that, an interface with which you can manipulate parameters that may be stored in .INI files, .CNF files, or the NT registry, depending upon implementation.

- If you flip to a particular implementation immediately upon completing this chapter, such as the Windows 3.1 Windows Web server, WHTTPd, you will understand the fundamental concepts and they won't have to be repeated for the WHTTPd implementation, or any other.

How HTTP Works

An essential Web concept to understand is how HTTP works. To get a hands-on rather than theoretical grasp, one way is to emulate a client. If you initiate a

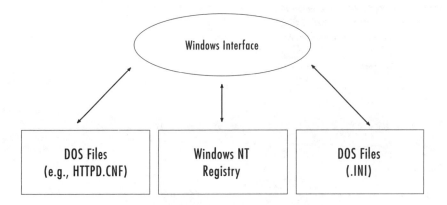

Figure 3.3 Windows Configuration Interface.

Telnet session and send to a server a GET request (the primary request command from a Web client) you'll see at first hand how the server responds. Try the example listed below.

In this example, we are sitting at the **cyber@CHARM.NET:>** prompt on a UNIX shell account and we type **telnet** to start the Telnet program. Next we pick a known Web server and execute the Telnet **Open** command, designating the server's Fully Qualified Domain Name (FQDN) and port 80, which is the default port where the server listens for HTTP connections. The message **trying 130.85.185.32...** appears, followed by **Connected to gumby.mis.umbc.edu**. The server accepted your connection and is waiting for your browser (that's you) to issue a command. You type **GET** and depress the **Enter** key twice and the server sends you the default home page because you did not specify a file. After it pumps the file down the line, it closes the connection. It's that simple!

```
cyber@CHARM.NET:> telnet
telnet> open gumby.mis.umbc.edu 80
Trying 130.85.185.32...
Connected to gumby.mis.umbc.edu.
Escape character is '^]'.
GET
```

```
<title>New MacHTTP Home Page</title>
<h1><simg src="Images/machttp.gif">Welcome to this MacHTTP Server!</h1>
This is the default home page for your server, contained in the file
"Index.html".
Put your welcome info here!<br>

<hr>

[... much more html deleted for the sake of brevity in this example...]

Connection closed by foreign host.
cyber@CHARM.NET:>
```

Directory Indexing

As you have just seen, when a client browser opens a URL on your server, a directory mapping takes place. If we consider the simple URL: http://host.site.com, the server will return the contents of a default index file called index.htm (or .html if you are not restricted to an 8.3 filename as in FAT file systems). This file is located in a directory most commonly known as the DocumentRoot (depending upon implementation it may be called the data directory). If no index.html file is available the server will generate a directory index (Figure 3.4) that resembles a gopher for FTP directory list. The DocumentRoot in the standard Windows 3.1 WinHTTPd implementation is located at C:\HTTPD\HTDOCS, and so one can say that the server's document-root directory is C:\HTTPD\HTDOCS. When one opens a URL to http://host.site.com, the directory C:\HTTPD\HTDOCS is searched for a file named INDEX.HTM. If found, it is served to the browser; if not, a directory index is created and served.

Notice that the default index file may have a different designation on some implementations, such as default.htm or home.htm. We won't worry about where these parameters are configured; that's for later chapters. If you wish to designate a file other than index.htm as the default index file, you can. You may also not wish to let people browse directories, generating directory lists on the fly. For the entire server or for designated directories, you can mark directories for no browsing.

If in fact you do allow browsing, you can create rather attractive directory lists, complete with custom icons, mapped to specific file types, and accompanied by descriptive text. Again, see the example in Figure 3.4. This technique is

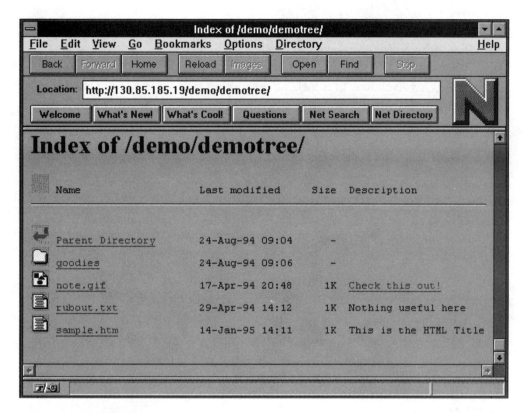

Figure 3.4 Directory index.

often referred to as *Fancy Indexing*. For the moment we'll consider only some
of the more important options and parameters. Remember, not all features are
available on every server. The discussion here covers a range of important
features that are implemented on most WWW servers, which are detailed in
later chapters.

Aliased Directories

While we're on the subject of directory mapping, consider the topic of *virtual*,
or *aliased* directories. If the server finds a defined alias in a URL, it will map to
the defined directory. A frequent example is using an icon directory to house
all your .GIF files. The mapping of the alias to the DOS directory would look
like this, for example:

```
Alias     /icons/  C:/HTTPD/ICONS/
```

If someone requested /icons/warning.gif, the server would return

```
C:\HTTPD\ICONS\WARNING.GIF.
```

Port Numbers

As previously explained, we have the well-known ports concept in TCP/IP and the default port for HTTP is 80. The minimal URL, http://host.site.com defaults to port 80. If you choose to run HTTP on another port you will then need to include the port in the URL. An example would be: http://host.site.com:8001.

Log Files

Most servers generate useful log files so that you can troubleshoot errors, maintain an audit trail of requests, and produce statistics on the server's performance. Access logs track each request for a file and can be analyzed to let you know which of your pages are popular, who is looking at them, and when. The log file record generally includes the host from which the request originated, the date and time of the request, the type of request (e.g., **GET**), a status code, and the number of bytes transferred. Most implementations of HTTP servers generate a common log format, as just described, providing a great deal of flexibility in processing your log files, because many utilities are available to process your files if they conform to this common format. And utilities are also available (although fewer) for log files not conforming to the common format.

Utilities

Supporting utilities is one area in which we will see tremendous advantages for system administration and overall organizational benefit. Utilities for analyzing log files that generate attractive charts and graphs are readily available. Easily configurable Windows-based utilities that provide automatic e-mail response, guestbooks, order forms, and customer-feedback mechanisms are arriving in the server marketplace. Hooks to back-end databases currently can be programmed with minimal knowledge of languages like Visual Basic, and are becoming even easier, requiring no programming because public-domain and commercial utilities are becoming readily available. Here, Windows 3.1 and Windows NT servers probably will distinguish themselves from their UNIX counterparts. We will find a wealth of public-domain and commercial utilities, either packaged with the product or as add-ons, extending the server's functionality to remarkable limits. In the very near future we'll see complete, turnkey office systems connected to the Internet that take orders through browsers, retrieve product information from back-end databases, and update customer information, all through the Web server model, complemented by a full suite of integrated utilities.

Controlling Access

It is unfortunate, and very much a fact of life, that as soon as you announce your server, someone will try to crack it. If you wish to restrict access to some or all the pages on your server to some or all of the world's population, you will need to think about Web security and access control. Security for your server and its documents can be administered at various levels. With careful planning and configuration you can provide adequate security for your server. Security can be configured at various levels, including globally (who can access my server), by directory (who can access a directory), and by file. You can also authenticate users by user name and password.

Global Server Security

You can control access to your server with configuration parameters in a server access configuration file that will either allow or deny access to specific hosts or groups of hosts. You specify the IP address of the hosts you wish to allow or restrict. Generally, the default configuration of the server allows unrestricted access and a configuration file holds a reference to the document-root directory and a fairly understandable statement like *allow from all*. Not only can you specify restrictions on the document root, but you may indicate other directories carrying restrictions in the access configuration file.

Directory Security

Security of directories can be configured through a server access configuration file or at the individual directory level. The UNIX convention for this directory security file is a file named .htaccess by default. Likewise, for example, with the WinHTTPd server the file is called #haccess.ctl. Within this file you may specify restrictions with the **allow** and **deny** commands. Again, you would specify the IP addresses of hosts or masks of groups of hosts you wish to restrict.

File Security

You can configure security for individual files on some server implementations, but not on all. On some servers one method for providing file-level security is to put the file requiring restrictions in a directory of its own. On other servers, this step is unnecessary and the file can be individually configured for protection.

Authenticating Users

You can set up names and passwords of individual users so that authentication will be required when someone tries to access a directory or file. Keep in mind that this user name and password almost never correspond to individual accounts on the system. This method for authenticating the user's name and password is at the server application level without hooks to operating-system accounts. The password information is generated by an accompanying user-name/password program (such as htpasswd.exe), and the password is stored in encrypted form. The browser that accesses these protected directories must be capable of handling authentication. Figure 3.5 shows Netscape in an authentication sequence. Be sure to remember that passwords are stored on the server in encrypted form, but travel the network in unencrypted form. The format used for transmitting the username/password pair is uuencoding, the same as Telnet-based connections.

MIME Typing

MIME (Multipurpose Internet Mail Extensions) is a standardized method for organizing file formats. The files are organized according to each file's MIME type. When Netscape software retrieves a file from a server, the server provides the MIME type of the file. Netscape uses that type to establish whether the file format can be read by the software's built-in capabilities or, if not, whether a suitable helper application is available to read the file.

Figure 3.5 Authenticating users via Netscape.

For servers that do not provide a MIME type with a file, Netscape interprets the file's extension (a suffix appended to a file name). For example, the .html extension in the file name welcome.html suggests a file in the HTML format. Likewise, a .zip extension suggests a compressed file, an .rtf extension suggests a file in the Rich Text Format, and so on. With most Web browsers you can use a preferences or options menu choice to view and configure the mapping of all MIME types to helper applications.

Image Maps

One useful way to depict your information on a Web server is with clickable *image maps*, which can be traditional cartographic representations such as a map of the United States. Once the map is displayed, you can click on a state and link to an HTML file that displays interesting information about that state. The clickable image technique has numerous applications beyond cartography.

To create an image map, you have to do a number of things:

- Create or acquire a graphical image that will be your map.

- Determine which areas will be defined as *hotspots*.

- Identify URLs to be associated with the hotspots.

- Identify the image-map file for the server.

- Create an HTML document with the image map.

- Creating image maps is somewhat tedious if you do it by hand. Tools such as Mapedit streamline the mapmaking. We cover in a later chapter specific details about creating image maps.

Common Gateway Interface (CGI)

You may want to make some resources on your server available to others through the World Wide Web. These could be files in formats other than HTML or from back-end databases. This information can be accessed via gateways that you develop or acquire in the form of executable programs. The Common Gateway Interface (CGI) is a means for connecting your Web server to these gateway programs.

The gateway program can be written in various languages and batch files, including products as diverse as the DOS shell to Visual Basic and Perl. In fact, a gateway can be constructed with just about anything that can create an executable program. One of the more useful languages for developing back-end applications is Microsoft Visual Basic, which supports many features for accessing data in the Windows environment, such as OLE, DDE, Sockets, and ODBC. Of course, ODBC permits accessing data in various databases.

File Transfer Protocol (FTP)

The most prolific application in network traffic, FTP, puts the largest number of packets out on the Internet. The application protocol's basic function is to copy files from one machine to another. For a thorough definition and examination of the FTP protocol, refer to RFC 959. The sample FTP session in the Appendix shows you how to retrieve RFCs. As you will see, the FTP character-based interface is laden with rather cryptic commands. By comparison, the sample Windows-based FTP client session shown in Figure 3.6 is significantly easier to use and requires no understanding of FTP's cryptic syntax. Of course with FTP you need a client machine running FTP as well as a server running an FTP server process from which you wish to retrieve files. You will also need some knowledge about directory structure so that you can locate your chosen file. You have several ways of locating interesting and useful files: you might see a reference in a book or journal article, or learn of a file from a friend. To connect to a server, you identify the host, either with a host name (such as ftp.novell.com) or via a numeric address (such as **130.85.185.98**). Once connected, you will be asked to supply a user name and password.

In most circumstances you can use a name that closely parallels the guest account, the user name *anonymous*. This name is referred to as *anonymous FTP* and will give you read access to files that are made available for general distribution from the server. Once you provide the anonymous user name, you will be prompted for a password. Enter your full e-mail address as the password. For example, **john@ajax.com**. Many servers will not check the mail address for validity, but some will validate the domain name provided with the address from which you are connecting.

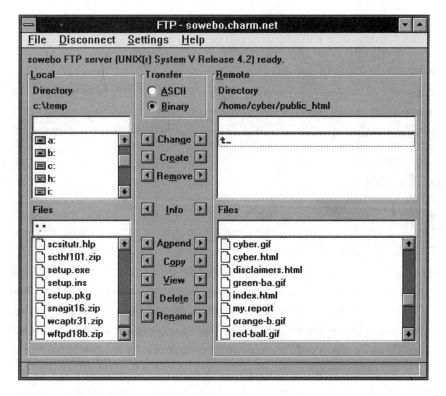

Figure 3.6 Windows FTP client.

Here are several general considerations from the server perspective that you will need for administering the system.

Multiple Logins

Give due consideration to the size of your machine and the maximum number of logins you will allow. With each of the implementations described later, this is a configurable option.

Security

You will need to amply plan your configuration of security options. Many servers offer configurable user-password lists, user-directory restrictions, and logging to a file. You will have to decide whether you will allow anonymous access to your server and also which parts of your server's directory structure you will make accessible, and to whom it will be accessible. On some server implementations you can also control who is allowed or denied access to your server. You can allow access to specific sites and therefore negate access by all others, or you can deny specific sites and permit others to log in.

Messages

Some FTP server implementations offer easily configurable greetings and informational messages at the directory level. These aids, when used properly, can go a long way in assisting the user in navigating your server while retrieving files.

Finger Server

Finger, as defined in RFC1288, is used to retrieve information about users on both local and remote systems. The Finger client opens a connection to a specified machine and sends a simple one-line query to the Finger server. The server reads the query, generates a response (see Figure 3.7), and closes the TCP/IP connection. The Finger command can tell you who is logged in on local and remote machines, together with information about each user, including the user's real name, when they logged in, and so on. If you identify a specific user, as in **finger john@ajax.com,** more detailed information is revealed, including the user's home directory, the UNIX shell they use, and a plan file, if they have one. You can set up the *plan* file with any information that you would like presented to the client when someone fingers you. Plan files carry all sorts of information, serving the purpose of billboards, bumper stickers, and other media of communication.

Under its normal operation, Finger can present security problems. Because Finger provides information valuable to crackers (those who wish to crack or break into your system), many sites have disabled the Finger server. Finger gives the cracker information with which to begin to direct an attack, including user names, directory information, and information about inactive accounts. For this reason some sites disable Finger or restrict its use.

Wide Area Information Server (WAIS)

WAIS (pronounced ways) is a networked information-retrieval system developed jointly by Thinking Machines, Dow Jones, Apple, and KPMG Peat Marwick. The principle behind it is that WAIS clients can retrieve text or multi-

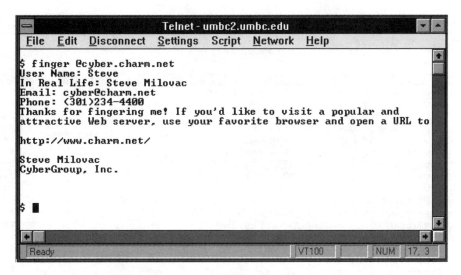

Figure 3.7 Finger.

media documents stored on WAIS servers. The client uses *keywords* or *search terms*. The servers then search a full-text index for the documents and return a list of documents that include the keyword. The client can further request the full text of any document found. This communication between client and server takes place using the Z39.50 protocol.

Before you delve into WAIS by setting up a server, you may want to try it out, which you can do using Telnet and connecting to one of the sites listed below. Then you can use a character-based version of WAIS to become familiar with the WAIS model (Figure 3.8). Table 3.2 shows where you can login to a WAIS Client.

Table 3.2 WAIS Clients	
WAIS Client	**Login as:**
quake.think.com	wais
sunsite.unc.edu	swais
wais.com	swais
info.funet.fi	swais

```
━                    Telnet - quake.think.com                    ▼
 Connect  Edit  Terminal  Help
SWAIS                     Source Selection              Sources: 549
  #           Server                    Source                  Cost
001:   [ wais.access.gpo.gov]  103_cong_bills                   Free
002:   [ wais.access.gpo.gov]  104_cong_bills                   Free
003:   [ wais.access.gpo.gov]  1992_cri                         Free
004:   [ wais.access.gpo.gov]  1993_cri                         Free
005:   [ wais.access.gpo.gov]  1994_cri                         Free
006:   [ wais.access.gpo.gov]  1994_hob                         Free
007:   [ wais.access.gpo.gov]  1994_record                      Free
008:   [ wais.access.gpo.gov]  1994_register                    Free
009:   [ wais.access.gpo.gov]  1994_unified_agenda              Free
010:   [ wais.access.gpo.gov]  1995_cri                         Free
011:   [ wais.access.gpo.gov]  1995_hob                         Free
012:   [ wais.access.gpo.gov]  1995_record                      Free
013:   [ wais.access.gpo.gov]  1995_register                    Free
014:   [ wais.access.gpo.gov]  1995_unified_agenda              Free
015:   [            archie.au]  aarnet-resource-guide           Free
016:   [ndadsb.gsfc.nasa.gov]  AAS_jobs                         Free
017:   [ndadsb.gsfc.nasa.gov]  AAS_meeting                      Free
018:   [       munin.ub2.lu.se]  academic_email_conf            Free

Keywords:

<space> selects, w for keywords, arrows move, <return> searches, q quits, or ?
```

Figure 3.8 WAIS client.

You can get further information on WAIS from these sources:

- A white paper on WAIS is available at
  ftp://ftp.think.com/wais/wais-corporate-paper.text.

- A good bibliography on WAIS can be found at:
  ftp://ftp.wais.com/pub/wais-inc-doc/bibliography.txt.

- The newsgroup, **comp.infosystems.wais,** is a good place to keep current and get your questions answered on-line.

- The United States Geological Survey has training videos on WAIS available at
  http://billings.nlm.nih.gov/current_news.dir/wais_tapes.html.

WAIS Operation

The Wide Area Information Server (WAIS) provides an easy and simple way for indexing large quantities of data on servers and making them available to clients. WAIS has three distinct components: clients, servers, and the protocol that handles communication between them. The client is the interface presented to the user, the server does the indexing and retrieval of documents, and the protocol is used to communicate between client and server.

WAIS, like many Internet tools, is fashioned on the client-server model. On the client side, search terms are formulated as English-language queries and the client application then uses the WAIS protocol and transmits the query over a network to a server. The server receives the query, translates the information received into its own query language, and searches for documents matching the query. The list of relevant documents is then transmitted back to the client. The client decodes the response and displays the list for the user. The documents can then be retrieved from the server in their entirety.

WAIS offers a number of features to those who wish to make information available on the Internet or on local networks:

Simple Client-Server Interface

The WAIS client is a user-interface program that sends requests for information to local or remote servers. A number of clients are available for the popular desktop platforms. A server implementation is available for Windows NT.

Full-Text and Image Retrieval

The system allows users to retrieve local, enterprise-wide, and wide-area text and images through one easy-to-use interface.

Relevance Feedback

The WAIS system uses English-language queries supplemented by relevance feedback. This feedback allows the user to mark documents that are interesting, and the system will then look for others with similar content.

An Open Protocol

A primary emphasis in the original WAIS architecture was to provide an open, publicly available protocol. The WAIS protocol, an extension of the existing Z39.50 standard from NISO, has been supplemented and now includes many requirements of a full-text retrieval system.

Communication over TCP/IP

The WAIS server can be located anywhere to which the client workstation has access: on a local machine, on a local network, or on some distant machine on the Internet. The user's workstation keeps track of varied information about each server.

Thinking Machines supports a directory-of-servers.src on its WAIS server and will list other servers that you can access. Additional information is available at:

```
ftp://think.com/public/wais
```

and

```
ftp://quake.think.com/pub/wais/wais-discussion/bibliography.txt
```

SMTP Mail

SMTP stands for Simple Mail Transfer Protocol and is defined in RFC 821. Its objective is to transfer mail reliably and efficiently between computers on the Internet. SMTP defines the interaction between mail systems to facilitate transfer of electronic mail even if the mail systems are not alike. This definition includes verification to ensure proper connection between mail servers, identification of message sender, negotiation of the set of recipients, and actual delivery of the message. The typical user, like you and me, doesn't generally deal at the level of an SMTP transaction. Instead, mail is exchanged and reconciled by servers, but we deal with delivered mail with graphically based mail clients.

An SMTP server offers you the opportunity to run a mail system on your PC. With SMTP you can send and receive e-mail messages to and from your PC; the PC acts as a mail server. You can also set up mailboxes on your PC for others within your organization.

POP3 Mail

POP3 stands for Post Office Protocol version 3 and is defined in Request for Comments RFC 1725. POP3 is intended to permit a user to easily access a mailbox on a server. The SMTP server has handled delivery of the mail and the POP3 server holds the mail for pickup by the individual client.

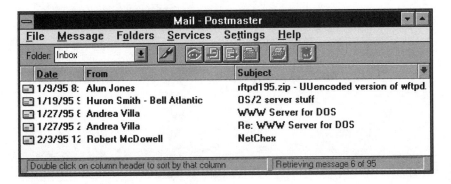

Figure 3.9 Windows mail client.

When the client contacts the POP3 server, the server will authenticate the user with a password prompt, and upon instructions from the client mail application, mail is transferred from the server mailbox to the client. You then have the advantage of using a graphically based mail client (Figure 3.9) instead of UNIX mail capabilities. Another feature is that mail can be deleted from the host after the mail transfer, freeing up space on the server. Just remember that if you wish to run a mail server, you'll have to run your server twenty-four hours a day because you never know when mail will arrive.

FTP Servers

You have undoubtedly had occasion to use File Transfer Protocol (FTP), either through a UNIX shell account or perhaps through a graphically based Windows client. You've probably retrieved a wealth of software from many sites, and even retrieved an Internet server package or two. Why, then, would you set up an FTP server?

Not all dissemination and distribution of information fits well with the Gopher or the Web models. Perhaps you have software that you wish to distribute to internal or external clients, but would like to leave that distribution up to the client side, allowing them to pick and choose from an archive or collection of files. Possibly your work involves producing written policies, procedures, brochures, price sheets, product specifications, and the like that need to be distributed to remote sites. Now, with the products covered in this chapter, you can make this information available for retrieval via FTP.

In this chapter a number of FTP servers are reviewed. Each has features and benefits that may address your individual requirements. These servers are:

- **WinQVT**. A shareware package that not only includes an FTP server, but provides a mail reader, Telnet client, and Usenet news reader. If you need a suite of client applications and an FTP server for casual use at an excellent price, this package is a good choice.

- **WFTPD**. This product offers significant features if you want a fully featured FTP server. The package includes security features, configurable greetings, and other benefits that match most Unix implementations.

- **SERV-U**. Like WFTPD, this shareware server allows you to enjoy sophisticated features on the Windows 3.1 platform.

- **Beame & Whiteside**. If you need a commercial product with a full complement of server applications, this software will be a good investment. The servers are easily configurable, run on the Beame & Whiteside TCP/IP stack, and utilize the Unix inetd paradigm.

- **Microsoft NT FTP**. If you're expecting high volume FTP activity, NT FTP offers both a solid operating system and an industrial strength FTP server. The major benefit of the NT FTP server is its tight integration with the NT operating system.

WinQVT/Net

WinQVT/Net is a suite of TCP/IP client and server applications for the Microsoft Windows environment, provided by QPC Software as a shareware product. Our immediate interest is in the FTP Server, but you may want to investigate the rcp server or the full complement of client applications.

The Windows Sockets version of WinQVT/Net can be retrieved from:

```
ftp://biochemistry.bioc.cwru.edu/gopher/pub/winqvt
```

The zipped file is QVTWS397.ZIP.

This version is written for Windows 3.1 and Windows for Workgroups. If you wish to run under Windows NT, use the 32-bit version, which is distributed in the archive qvtnt396.zip, available at **biochemistry.cwru.edu**. Because no TCP/IP transport is included, use the Trumpet Winsock package or any of the commercial Winsock packages, such as Chameleon.

WinQVT/Net Services

Services provided by WinQVT/Net include:

- **Telnet**. The WinQVT/Net Telnet client will support up to fifteen simultaneous terminal (Telnet or rlogin) sessions. The software also offers DEC VT52, VT102, and VT220 emulation.

- **File Transfer Protocol (FTP)**. The software includes an FTP client with which you can transfer files to and from your PC. Because the FTP application runs in a separate window, you can run terminal sessions at the same time.

- **FTP and rcp Servers**. WinQVT/Net includes an FTP server, which allows remote users to log on to your PC and transfer files using the FTP protocol, and an rcp server, which allows files to be copied to and from the PC from the remote user's UNIX command line.

- **Mail Client**. Electronic mail is supported with a POP3 client, which allows you to send and receive mail from your PC. WinQVT/Net also allows mail to be sent using the SMTP protocol.

- **Usenet News**. If you have access to an NNTP server, WinQVT/Net includes a news-reading and posting client.

- **Network Printing**. With WinQVT/Net's lpr module, you can print PC files on printers and plotters that are attached to remote network hosts.

Installing WinQVT/Net

WinQVT/Net should be installed from the DOS prompt, with Windows not running because changes must be made to the runtime environment (i.e., AUTOEXEC.BAT).

To install WinQVT/Net:

1. First, create a directory on your hard drive called C:\WINQVT.

2. Move all files from the ZIP file into the WINQVT directory except for VT220.FON, which should be moved to the \WINDOWS\SYSTEM directory.

3. Next, make sure that your PC is represented in the HOSTS file in the C:trumpet directory. Entries in hosts are of this form:

```
<IP address>           <host name>
...
<Your IP address>      <Your PC's host name>
...
```

4. Modify your AUTOEXEC.BAT to include this statement in that file:

```
set QVTHOST_DIR=C:\TRUMPET
```

Only the directory path name is used, not the entire file name. WinQVT/Net assumes that the name of the hosts file is hosts.

Note: If you omit QVTHOST_DIR, WinQVT/Net will assume that the hosts file is located in the Windows directory.

5. Reboot the PC to install the QVTHOST_DIR variable that was set up in the preceding step.

6. Start Windows.

7. Create a Program Manager icon for the WinQVT/Net icon. The two fields that you must fill in are command line and working directory. The command line field should be filled in with the complete pathname of the WinQVT/Net executable for example:

```
C:\WINQVT\wnqvtwsk.exe
```

The working directory field should be filled in with the name of the WinQVT/Net directory, for example:

```
C:\WINQVT
```

8. Start WinQVT/Net by clicking on the program icon. WinQVT/Net will start by presenting a small console window in the upper-right corner of

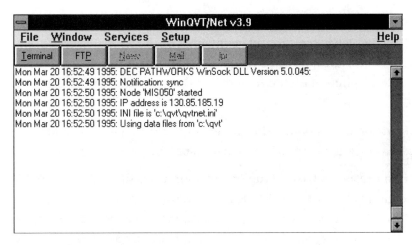

Figure 4.1 WinQVT console.

the screen (Figure 4.1). All the various application modules are started from the console.

If WinQVT/Net is unable to determine the local node name or IP address, the condition will be reported and the program will terminate. This condition can be corrected by making sure that your hosts file includes a reference for your PC, that the environment variable QVTHOST_DIR exists, and also that it points to the directory that includes the hosts file.

WinQVT/Net Support Files

WinQVT/Net uses these external configuration files:

QVTNET.INI	Main configuration for all applications.
QVTNET.RC	Alternate Terminal configurations.
QVTALIAS.RC	List of aliases for mail recipients.
QVTMAIL.SIG	Default signature file for mail messages.
NEWS.RC	List of subscribed Usenet newsgroups.
QVTNEWS.KIL	Kill file for news reader.
QVTNEWS.SIG	Default signature for news articles.
QVTNET.ACL	Access-control lists for FTP and rcp servers.
FTPSERV.HLO	Welcome message for FTP server.

The QVTNET.INI file is represented by a sample file in the distribution. Except for NEWS.RC, which is created and maintained by the News Reader application, you will create each file using an ASCII text editor (e.g., Notepad). A complete description of each is included in the software-distribution documentation.

All configuration files should reside in the same directory. This should be the Working Directory, as specified by Program Manager Properties dialog.

WinQVT/Net reads its basic setup information from the QVTNET.INI file. Constructing a valid QVTNET.INI file is critical to the proper functioning of WinQVT/Net. See the sample file for an explanation of the required setup parameters, as well as the optional ones that you can use to customize your environment.

The most important lines in QVTNET.INI are name= and ip=. Both statements are found in the [net] section of QVTNET.INI. Here is an example:

```
[net]
name=mypc
ip=198.17.243.184
...
```

Using WinQVT/Net Telnet

To start a Telnet session, simply press the **Terminal** button and wait for the Start Terminal Session dialog to appear. All host names defined in hosts will be shown in the left-hand listbox. The right-hand list box should have the sole entry, Default (unless you have already created a QVTNET.RC file, with some additional configurations).

To start the session, select a host from the Hosts list, and a configuration from the Configurations list, then press **OK**. WinQVT/Net will attempt to start a Telnet session on the selected host. As soon as a connection is made, a Terminal window will be displayed with the login prompt.

Using the FTP Client

To start an FTP session, go to the Console window and press the **FTP** button (or select FTP from the Services menu). Once the FTP window appears, you can use the Open menu item to begin an FTP session (Figure 4.2). The FTP login dialog box has a list box showing names of the hosts defined in your hosts file, and also provides fields for your login name and password. All three must be filled in before you can begin the FTP session.

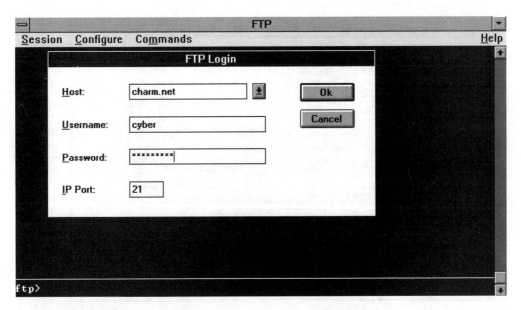

Figure 4.2 WinQVT FTP Client.

If you cancel the dialog, the login window will disappear, but the FTP window will remain, in a closed state.

When you are ready to close the FTP session, enter the command **bye** or **quit** at the ftp> prompt. This command will terminate the FTP connection and close the window. You can terminate an FTP session without closing the window by using the **close** command. All these commands are also available from the menu bar.

FTP runs concurrently with any terminal sessions that you may have started. You can switch back to one of them at any time.

Using the News Reader

If an NNTP server is running on your network, you can use WinQVT/Net to read Usenet articles directly from the server.

Using E-mail

If a POP3 server is available on your network, you can use WinQVT/Net to receive (and possibly send) electronic mail from your PC (Figure 4.3). If no POP3 server is available, you will not be able to use WinQVT/Net to read mail. You will still be able to send mail, however, using SMTP.

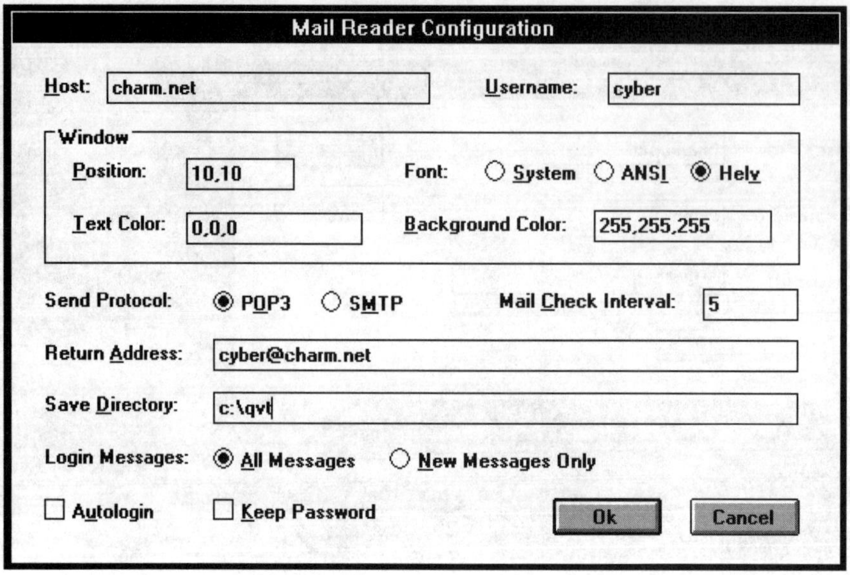

```
┌─────────────────────────────────────────────────────────────┐
│                    Mail Reader Configuration                  │
├─────────────────────────────────────────────────────────────┤
│  Host:  charm.net                  Username:   cyber          │
│  ┌Window──────────────────────────────────────────────────┐  │
│  │ Position:   10,10      Font:  ○ System ○ ANSI ● Helv    │  │
│  │ Text Color: 0,0,0      Background Color: 255,255,255     │  │
│  └─────────────────────────────────────────────────────────┘  │
│                                                                │
│  Send Protocol:  ● POP3  ○ SMTP    Mail Check Interval:  5    │
│  Return Address: cyber@charm.net                              │
│  Save Directory: c:\qvt                                       │
│  Login Messages: ● All Messages  ○ New Messages Only          │
│  □ Autologin   □ Keep Password          [ Ok ]  [ Cancel ]    │
└─────────────────────────────────────────────────────────────┘
```

Figure 4.3 WinQVT POP3 client configuration.

Server Applications

WinQVT/Net includes two server applications, FTP and rcp. These applications allow remote users on other systems to access your PC's file system. The server application window is shown in Figure 4.4.

FTP Server

WinQVT/Net provides a background FTP server facility. This feature allows remote users to access your PC remotely, using FTP. Only one logged-in user at a time is allowed.

You will have to modify several QVTNET.INI configuration parameters:

`passfile`

This is the file holding the list of authorized users and their passwords

`login_dir`

The directory that authorized users will be attached to at login time is:

`anonftp_dir`

This is the directory to which anonymous users will be attached. These users will not be able to log in to any other directories, except for subdirectories within the same tree.

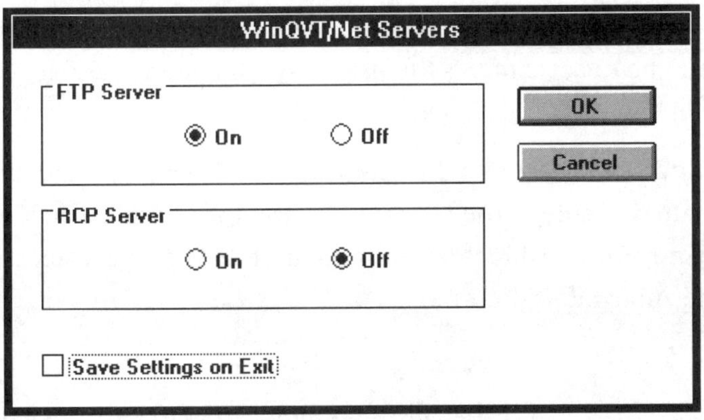

Figure 4.4 WinQVT enabling servers.

A small utility program, PASSWD.EXE, is provided for maintaining the password file.

Security for the FTP server depends on whether or not you have implemented a password file. If you supply no file, users can log in without passwords or restrictions on access (other than those indicated in QVTNET.ACL). If you do create a password file, then only users listed in this file will be allowed to log in.

If you provide a value for the anonftp_dir directive, WinQVT/Net will allow anonymous logins. Anonymous users operate under some restrictions:

Access is restricted to a single directory tree (as specified by anonftp_dir).

Anonymous users are not allowed to delete or overwrite files.

(If you don't specify an anonymous login directory, anonymous logins will not be permitted.)

Authorized users have fewer restrictions, but access-control lists can be used to protect some files and directories even from authorized users. Access-control lists are stored in the QVTNET.ACL file, which should be placed in the WinQVT/Net home directory. Each access-control list occupies a single line in QVTNET.ACL, and is of the form:

```
<directory name> [<username>,<username>,...]
```

The <directory name> is mandatory, and gives the name of the directory to which the ACL applies. The optional <username> entries identify users who are authorized to access the named directory. Each user name should be the name of a valid FTP user, as created by PASSWD.EXE. If <username> entries are present in an ACL, they should be separated from the <directory name> by one blank space. Separate the <username>'s themselves with commas, and leave no blanks anywhere in the list.

You can completely cut off access to a directory by creating an ACL with an empty list of user names. Achieve the inverse—a directory with no access control—by creating no ACL for a directory; any valid user will be able to access it (possibly excepting anonymous users).

rcp Server

WinQVT/Net also provides a server that allows remote users to copy files to and from the PC using the BSD **rcp** command. This server uses the same security features as does the FTP server, particularly the user-validation facility. Unlike FTP, however, it does not provide for anonymous users, admitting only documented users.

Information on WinQVT Registration

The registration fee for WinQVT/Net is $40, except for students, who can register for $20. For shipment outside North America, add $5. WinQVT/Net is a shareware product; if you decide to use it, forward your registration fee to:

> QPC Software
> P.O. Box 226
> Penfield, NY 14526
> (USA)

Registered users receive a printed user manual, a complete set of fonts, and free access to upgrades for one year.

You can contact QPC electronically via Internet mail at their e-mail address:

`djpk@troi.cc.rochester.edu`

WFTPD—An FTP Server for Windows

WFTPD is an FTP server, written by Alun Jones, which runs with the Trumpet Winsock and most other Windows Sockets TCP/IP stacks. This program will allow you to set up an FTP server under Microsoft Windows 3.1 and make your files available to FTP clients.

These are the program's main features:

- Support for most FTP commands.

- Multiple logins and simultaneous transfers.

- Runs over most Winsock drivers.

- Has security built in, with configurable user-password lists, user directory restrictions, and logging to a file.

- Can be run invisibly, through a command-line option (-h for hidden) and neither the Window nor the icon will appear.

- Has easily configurable greetings (in the registered version only).

Installing WFTPD

To install WFTPD:

1. The WFTPD server software may be retrieved from:

   `ftp://sunsite.unc.edu/pub/micro/pc-stuff/ms-windows/winsock/apps`

   The file name is WFTPD196.ZIP.

2. Create a directory on your PC for the server software (e.g., C:\WFTPD). Unzip the files with PKUNZIP and place them in the WFTPD directory. They include:

WFTPD.EXE	the program executable
WFTPD.HLP	the program help file
README.TXT	late news and installation instructions
CTL3DV2.DLL	Microsoft 3D control library

3. Copy the file CTL3DV2.DLL to the C:\WINDOWS\SYSTEM directory (if it's not already there) and delete it from the C:\WFTPD directory.

4. Start up the Trumpet Winsock (or your preferred TCP package) as in the section titled Installing Trumpet Winsock, if you don't already have it running.

5. From the Windows File Manager, select **Run**, and pick the WFTPd Server program, or set up a Program Item within a Program Group and click on the icon.

   The defaults for the out-of-the-box server include:

   • A setting of no log file and no logging to screen or disk.

   • User/password security enabled with no users defined.

   • Anonymous user access disabled and restricted to the C:\ directory (and beneath) if you enable it.

   • Host/Net security settings allow all hosts and networks to access the server.

   • No limit on the maximum number of users who can access the server simultaneously.

   • A greeting and farewell message showing that you're not registered.

   • No display of the informational file MESSAGE.FTP when one changes directories.

   • No time-out of idle connections.

   Therefore, you will either need to enable Anonymous access (and consider changing the directory that Anonymous users can access) and/or set up new users with passwords. Be sure to give adequate forethought to security to ensure proper access to files on your server. For testing, the steps that follow will help you set up a basic WFTPD configuration.

6. Once you are in the WFTPD Server program, go to the Menu Bar and select *Security*. Here you can add or change server security parameters. You have three options displayed under Security: General, User/Password, and Host/Net.

7. Select General from the Security menu. Check the boxes: Enable Security, Allow Anonymous, and turn off or uncheck the boxes for Allow Uploads and Allow Anonymous Uploads. Next, set the maximum number of users to 5 and the time out for inactive connections to 300 seconds (Figure 4.5).

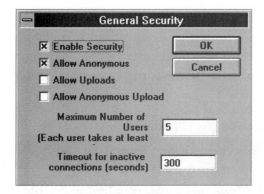

Figure 4.5 WFTPD General Security.

8. The User/Password option allows you to define users for your server. A new user would be defined by your selecting this option and completing the dialog box that appears (Figure 4.6). Here you'll enter the name the user will use to log in to the server in the User name box. For each user, define an associated password and FTP directory. If you wish to allow users access to their home directory and related subdirectories, check the box Restrict to Home. Once you have completed the necessary information the **Add/Update** button will become enabled (it was previously grayed out) and you may click on it to update the record. All entries will be stored in the WFTPD.INI file. The **Delete** button will remove the entry for the user record currently displayed.

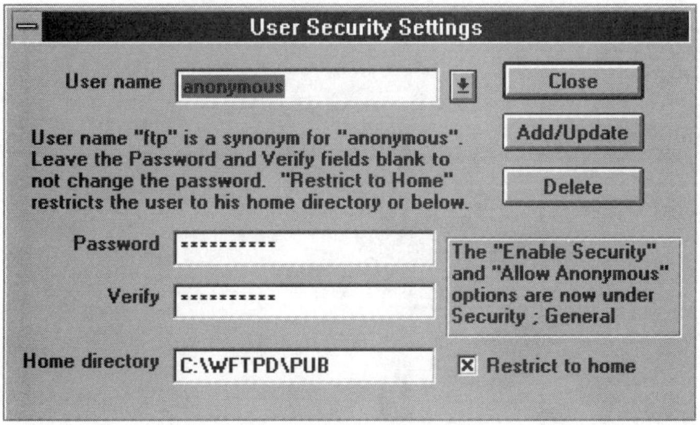

Figure 4.6 WFTPD User Security settings.

The Username box is clickable so that you can list and select from the users you have set up. For testing, click on the user-name box to display the default user Anonymous. Identify a home directory for the anonymous user. You can create the directory through DOS and reference it in this box (e.g., C:\WFTPD\PUB).

9. Through the Host/Net selection you can control who is allowed or denied access to your server. You can allow access to specific sites and therefore negate access by all others, or you can deny specific sites and permit others to log in. To specifically allow or deny a host or network, enter the IP address in the Host Address box. For testing, leave the default as is, which will allow any user access to the server (Figure 4.7).

10. Under the menu item Messages, you will not be able to modify the greetings unless you contact the author and purchase a registered copy. Otherwise you will have to live with the notice to users (Figure 4.8) that your copy is unregistered (check the Help/Registering menu choice for address, version, and fees).

    Registering the software will give you these advantages:

    • You'll be automatically notified about any new versions of the software.

    • All restrictions on the shareware version, including the impolite greeting and farewell messages, will be removed.

    • You get opportunities to give the author feedback about new and enhanced features.

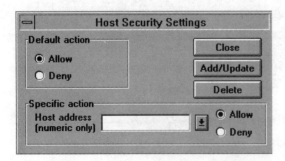

Figure 4.7 WFTPD Host Security settings.

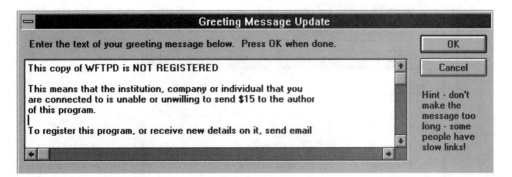

Figure 4.8 WFTPD Greeting message.

Beyond being able to change greetings and farewell messages, if you click on the MESSAGE.FTP option, you can set up a message that will be displayed each time a user enters a directory. You may place a file named MESSAGE.FTP in each directory in which you wish to provide an informational message. If you wish to make this a hidden file, go to the File Manager, select the file, MESSAGE.FTP, then click on Properties under the File menu. Next, check the "hidden box". This is an important step if you don't want users changing your informational messages or deleting the file.

11. Under the menu item File, you can open and close a Log file. When you select **Open**, you will be given the opportunity to create a new log file or to use an existing file. Select **Open** and create a file named FTP.LOG in the C:\WFTPD directory.

12. Under the menu option Logging (Figure 4.9), you can determine which of these items will be logged:

    • Gets—a record is written with each get.

    • Puts—a record is written with each put.

    • Logins—each time a user logs in, a record is written.

    • Anonymous—a record is written with each Anonymous login.

    • Commands—writes a record of each command received.

    • Winsock calls—not recommended for your use; primarily an aid to the software author.

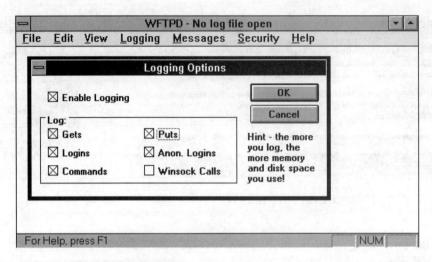

Figure 4.9 WFTPD logging.

Check Enable Logging and under the heading titled Log: check that you want to log Logins and Anon. Logins.

Format of the Log File   The log file is a simple text file with this format:

```
[X nnnn] mm/dd/yy hh:mm:ss<Message text>
```

X values can be:

L   login

C   command

G   get

P   put

A   Anonymous login

?   Debugging information

!   Warning / helpful information

nnnn This is a four-digit hexadecimal number for the connection number this record applies to. Connections are numbered from 0001 when the program is started. Each time the program is restarted, the counter is reset to 0001.

mm/dd/yy Transaction date.

hh:mm:ss Time the record was written.

message text Information such as, User anonymous logged in.

Records will be written to the LOG.FTP file and to the screen.

13. Once you have installed and configured the server, go to an FTP client and log in to the server to test WFTPD.

14. You can then minimize the WFTPD application.

Beyond the configuration options listed above, take the time to access the Help facility through the program Menu. Besides information about registering the software you'll find a number of helpful tips and hints.

Serv-U FTP Server

Serv-U is a shareware FTP server for Windows written by Rob Beckers. The software distribution is available from:

```
ftp://oak.oakland.edu/pub/winsock/ftpsr103.zip
```

The software is a fully functional FTP server but will expire after the thirty-day evaluation period. Therefore, you will want to review the information on shareware registration included with the distribution.

Serv-U Features

The FTP server includes:

- The ability to serve multiple clients at the same time, with a configurable limit on the number of users so that you can balance performance.

- Anonymous FTP access.

- Security, including ability to restrict access by IP address and ability to secure files and directories, as desired.

- Compliance with the FTP standard (RFC 959) with the necessary support for WWW browsers.

- Easy menu-assisted setup and configuration.

Serv-U Installation

To install and set up Serv-U, follow these steps:

1. Retrieve the zipped file, FTPSR103.ZIP, and unzip it into a directory of your choosing (e.g., C:\SERV-U).

2. Set up the server program, SERV-U.EXE, in the Program Manager so that you can click on an icon to start the program. Once you've done that, start the server program.

3. Select the Setup FTP Server menu item to configure the server (Figure 4.10). Most options for Serv-U can be configured via this setup routine, except for allowing users to access the server without a password and the option for making the program invisible. These options can be changed through the SERV-U.INI file, which is explained in the distribution's documentation files.

4. Set the Setup options that follow to configure the server:

   FTP Port Number This is the port on which Serv-U listens for incoming connections. The default is 21. If you wish to change it, make the port number greater than 1024 because TCP/IP well-known ports are in the range below 1024.

   Maximum number of users This setting should be at the maximum number of simultaneous users you wish to allow. The setting will vary

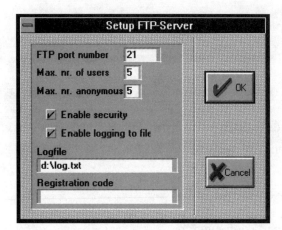

Figure 4.10 Serv-U FTP Server setup.

depending on a number of performance factors, such as the size of your machine and which other programs you have running. If you set this parameter to 0, no one will be able to access the server. Set it to blank and you'll allow unlimited access.

Maximum number of anonymous This setting limits the number of users who may log in anonymously.

Enable security This option, when checked, allows you to secure your server. We strongly recommend that you enable security and properly configure access restrictions.

Enable logging to file Checking this box will turn on logging to a disk file as well as the screen (which is always on).

Logfile Enter the proper path and file name for the file to which you wish to log server activity.

Registration code Once you register the software you will be given a code to enter here.

5. Next, select the Setup IP Access menu item (Figure 4.11). The IP restrictions that you can enforce are set up like many other servers, using the *allow* and *deny* concept. And, as with other servers, order is important.

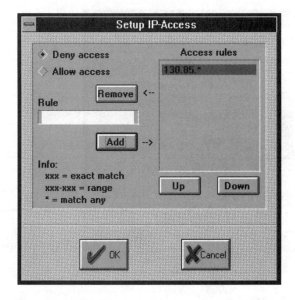

Figure 4.11 Serv-U Setup IP Access.

The server will first evaluate all deny rules, and then evaluate the allows. When a match is found, the restriction is enforced and the evaluation ceases. If you don't set up any IP restrictions, all access is allowed. Rules can be Added or Removed, and order can be changed by moving rules Up and Down the list. IP masks can be used to wildcard specified addresses. For example, denying hosts from 198.69.33.* would mean that any host starting with 198.69.33 would be denied access to the server. A hyphen (-) can also be used to designate a range of hosts to allow or deny. For example, 198.69.33.75-77 would indicate a rule for hosts 198.69.33.75, 198.69.33.76, and 198.69.33.77.

6. Welcome messages can be configured by selecting the Setup Signon/Signoff option. You can set up an informative message that tells your visitors things like the purpose of your server or location of files. And you can post a goodbye message to leave them as they sign off.

7. Because we have enabled security above, we will have to set up users. Select the Setup Users menu item (Figure 4.12). Click on **Edit** to set up new users (the Setup groups works similarly). The fields to configure include:

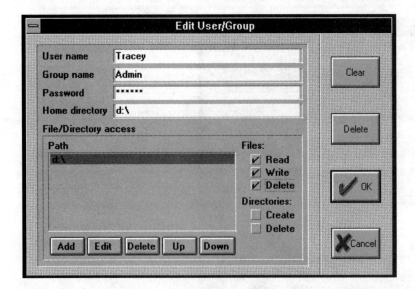

Figure 4.12 Serv-U Setup Users.

User name Set up each user with a user name.

Group name You can separate users into groups and establish settings applicable to each group.

Password Passwords are stored in UNIX crypt format and cannot be viewed as plain text.

Home directory You can (and should) specify a home directory for each user. If the user is part of a group and you fail to specify a user home directory, the group's home directory will be used.

File/directory access This list of rules for access defines a number of paths with access information tied to each path. You must identify access paths to ensure access. You will at least want to identify a path for the user's home directory. When a user tries to retrieve a file, for example, the user's path list is evaluated to see if the command can be executed. Again, order is important in the list of rules governing the five types of access:

Read Allows you to **Get** files from the server.

Write Enables you to **Put** files on the server, but not change, delete, or rename files.

Delete Allows you to **Change**, **Delete**, or **Rename** files (includes **Write**).

Create At this path you can create directories.

Delete You can **Delete** directories.

Any rights on a path are also applicable to subdirectories. If you wish to override this right, you specify the subdirectory and its rights before the parent.

Next, set up this rule for access paths:

```
C:\ANONFTP          read rights
```

For more detailed examples of rules for access paths and restrictions on access to files, consult the documentation.

Anonymous user The Serv-U server will ask for the anonymous user's e-mail address when they log in. The Password setup is ignored for the anonymous user. When that user logs in, he or she will be put in C:\ANONFTP but will see \ as the current path.

User ALL The other special user name is user ALL. If no settings have been planned for a user at the user or group level, checking reverts to the settings established for user ALL. If user ALL exists, then the settings will be applied. Be especially careful if you set up user ALL because it is a potential security risk.

Beame & Whiteside FTP Server

The BW-Connect TCP/IP package for DOS and Windows 3.1 is a very full-featured suite of TCP/IP client and server programs available as commercial products from Beame & Whiteside Software of Raleigh, North Carolina. The client software includes Telnet, Finger, Ping, Talk, a POP/SMTP mail reader, graphical FTP, and other programs. The client side is just about everything you need to navigate the Net. But that's not our main focus, of course. Besides fine client programs, Beame & Whiteside has developed a personal publishing initiative, which includes a number of useful Windows 3.1 server products.

Be aware that the package also handles all your TCP/IP connectivity, whether you are using SLIP, PPP, or a direct connection to the Internet. If you use this software you'll have no need for Chameleon, Trumpet, or any other TCP/IP implementation, although you'll have to contend with the normal TCP/IP configuration issues while you're installing and configuring software.

Daemons

The package includes a processing model from the UNIX side, incorporating the first inetd daemon for Windows. inetd provides server-based functions for TCP/IP. Resources are then consumed as needed, resulting in lower server overhead. These are the servers included in the Beame & Whiteside software distribution:

- An FTP server, with full password protection and access rights, so that remote users can retrieve files from your machine.

- A Finger server, which allows client machines to look up information about your machine.

- A Gopher server, which allows your Windows PC to serve up Gopher documents.

• A World Wide Web server that will handle requests from clients such as Mosaic and Netscape and deliver HTML documents to those browsers. The Web server runs as a stand-alone server, rather than under the inetd daemon.

inetd

One of the novel approaches to Windows server programs comes from an older UNIX concept, inetd. Instead of running separate server applications for many of the servers in the Beame & Whiteside package, inetd will listen to the network and initiate the appropriate server task to handle incoming requests. The inetd daemon provides services by running in the background listening for attempts at connection. When an attempt is detected, the inetd daemon looks to see the port number being used and whether a daemon (e.g., ftpd daemon) is enabled on that port. If not, then the connection is refused. If the daemon requested is started, an icon appears on the Windows desktop. The software-installation procedure places inetd in the Startup program group so that it will automatically run when you start Windows. To start or stop any of the programs that run under inetd, maximize the inetd program to access the Main Menu Screen, as shown in Figure 4.13.

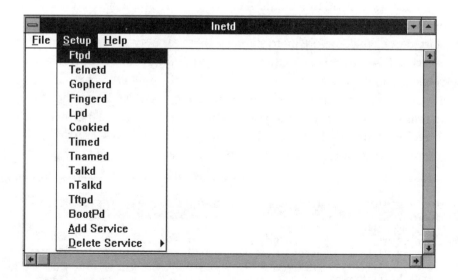

Figure 4.13 Beame & Whiteside Available Daemons.

inetd Configuration

These items can be configured through the inetd File Menu:

- **Defaults**. Select the Defaults options if you have lost or corrupted your INETD.CFG configuration file. Default programs such as FTP, Gopher, Finger, and others will be inserted in your INETD.CFG file. For inetd to listen for requests for a specific service, that service must be enabled. See the Beame & Whiteside documentation for a complete listing of the default services.

- **Logging**. When logging is enabled, all information written to the inetd window (Figure 4.14) is also appended to the file INETD.LOG in the C:\BWTCP directory.

These options can be configured through the Setup menu:

- A list of various services (Figure 4.13)
- Add Service
- Delete Service

Selected Services

Each service is identified by a unique name (e.g., ftpd). The service is defined by a combination of the port, protocol, and program to be run. Each service must be started or enabled before inetd starts listening for network connections for the service. For performance reasons, you can limit the number of concurrent sessions that a server will allow at one time. When the limit is reached, a remote user will receive a message indicating that their connection was refused. When inetd is installed, default services are listed but none are enabled. Because each enabled service uses valuable buffer memory, start only the servers that you need. Important note: If you plan to have many services and remote

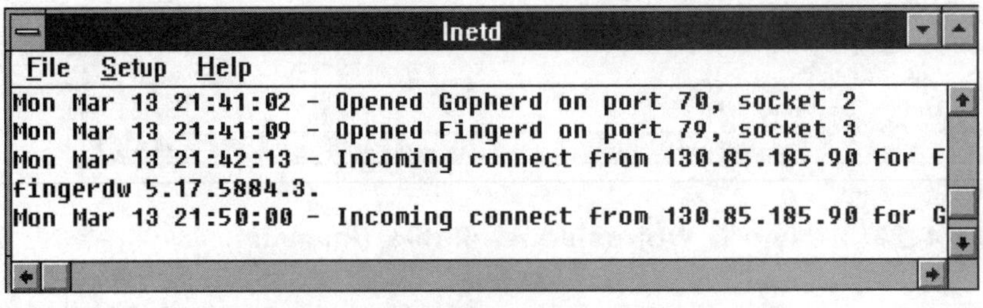

Figure 4.14 Beame & Whiteside inetd logging.

connections active all at once, increase the buffer memory with the program BWCUSTOM or BWCUSTOMW.

Starting a Server under inetd

To start a service, or to edit any of the configuration options, select the desired service. The Setup screen appears as shown in Figure 4.15.

The various options are:

1. **Enabled**. Checking this box indicates that the service is enabled.

2. **Name**. This field includes the name of the service, such as ftpd.

3. **Program Filename**. This field holds the name of the file for the service daemon, such as FTPDW.

4. **Optional Parameters**. This field has the optional parameters. Refer to the program in the software-distribution documentation for details about the various options. In the example shown, the -v parameter is included, indicating that FTPDW should log data to the screen.

5. **Port**. This is the Port that is used for this service (e.g., 21 = FTP).

6. **Maximum Servers**. UDP services can have only one instance of the

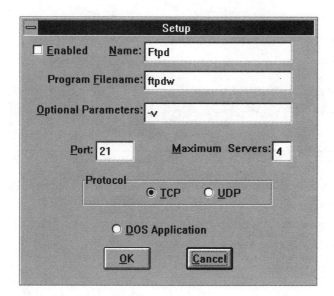

Figure 4.15 Beame & Whiteside starting a server.

server application running at a time, but TCP services can have up to sixty-four instances active at once.

7. **Protocols**. The User Datagram Protocol (UDP) and Transmission Control Protocol (TCP) are supported by BW-Connect TCP and BW-Connect NFS.

8. **DOS Application**. A special application (Telnetd) allows either interactive DOS sessions or execution of specific character-based DOS programs to be provided on arbitrary TCP ports. Note: Only if the program being run is Telnetd should this radio button be selected.

9. **OK/Cancel**. If no changes are made, click on **Cancel** rather than **OK**. Clicking on **OK** will shut the service down and restart it.

10. **Add Service**. Select the Add Service option from the Setup menu if any other server is to be added. The same Setup screen appears as shown in Figure 4.15 above, but all the fields are empty. Any of the existing servers can be configured to run on any port, and servers can be added so that a server runs on more than one port at a time.

11. **Delete Service**. Select this option if you want to remove any of the services from the list of available services. When this option is selected, a second menu appears with the services currently available. Select the service to be deleted, or select the All Services option if you wish to delete all.

Installing the Product Suite

The software comes with an installation guide covering the many client and server options that are included. If you follow the steps below, you can be up and running with your choice of servers in short order:

1. Be sure to collect the necessary information on the TCP/IP Parameters Form in the Appendix, or use the Preliminary Worksheet from the Appendix in the Beame & Whiteside Installation Guide. Some aspects of the installation get into rather heavy networking and PC issues, such as choice of IRQs and network drivers. You may want to get assistance

from your friendly network administrator. If friendly network administrator is an oxymoron in your organization, you probably can accomplish the installation by following these steps, which generally rely on defaults. Complications usually arise when you're dealing with multiple protocol stacks. In other words, perhaps you're currently running Netware and wish to install TCP/IP. If so, the defaults will not always work and you may do best by throwing the network administrator a bone and getting some help.

2. Insert the first disk from the disk set of Beame & Whiteside software and, from the Windows Program Manager, select **Run** and click on the SETUP.EXE program on your A or B drive.

3. A screen appears (Figure 4.16), asking you the type of installation you wish to perform. The example here uses the Windows Only TCP/IP installation option. Make your selection and click on **Install**. An informational screen describing source and destination paths (Figure 4.17) will appear. Click on **Continue**.

4. Select the source disk (Figure 4.18) and click on **OK**. Next, select the destination disk (Figure 4.19) and click on **OK**. Files will be copied to disk.

5. Figure 4.20 shows some of the many network adapter types that you can choose from. Indicate your network adapter type and click on **OK**.

6. Next, choose your driver type from the screen shown in Figure 4.21. NDIS drivers are provided with the software distribution. If you are

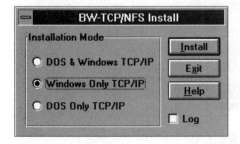

Figure 4.16 Beame & Whiteside TCP/NFS install.

124 *Chapter 4*

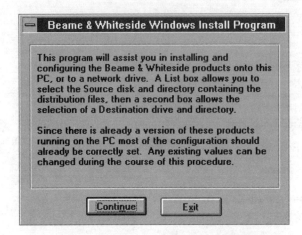

Figure 4.17 Beame & Whiteside paths.

running another networking package, such as Netware, choose ODI driver or Packet Driver, whichever is appropriate for your installation, and click on **OK**. The system will prompt you for additional disks as it loads the series of disks.

7. Once all disks are loaded, the Customization Menu screen in Figure 4.22 will appear. Take the values for IP Address, Netmask, and Default Gateway from the TCP/IP Form or the Beame & Whiteside Preliminary Worksheet and key them into this screen. For this installation, leave the Authorization field blank.

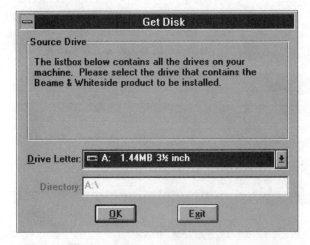

Figure 4.18 Beame & Whiteside source disk.

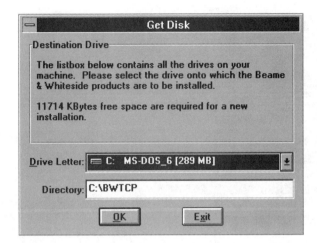

Figure 4.19 Beame & Whiteside destination disk.

8. Click on the **Load Options** button on the Customization Menu screen and the Windows Configuration screen in Figure 4.23 appears. Select an available Hardware Interrupt (IRQ), I/O address, and Shared Memory, Buffer Size, and Software Interrupt, as shown on the screen. Click on **OK**.

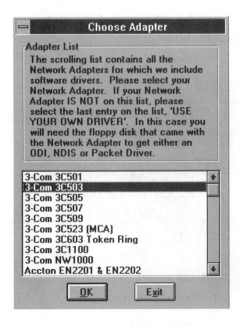

Figure 4.20 Beame & Whiteside network adapter choices.

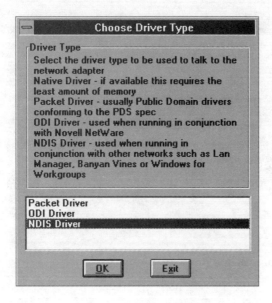

Figure 4.21 Beame & Whiteside choose driver type.

9. Next, click on **Name Services** and Figure 4.24 will appear. Enter the numeric IP address of a Domain Name Server and click on **Add>**. Once you've identified the server(s), click on **OK**.

10. Once you have completed these steps, click on **Done** on the Customization Menu and a screen will appear asking for your PC's

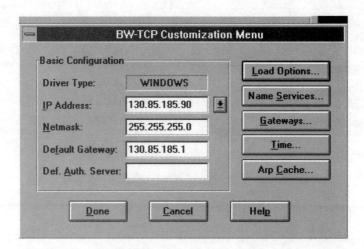

Figure 4.22 Beame & Whiteside customization menu.

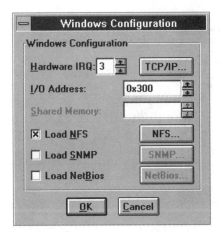

Figure 4.23 Beame & Whiteside Windows configuration.

machine name. You should have received this name from your network administrator or your Internet service provider; it will be something like: fido.ajax.com. Enter the name and click on **OK**.

11. You will be asked if you want to run NIS Services when the screen in Figure 4.25 appears. Click on **OK** if you're not currently using NIS and proceed to the next step.

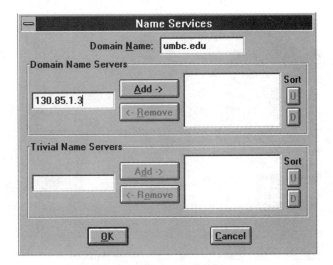

Figure 4.24 Beame & Whiteside Name Services.

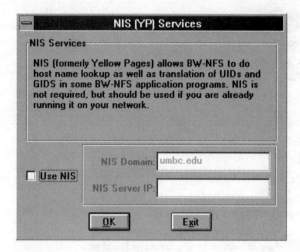

Figure 4.25 NIS Services.

12. You will now be asked whether the installation procedure can change your AUTOEXEC.BAT and CONFIG.SYS files (Figure 4.26). Your old files will be saved with a .BW extension (e.g., AUTOEXEC.BW). Click on **Yes** to modify these files.

13. The installation procedure now says it will create two program groups in the Windows Program Manager. Click on **OK** to create these groups.

14. You will now be asked if you want to install the BW-NFS Windows Network Driver (Figure 4.27). If you will be running multiple

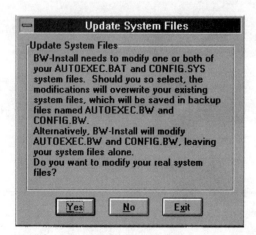

Figure 4.26 Beame & Whiteside Update System files.

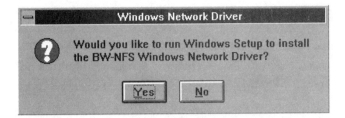

Figure 4.27 Beame & Whiteside Windows Network Driver.

network operating systems, such as BW-Connect NFS and Netware, you must first complete Netware's installation instructions. You can then run Windows Setup to install the Beame & Whiteside NFS network driver. If you don't want to install the network driver at this time, or if you're a SLIP user, click on **No**. If you wish to continue with the Windows Driver installation, click on **Yes**. Through the Windows Setup screen you can select Network: and click on **Other Network**. You can then supply the NFS disk for Installation.

15. Once you have completed these steps, a screen will be displayed, as in Figure 4.28, indicating that the installation is complete. Click on **Reboot** to restart your PC with the necessary changes to allow you to run the Beame & Whiteside software. On reboot, inetd will run from the Startup file. Refer to the chapters on Gopher, FTP, and the World Wide Web for specific information about each of those Beame & Whiteside servers.

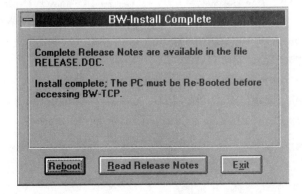

Figure 4.28 Beame & Whiteside Install Complete.

BW-Connect FTP Server

FTPDW is a Windows-based file-transfer server daemon that allows your PC to function as an FTP server for remote users. The program allows multiple FTP connections to be serviced by your PC with full password protection and access rights on your drives or directories. The program runs in the background, and is enabled through the inetd program. Figure 4.15 shows your options for running the FTP server through inetd. To start up the FTP server from the inetd menu, select Setup and then ftpd. Click on the **Enable** box to start the ftpd daemon. The following options are also configured through the Optional Parameters field in the inetd Setup dialog box:

1. **-v** A verbose (-v) setting will cause the program to log all logging data to the screen.

2. **-p** A password flag (-p) defines the location and name of the password file that is used to validate user access. The default is C:\BWTCP\PASS-WORD.BW. If you define an entry in the password file for a user name FTP, with a password of FTP, anonymous FTP access will be available. Then any user can connect to your PC, specifying the user name anonymous and anything for the password.

Note well: If you set up your machine for anonymous FTP access, pay particular attention to the definitions of access and permissions on drives and directories, and follow closely the examples that follow here.

Setting Up Users and Permissions

The ADMINW program is used to create and modify IDs for users who can access your PC resources through inetd server programs. The ADMINW program is selected by clicking on the **Admin** icon from within the Windows Program Group, BWApps. The program provides a Windows-based interface to the PASSWORD.BW file used by the FTP and Telnet daemons when remote users attempt to connect to your PC. Each entry in the password file includes a user name and password as well as other setup and permission information.

To set up users:

1. Select the ADMINW program from the Windows BWApps group. The Open Beame & Whiteside Software Password File window appears as shown in Figure 4.29.

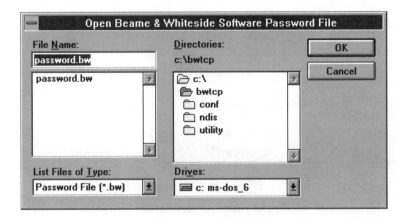

Figure 4.29 Beame & Whiteside Password File.

2. Select the name of the password file to be edited. The default password file is PASSWORD.BW.

When the password file is selected, click on **OK** to access the Password Administration screen, as shown in Figure 4.30. The record displayed shows the name for the first user on the list. The first time you run the program, the only user listed is ftp. The FTP user is there to allow Anonymous FTP. If you have a user FTP set up and a password of ftp, your machine will be available for Anonymous FTP. You may click on the **Delete** button to remove this user if you wish to disable Anonymous FTP. Click on the **Add** button to add new users to the list for those you wish to have access. The Admin -Add Username screen appears as shown in Figure 4.31.

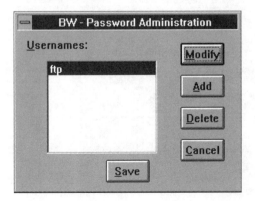

Figure 4.30 Beame & Whiteside Password Administration.

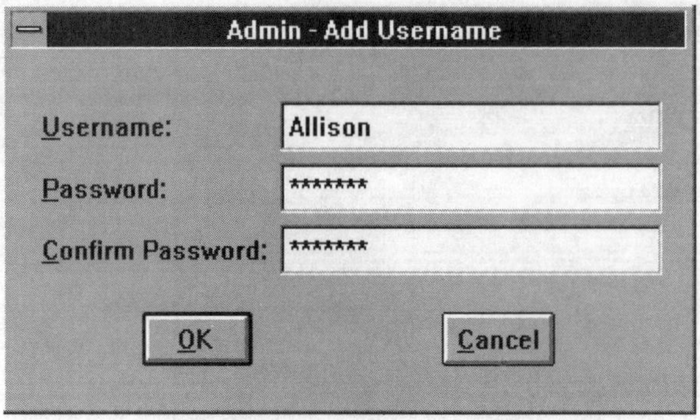

Figure 4.31 Beame & Whiteside Add Username.

3. Type the new user name in the first field and then tab to the Password: field. Enter a password for the new user. Tab to the Confirm: field and type the password again. When the fields are completed, click on **OK**. The User Access Rights dialog box appears as shown in Figure 4.32. The services and directories to which the user has access will be displayed. The default directory, temporary directory, and shell (COMSPEC) that the user runs when Telneting to your PC are included in each user authorization record. The user's file access rights are assigned on a directory basis and allow for full Read, Write, Create, Delete, Modify, and Execute control.

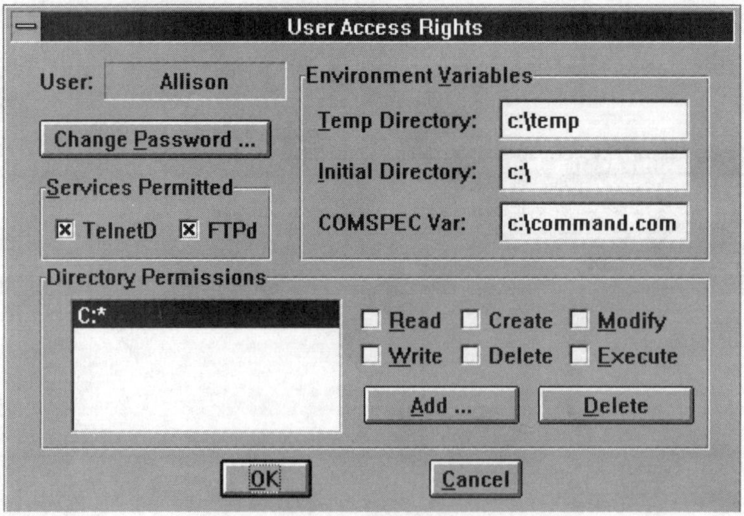

Figure 4.32 Beame & Whiteside User Access Rights.

These options are available from this screen:

- **Change Password**. You may change the user's password at this screen.

- **Services Permitted**. To access the FTP or Telnet daemons, the user must have the service (FTP, TELNET) enabled in the Services Permitted: section. If the service the user is attempting to access is not enabled under inetd, the user will not be logged in and the connection will be terminated. You may add or delete services in the user's record by checking the appropriate box.

- **Temporary Directory (Environment Variable)**. The temporary directory is pointed to by the DOS TEMP environment variable and telnetd points to it when starting. This directory should be set to full Read/Write access if temporary files are required. You can change this directory by tabbing to or clicking on this field. Delete the current entry and enter the desired directory.

- **Default Directory (Environment Variable)**. This is the directory that is changed to when the ftpd or telnetd daemon applications start. You must have permission to access this directory, or your connection will be terminated. You can change the directory by tabbing to or clicking on this field. Delete the current entry and enter the desired directory.

- **COMSPEC or Shell (Environment Variable)**. This is the full file specification of the DOS shell that is started when no -e parameter is used. The COMSPEC environment variable is also set to this value (normally C:\command.com), although other shells can be used. Unfortunately, the DOS command.com shell requires that it have full Read and Write access to the directory in which it resides. Move the command shell to a specific directory and give Read/Write access to that directory instead of C:. You can change this file specification by tabbing to or clicking on this field. Delete the current entry and enter the desired file specification.

- **Directory Permissions (Environment Variable)**. You may add directories with the **Add** button and delete directories with the **Delete** button. Ten directories may be identified here with appropriate permissions. A directory specification should not end in a backslash (\). Only the specified directory has the listed permissions. To include all subdirectories, append a backslash asterisk (*) to the directory name. Permissions for the directory may be added or deleted by clicking on the box next to each permission option. These permissions can be defined:

Permission   Access Rights.

Read   Files can be opened for reading and directories searched.

Write   Files can be opened for writing.

Create   New files and subdirectories can be created.

Delete   Files and subdirectories can be deleted.

Modify   File attributes can be changed.

Execute   Programs can be executed.

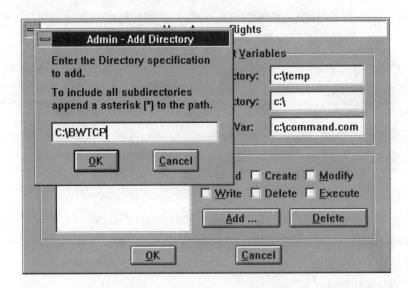

Figure 4.33 Beame & Whiteside Add Directory.

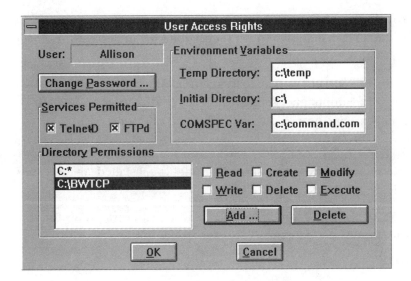

Figure 4.34 Beame & Whiteside User Access Rights new directory.

To add new directories to the list, click on the **Add** button to access the Add Directory dialog box, as shown in Figure 4.33.

Enter the new drive/directory information. When you click on **OK** you are returned to the User Access Rights screen shown in Figure 4.34. The new directory is now listed in the directory window. You may now assign permissions for that directory.

When all the changes have been made to your password file, click on **OK** to exit the ADMINW program.

NT FTP Server

The NT FTP Server allows other computers using FTP clients to connect to your computer and transfer files. The FTP Server service supports all Windows NT FTP client commands. Non-Microsoft versions of FTP clients may include commands that are not supported. The FTP specification is defined in Requests for Comments (RFCs) 959 and 1123.

The FTP Server service is integrated with the Windows NT security model. Users connecting to the FTP Server service are authenticated if they have valid Windows NT user accounts and receive access if they have approved user profiles. For this reason it is recommended that the FTP Server service be installed on an NTFS partition so as to secure the files and directories made available via FTP.

Notice that the FTP Server protocol relies on the ability to pass user passwords over the network without encrypting data. A user with physical access to the network could examine user passwords during FTP validation.

Installing the NT FTP Server

Outlining these procedures, we assume that you have installed any necessary devices and device drivers.

You must be logged on as a member of the Administrators group for your system to install and configure the FTP Server service.

To install the FTP Server service:

1. Click on the Network option in Control Panel (Figure 4.35).

2. In the Network Settings dialog box (Figure 4.36), click on the **Add Software** Button to display the Add Network Software dialog box.

3. In the Network Software box (Figure 4.37), select TCP/IP Protocol and Related Components, and then click on the **Continue** button. When the Windows NT TCP/IP Installation Options dialog box appears (Figure 4.38), check the FTP Server service option, and then click on the **OK** button.

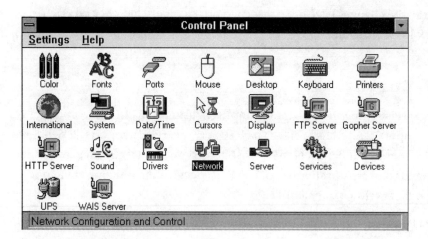

Figure 4.35 NT Control Panel network option.

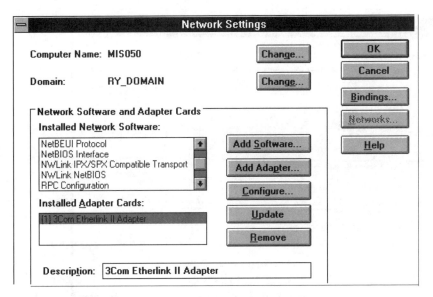

Figure 4.36 NT Network Settings dialog box.

4. When the message prompts you to confirm that you are familiar with
   FTP security, click on the **Yes** button to continue with FTP Server
   service installation.

5. When prompted for the full path to the Windows NT distribution files,
   provide the appropriate location and then click on the **Continue** button.

6. After the necessary files are copied to your computer, the FTP Service
   dialog box appears so that you can continue with the configuration
   procedure as described in the next section. To operate, the FTP Server
   service must be configured.

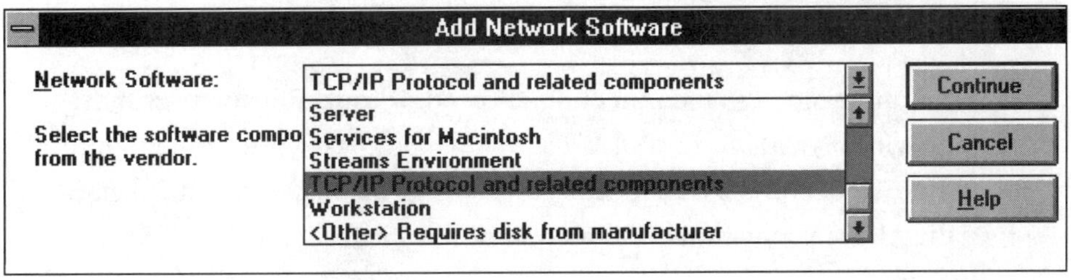

Figure 4.37 NT Add Network software.

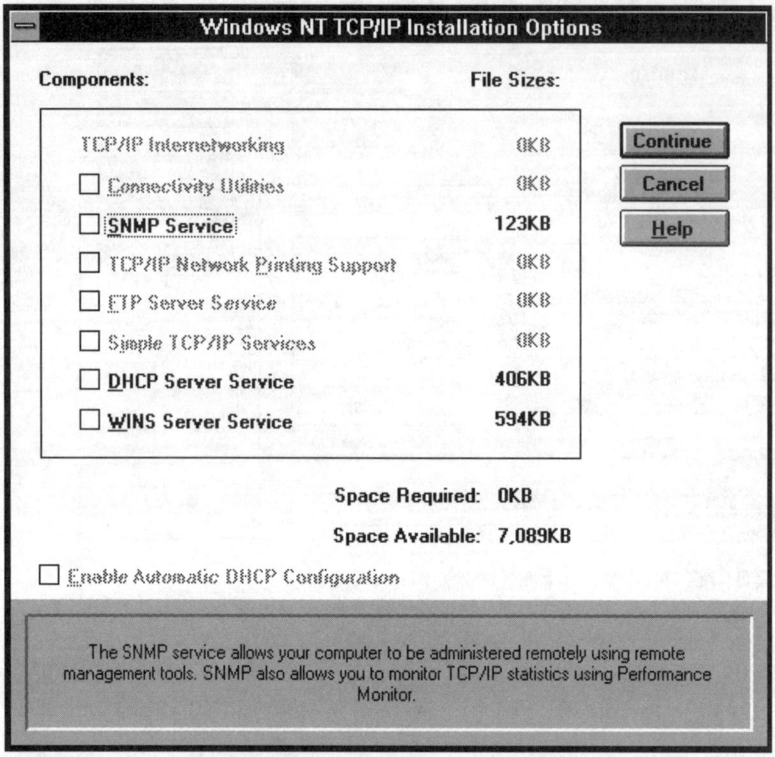

Figure 4.38 NT TCP/IP installation options.

For disk partitions that do not use the Windows NT file system (NTFS), you can apply Read/Write security simply by using the FTP Server tool in the Control Panel, as described in the following section.

Configuring the NT FTP Server

After the FTP Server service software is installed on your computer, you must configure it to operate. When you configure it, your settings result in one of these:

- No anonymous FTP connection allowed. To qualify, each user must provide a valid Windows NT user name and password. To configure the FTP Server service for this authentication, make sure that only the Allow Anonymous Connection box is cleared in the FTP Service dialog box.

- Allow both anonymous and Windows NT users to connect. A user can choose either an anonymous connection or a Windows NT user name and password. To configure the FTP Server service, make sure only the Allow Anonymous Connection box is checked in the FTP Service dialog box.

- Allow only anonymous FTP connections. A user cannot connect using a Windows NT user name and password. To configure the FTP Server service, make sure both the Allow Anonymous Connections and the Allow Anonymous Connections Only boxes are checked in the FTP Service dialog box.

If anonymous connections are allowed, you must apply the Windows NT user name and password to be used for anonymous FTP. When an anonymous FTP transfer takes place, Windows NT will check the user name assigned in this dialog box to determine whether access to the files is allowed.

To configure or reconfigure the FTP Server service:

1. The FTP Service dialog box appears automatically after the FTP Server service software is installed on your computer or, if you are reconfiguring the FTP Server service, click on the **Network** option in Control Panel. In the Installed Network Software box, select FTP Server and then click on the **Configure** button.

   The FTP Service dialog box (Figure 4.39) displays these options:

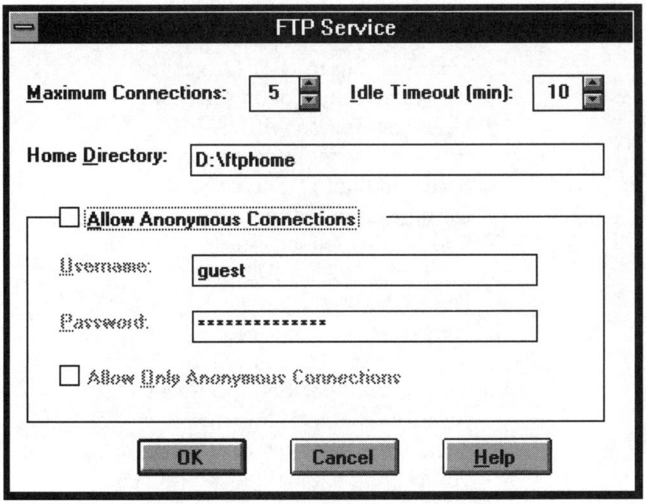

Figure 4.39 NT FTP Services dialog box.

Table 4.1 Options in the FTP Service Dialog Box

Item	Description
Maximum Connections	Specifies the maximum number of FTP users who can connect to the system simultaneously. The default value is 20; the maximum is 50. A value of 0 means no maximum—that is, an unlimited number of simultaneous users.
Idle Timeout	Specifies how many minutes an inactive user can remain connected to the FTP Server service. The default value is 10 minutes; the maximum is 60 minutes. If the value is 0, users are never automatically disconnected.
Home Directory	Specifies the initial directory for users.
Allow Anonymous Connections	Enables users to connect to the FTP Server using the user name Anonymous (or FTP, which is a synonym for Anonymous). A password is not necessary, but the user will be prompted to supply a mail address as the password. By default, anonymous connections are not allowed. Notice that you cannot use a Windows NT user account with the name Anonymous with the FTP Server. The Anonymous user name is reserved in the FTP Server for the Anonymous logon function. Users logging on with the user name Anonymous receive permissions based on the FTP Server configuration for anonymous logons.
Username	Specifies which local-user account to use for FTP Server users who log on under Anonymous. Access permissions for the anonymous FTP user will be the same as the specified local-user account. The default is the standard Guest system account. If you change this name, you must also change the password.

Table 4.1 *Continued*	
Item	Description
Password	Specifies the password for the user account specified in the Username box.
Allow Only Anonymous Connections	Allows only the user name Anonymous to be accepted. This option is useful if you do not want users to log on using their own user names and passwords because FTP passwords are unencrypted. However, all users will have the same access privilege, defined by the Anonymous account. By default, this option is not enabled.

2. Default values are provided for Maximum Connections, Idle Timeout, and Home Directory. Accept the default values, or change values for each field as necessary.

3. Click on the **OK** button to close the FTP Service dialog box and return to the Network Settings dialog box.

4. To complete initial FTP Server service installation and configuration, click on the **OK** button. A message reminds you that you must restart the computer so that the changes you made will take effect.

When you first install the FTP Server service, you must also complete the security configuration (as described in the following procedure) for users to access volumes on your computer.

NT FTP Security Configuration

To configure FTP Server security:

1. After the FTP Server has been installed and you have restarted the Control Panel, start the FTP Server option in the Control Panel (Figure 4.40). Windows NT Server users can also use the FTP menu in Server Manager.

2. In the FTP User Sessions dialog box (Figure 4.41), click on the **Security** button.

3. In the Partition box of the FTP Server Security dialog box (Figure 4.42), select the drive letter on which you want to set security, and then check

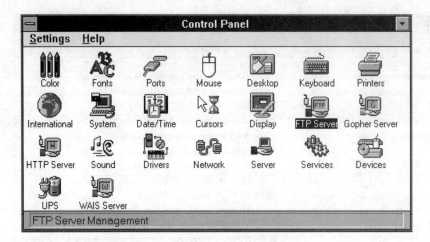

Figure 4.40 NT Control Panel FTP server.

the Allow Read or Allow Write check box, or both check boxes, depending on the security you want for the selected partition. Repeat this step for each partition.

Setting these permissions will affect all files across the entire partition on file allocation table (FAT) and high-performance file system (HPFS) partitions. On NTFS partitions, this feature can be used to remove Read or Write access (or both) on the entire partition.

Any restrictions set in this dialog box are enforced in addition to any security that may be part of the file system. That is, an administrator can use this dialog box to remove permissions on specific volumes but cannot use it to grant

Figure 4.41 NT FTP User Sessions dialog box.

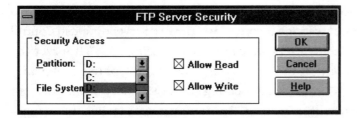

Figure 4.42 NT FTP Server security.

permissions beyond those maintained by the file system. For example, if a partition is marked Read only, no one can write to the partition via FTP, regardless of any permissions set in this dialog box.

4. Click on the **OK** button when you have finished setting security access on partitions. The changes take effect immediately. The FTP Server service is now ready to operate.

Administering the NT FTP Server

After initial installation is complete, each time the computer is started the FTP Server service is automatically started in the background. *Remove computers* can initiate an FTP session while the FTP Server service is running on your Windows NT computer. Both computers must be running the TCP/IP protocol.

You must be logged on as a member of the Administrators group to administer the FTP Server.

Remote users can connect to the FTP Server using their account on the FTP Server, an account on the FTP Server's domain or trusted domains (Windows NT Server only), or the Anonymous account if the FTP Server service is configured to allow anonymous logons.

When making any configuration changes to the FTP Server (except for security configuration), you must restart the FTP Server by either restarting the computer or manually stopping and restarting the server, using the net command or Services icon in Control Panel. To start or stop the FTP Server service use the Services option in Control Panel, or at the command prompt use the commands **net stop ftpsvc** followed by **net start ftpsvc**.

Restarting the service in this way disconnects any users presently connected to the FTP Server without warning therefore, use the FTP Server option in Control Panel to determine if any users are connected. Pausing the FTP Server (by using the Services option in Control Panel or the net **pause** command) prevents any more users from connecting to the FTP Server but does not disconnect users currently logged on. This feature is useful when the administrator wants to restart the server without disconnecting the current users. After the users disconnect on their own, the administrator can safely shut down the server without worrying that users will lose work. When attempting to connect to a Windows NT FTP Server that has been paused, clients receive the message "421 Service is not available," closing control connection.

Using FTP Commands

When you install the FTP service, a set of client FTP commands are automatically installed that you can use at the command prompt.

To get help on FTP commands:

1. Double-click the Windows **NT Help** icon in the Program Manager group.

2. In the Windows NT help window, click the Command Reference **Help** button.

3. Click the FTP commands name in the Commands window (Figure 4.43).

4. Click an FTP command name in the Command Reference window to see a description of the command, plus its syntax and parameter definitions (Figure 4.44).

Managing NT FTP Users

Use the FTP Server option in the Control Panel to manage users connected to the FTP Server and to set security for each volume on the FTP Server. For convenience on Windows NT Server computers, the same dialog box can be reached from Server Manager by choosing the FTP menu command.

In the FTP User Sessions dialog box, the Connected Users box displays the names of connected users, their system's IP addresses, and how long they have been connected. For users who logged on using the Anonymous user name, the display shows the passwords used when they logged on as their user names. If the user name included a mail host name (for example, greg@mis050.mis. umbc.edu), only the user name (greg) appears.

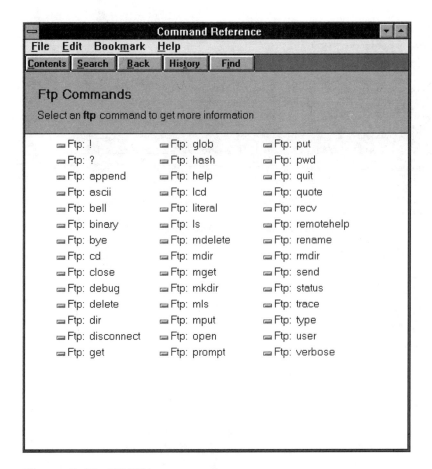

Figure 4.43 NT FTP commands.

Anonymous users also have a question mark (?) over their user icons. Users who have been authenticated by Windows NT security have no question mark.

The FTP Server allows you to disconnect one or all users with the **Disconnect** buttons. Users are not warned if you disconnect them.

The FTP Server displays users' names as they connect but does not update the display when users disconnect or when their connect time elapses. The **Refresh** button allows you to update the display to show only users who are currently connected.

Choosing the **Security** button displays the FTP Service Security dialog box, where you can set Read and Write permissions for each partition on the FTP

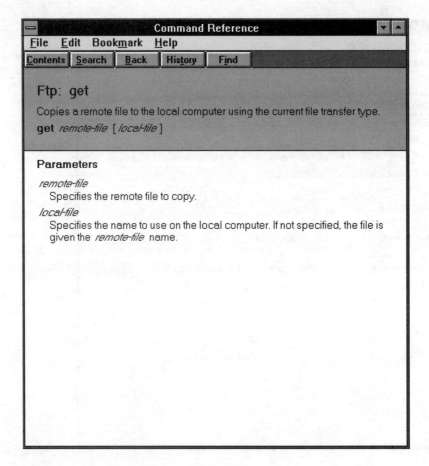

Figure 4.44 NT FTP command—Get.

Server, as described earlier in this chapter. You must set the permissions for each partition to which you want FTP users to have access. If you do not set partition parameters, no users will be able to access files. If the partition uses a secure file system, such as NTFS, file-system restrictions are also in effect.

In addition to FTP Server partition security, if a user logs on using a Windows NT account, access permissions for that account are in effect.

Controlling the Number of Users

A network administrator can control several variables in the FTP Server configuration. One such variable, Maximum Connections, can be set by using the Network option in Control Panel to define a value between 0 and 50. Any value from 1 to 50 restricts concurrent FTP sessions to the value specified. A value of 0 allows unlimited connections to be established to the FTP Server until the system exhausts the available memory.

You can specify a custom message to be displayed when the maximum number of concurrent connections is reached. Enter a new value for MaxClients Message in the Registry, as described in Advanced Configuration Parameters for FTP Server Service later in this chapter.

Annotating Directories

You can add directory descriptions to inform FTP users of the contents of a directory on the server by creating a file called FTPSVC-CKM in the directory that you want to annotate. Usually you want to make this a hidden file so that directory listings do not display it. Use File Manager or type the command **attrib+h~ftpsvc~.ckm** at the command prompt.

Directory annotation can be toggled by FTP users user by user, with the built-in, site-specific command **ckm**. On most FTP client implementations (including the Windows NT FTP client), users type a command at the command prompt similar to **quote site ckm** to get this effect.

You can set the default behavior for directory annotation by setting a value for AnnotateDirectories in the Registry, as described in Advanced Configuration Parameters for FTP Server Service later in this chapter.

DOS and UNIX Style Directory Listings

Some FTP client software makes assumptions based on the formatting of directory list information. The Windows NT FTP Server provides some flexibility for client software that requires directory listing similar to that of UNIX systems. Users can use the command **dirstyle** to toggle directory-listing format between MS-DOS-style (the default) and UNIX-style listings. On most FTP client implementations (including the Windows NT FTP client), users type a command at the command prompt similar to **quote site dirstyle** to get this effect.

You can set the default style for directory-listing format by setting a value for MsDosDirOutput in the Registry, as described in Advanced Configuration Parameters for FTP Server Service later in this chapter.

Custom Greeting and Exit Messages

You can create customized greeting and exit messages by setting values for GreetingMessage and ExitMessage in the Registry, as described in Advanced Configuration Parameters for FTP Server Service below. By default, these value entries are not in the Registry, and so you must add them to customize the message text.

Greeting and exit messages are sent to users when they connect or disconnect from the FTP Server. When you create custom messages, you can add multiline messages of your choice.

Logging FTP Connections

You can log incoming FTP connections in the System event log by setting values for LogAnonymous and LogNonAnonymous in the Registry, as described in Advanced Configuration Parameters for FTP Server Service below. By default, these value entries are not in the Registry, and so you must add them to log incoming connections.

You can specify whether event log entries are made for both anonymous and nonanonymous users connecting to the FTP Server. You can view such entries in the System event log by using Event Viewer.

Advanced Configuration Parameters

In this section I present configuration parameters which affect the behavior of the FTP Server service and which can be modified only through the Registry Editor. After you modify any of these value entries, you must restart the FTP Server service for the changes to take effect.

Caution: You can impair or disable Windows NT if you make incorrect changes in the Registry while using Registry Editor. Whenever possible, use administrative tools such as Control Panel rather than Registry Editor to make configuration changes. If you make errors while changing values with Registry Editor, you will not be warned, because it does not recognize semantic errors.

To make changes to the FTP Server service configuration using Registry Editor:

1. Run \WINNT35\SYSTEM32\REGEDT32.EXE from File Manager or Program Manager, or at a command prompt, type **start regedt32** and press **Enter**.

When the Registry Editor window appears, you can press **F1** to get Help on how to make changes in Registry Editor.

2. In Registry Editor, click the window titled **HKEY_LOCAL_MACHINE** on Local Machine, and then click the icons for the **SYSTEM** subtree until you reach this subkey (see Figure 4.45):

    `..\SYSTEM\CurrentControlSet\Services\FTPSVC\Parameters`

All the parameters described here are located under this Registry subkey (Figure 4.46).

We next describe the value entries for FTP Server service parameters that can be set only by adding an entry or changing their values in Registry Editor. These value entries do not appear by default in the Registry, and so you must add an entry if you want to change its default value.

AnnotateDirectories

Data type = REG_DWORD

Range = 0 or 1

Default = 0 (false that is, directory annotation is off)

This value entry defines the default behavior of directory annotation for newly connected users. Directory descriptions are used to inform FTP users about the

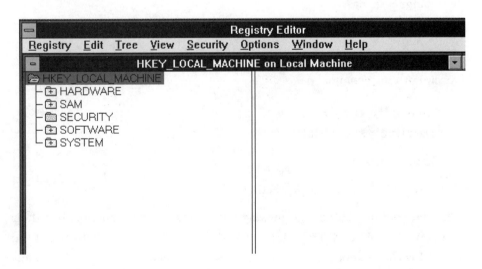

Figure 4.45 NT Registry Editor.

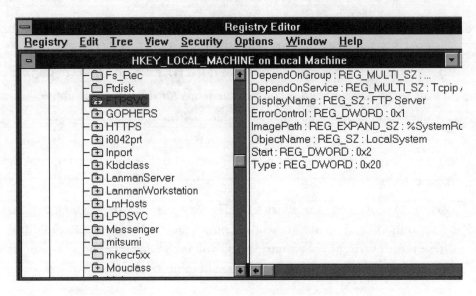

Figure 4.46 NT Registry Editor.

contents of a directory on the server. The directory description is saved in the file names~FTPSVC~.CKM, which is usually a hidden file. When this value is 1, directory annotation is on.

ExitMessage

>   Data type = REG_SZ

>   Range = String

>   Default = Goodbye.

This value entry defines a signoff message that will be sent to FTP clients upon receipt of a **quit** command.

GreetingMessage

>   Data type = REG_MULTI_SZ

>   Range = String

>   Default None (no special greeting message)

This value entry defines the message to be sent to new clients after their accounts have been validated. In accordance with Internet behavior, if the client logs on as anonymous and specifies an identity that starts with a minus sign ( ), this greeting message is not sent.

LogAnonymous

> Data type = REG_DWORD
>
> Range = 0 or 1
>
> Default = 0 (false that is, do not log successful anonymous logons)

This value entry enables or disables logging of anonymous logons in the System event log.

LogNonAnonymous

> Data type = REG_DWORD
>
> Range = 0 or 1
>
> Default = 0 (false that is, do not log successful nonanonymous logons)

This value entry enables or disables logging of nonanonymous logons in the System event log.

LogFileAccess

> Data type = REG_DWORD
>
> Range = 0 or 1
>
> Default = 0 (do not log file accesses to FTPSVC.LOG)

If this value is nonzero, all file accesses are logged to the file FTPSVC.LOG in the service's current directory (typically \systemroot\SYSTEM32). For each file opened by the FTP Server, FTPSVC.LOG will have a single line entry in this format:

> IPAddress username action path date_time

- **ip_address** is the client computer's IP address.

- **username** is the user's name (or password for anonymous logons).

- **action** is opened, created, or appended.

- **path** is the fully qualified path of the file acted upon.

- **date_time** is the date and time the action took place.

> Entries are also written to the log whenever the FTP Server starts or stops.

LowercaseFiles

Data type = REG_DWORD

Range = 0 or 1

Default = 0 (do not map file names to lowercase)

If this value is nonzero, all file names returned by the list and list commands will be mapped to lowercase for noncase-preserving file systems. This mapping occurs only when a directory listing is requested on a noncase-preserving file system. If this value is 0, case in all file names will be unaltered. Currently, FAT is the only noncase-preserving file system supported under Windows NT, and so this flag has no effect when retrieving listings on HPFS or NTFS partitions.

MaxClientsMessage

Data type = REG_SZ

Range = String

Default = Maximum clients reached, service unavailable.

This value entry specifies the message to be sent to an FTP client if the maximum number of clients has been reached or exceeded. This message indicates that the server is refusing additional clients because it is currently servicing the maximum number of connections (as specified in the FTP Service dialog box or the MaxConnections value in the Registry).

MsdosDirOutput

Data type = REG_DWORD

Range = 0 or 1

Default = 1 (true that is, directory listings will look like MS-DOS)

This value entry specifies the default behavior for whether the output of the list command will look like the output of the MS-DOS **dir** command or the output of the UNIX **ls** command. This value also controls the direction of slashes in paths sent by the **pwd** command.

When this value is 1, directory listings will look like MS_DOS listings, and the path will have backward slashes (\). If this value is 0, listings will look like UNIX listings, and the path will have forward slashes (/).

These Registry parameters can be set using the options available when config-uring the FTP Server service in the Network Settings dialog box:

- AllowAnonymous

- AnonymousOnly

- AnonymousUsername

- ConnectionTimeout

- HomeDirectory

- MaxConnections

These Registry parameters can be set using the options available when you select the FTP Server icon in Control Panel and then click on the **Security** button:

- ReadAccessMask

- Write AccessMask

The ranges of values that can be entered for these parameters in Registry Editor are the same as those described in the related dialog boxes earlier in this chapter. Use only the FTP Server service dialog boxes to set these values.

Gopher Servers

Is Gopher dead? The World Wide Web's explosive growth and wide popularity make that a popular question. But just as the furry little creature in the movie *Caddyshack* had staying power, Gopher has managed to survive and continues to prosper as an efficient and effective tool for delivering information. In this chapter I describe three highly viable options for running a Gopher server, two of them on Windows 3.1 and one on Windows NT 3.5. If the Gopher model for delivering information is your choice, this software offers the same features as the UNIX counterparts, with flexibility added by menu editors and comfort contributed by a graphical interface for administering and configuring systems. Advanced features include the ability to interface with WAIS information servers, relational databases, and the security to protect your information.

Windows 3.1 Gopher Server

The Hamburg Gopher Server for Windows 3.1, written by Gunter Hille of the University of Hamburg in Germany, originally came out as a Microsoft DOS-based server and was eventually rewritten for Windows. Because it requires a Winsock implementation, you should have Trumpet, Chameleon, or some other Winsock product installed, configured, and running to test the server.

The program's features include:

- Allows you to serve varied information and file types (e.g., text, images) to Gopher and other browsers.

- Provides a secure server mode in which you have to specify the names of programs that can be executed by the server.

- Ability to restrict access to files above the working directory.

- The server can run application or utility programs from Gopher menus and includes examples in the distribution.

Some may feel that this server does not have industrial strength. The limitations on number and kinds of Gopher types it supports are obvious. Then too, since 1993, the software's author has not had the opportunity to work on it, but has spent time on such other good endeavors as the Web4Ham Windows Web Server (discussed in a later chapter). Once you consider these limitations, if you are a Windows 3.1 user and have a 386 or better, this is a very useful alternative for serving information, especially with the full-text search engine. Perhaps your organization needs to provide information to a specific clientele but has limited resources. Or your more critical needs might be met by some form of text indexing and search engine or keyword retrieval mechanism that this product provides.

Installing the Windows Gopher Server

To get a basic idea about what the server can do and how it does so, install and run it by following these steps.

1. You can retrieve the GO4HAM package from the University of Hamburg: **ftp://ftp.informatik.unihamburg.de/pub/net/gopher/ pc/go4ham.** The GO4HAM files, go4ham.doc and go4ham.zip, can be found in the go4ham directory.

2. On your PC, set up a Gopher directory (e.g., C:\GO4HAM) and unzip the files into the GO4HAM directory.

3. Print out each of the *.DOC files for additional reference.

4. The software distribution comes with sample files. Files with the extension .GOP include directory entries. We will modify these entries to use the sample data provided for setting up our server. Modify the file named 000ROOT.GOP in the GO4HAM directory and change the IP address in each line to your IP address. You'll also need to change the path names for the location of the Go4ham documentation and the Search Engine (Figure 5.1). It is very important to remember here that tabs *must* separate each field in the .GOP files. If you fail to insert tabs you will get unpredictable displays on your client browser. You should also modify the IP addresses in the file 00GOPHER.GOP to match your address. The first line, for example (if you have all the files in the GO4HAM directory) will then be changed to:

```
0 1KB The Database Information Engine    OGOPHINFO.DOC    198.69.33.75    70
```

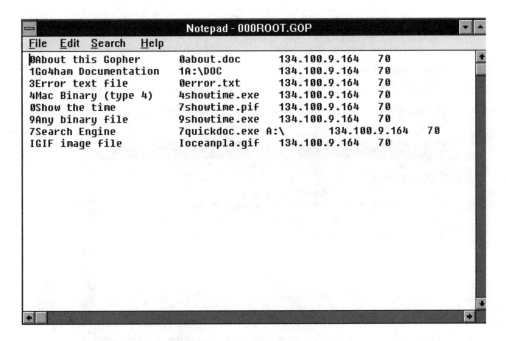

Figure 5.1 GO4HAM sample file.

Each line has the fields listed here. The sample values are from the line above.

Gopher Item Type   0

User Display String   1 Kb The Database Information Engine

Selector String   7GOPHINFO.DOC

IP Address of Server   198.69.33.75 (place your IP address in this field)

Port Number   70

5. You can now start the Gopher Server by selecting the Windows File Manager and selecting **Run** from the File Menu. Select the program SERVER.EXE in the GO4HAM directory. From the Go4ham server windows (Figure 5.2), select File and Start Server.

6. Go to Netscape or any Gopher client and point to your server. With Netscape, you would select Open Location from the menu, and enter a URL such as:

```
gopher://198.69.33.75
```

Just substitute your IP address for the one above. You should now see the home Gopher screen as shown in Figure 5.3.

Creating Directory Files

Included in the distribution is a program that can create .GOP files for you. GOPBROWS.EXE creates a file 00GOPHER.GOP with all the files specified in

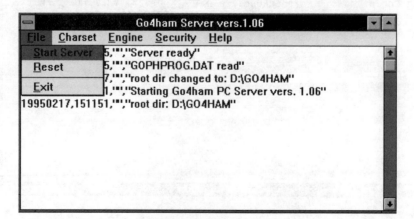

Figure 5.2 GO4HAM starting the server.

the command-line parameters. This program works recursively in all the subdi-rectories, starting at the specified root directory.

If you later create a DOC directory off the GO4HAM directory, to store the DOC files and perhaps some .TXT files you have set up, you could create the .GOP file for the DOC directory by typing this line at the DOS prompt:

```
GOPBROWS 198.69.3.75 C:\GO4HAM\DOC *.DOC *.TXT
```

This instruction will examine each file with a .DOC or .TXT extension, insert your IP address, grab the first line of text from each file for the gopher menu-item description, size the file (e.g., 2 Kb), and type the file (e.g., Gopher type 0). Thus you can use this program to search each directory, creating the necessary directory entries in the 00GOPHER.GOP file.

Executing Programs

As you can see from the sample menu items (Figure 5.3), you can execute programs from the menus. Of course, this choice opens up a potential security

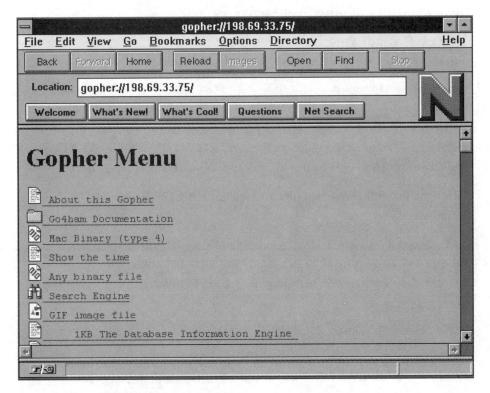

Figure 5.3 GO4HAM gopher menu.

hole. Be extremely careful which programs you allow people to execute. A tame example is included with the menu item Show the Time. The PIF file SHOWTIME.PIF is executed and, in turn, runs SHOWTIME.EXE, which will return the time to the client browser. The server is able to execute any program that does not call for user input. and sends its results to a file. After the program is executed, the server looks for a file called RESULTS.PDX and sends its contents to the Gopher client. As you can see in the SHOWTIME example, you need only use the item type of zero and the selector string of 7. Create a PIF file for every DOS executable that calls a batch file. The distribution has several examples.

Secure Server Mode

To maintain adequate security, you must specify the names of programs that can be executed in the file GOPHPROG.DAT. If the program is not listed in this file, it will not be executed and no access will be granted to files above the working directory. In our example, the working directory is GO4HAM. A logging file, GOPHSERV.LOG, will track accesses to the server and log to disk the information that is displayed in the server window.

Full-Text Searching

You can index your text files very easily with this procedure:

1. You will probably want to exit to DOS or select the MSDOS icon from the MAIN program group and shell out to DOS to do this step and those which follow. The first task is to set an environment variable that the indexing program requires. Insert the line: **SET MYIP = 198.69.33.75** (replace this value with your address) into the AUTOEXEC.BAT file.

2. Purge the (sample) database files by typing in **00CLEAR** at the DOS prompt.

3. Next, create the database files by typing in **00MAKE** at the DOS prompt. You can set up the documentation files that come with the GO4HAM distribution for searching by typing in this command:

   ```
   QUICKNDX C:\GO4HAM\*.DOC
   ```

   These database files will be updated:

WORDS	Dictionary of words.
REFS	Occurrences of words in documents.
WHERE	Location of documents.

STOPW	List of stopwords.
HITS	Hitlist of frequent words.
TEMP	Used by the search engine.

This updating will take a few moments and progress messages will be displayed showing you which files are processed.

4. Once the indexing is complete, you can return to Windows and **Run** the SERVER.EXE program from the File menu. Once the program starts, go to the File menu and select Start Server (Figure 5.2).

5. Next, go to your Gopher client or Netscape, access the server, select the Search Engine menu item, and try it (Figure 5.4). Key in the keyword **gopher** and you should have a screen as shown in Figure 5.5. The Information menu item will hold the summary results of your search (Figure 5.6), and the other items listed on the menu (e.g., 1KB This is a

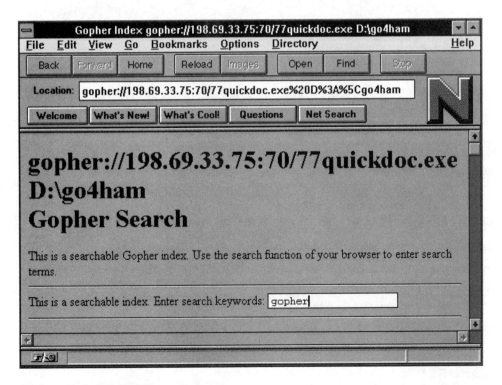

Figure 5.4 GO4HAM search screen.

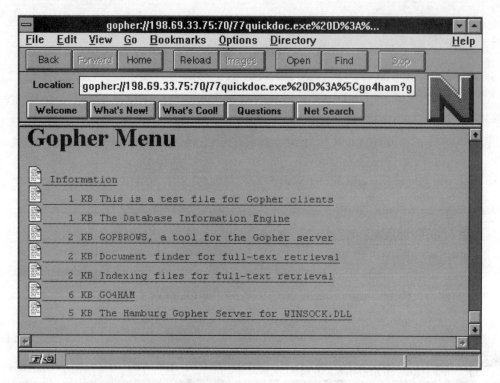

Figure 5.5 GO4HAM search results.

test file...) are links to the documents that include the keyword you entered.

These steps can be done from DOS or from within the server program itself, as illustrated in Figures 5.7 and 5.8.

Beame & Whiteside Gopher Server

The Beame & Whiteside Gopher server is part of an entire suite of client and server products available for Windows 3.1. The Gopher application runs as a server under the Beame & Whiteside inetd server. Installing the Beame & Whiteside client and server product suite, including their TCP/IP implementation, is covered in detail in Chapter 4 and is required reading for installing and supporting their Gopher server.

GOPHERDW

GOPHERDW is a daemon program, available through Beame & Whiteside Software, running under the inetd daemon (or program). It allows a remote

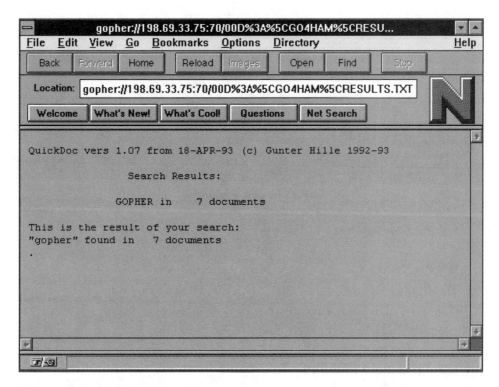

Figure 5.6 GO4HAM search summary.

user to access informational menus and other Gopher item types that have
been set up on your PC, using the Gopher model of information delivery. To
start up the Beame & Whiteside Gopher server from the inetd menu, select
Setup and then gopherd. Click on the **Enable** box to start the gopherd
daemon. Figure 5.9 shows your options for running the Gopher server through
inetd.

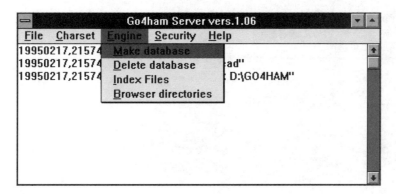

Figure 5.7 GO4HAM make database.

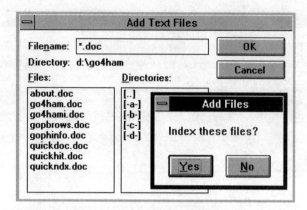

Figure 5.8 GO4HAM index files.

GOPHMNU

The Gopher Menu utility, GOPHMNU, is a Windows-based utility used to create and edit the menus used by the Beame & Whiteside gopherdw Gopher server program. You can use a text editor (such as Windows Notepad) to create and modify Gopher menus, but this handy interface makes creating and maintaining Gopher menus a snap.

To use the Gopher Menu utility, double-click on the GOPHMNU icon in the BW-Apps group in the Windows Program Manager to display the Gopher Menu

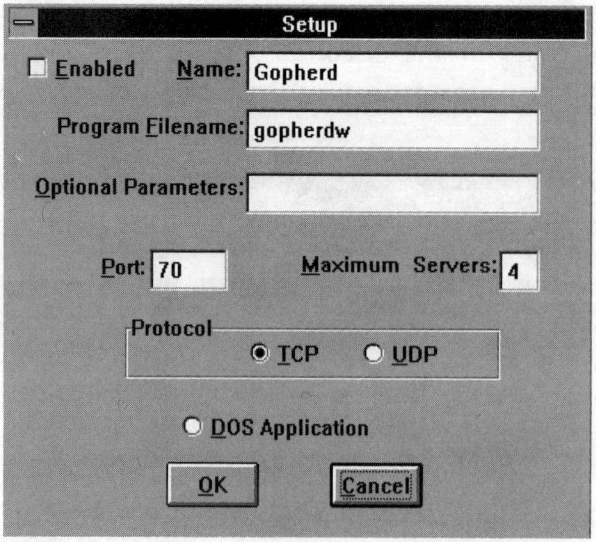

Figure 5.9 Beame & Whiteside starting the Gopher daemon.

screen as shown in Figure 5.10. The functions discussed in the following sections will be available to you.

File Options Gopher Menu Editor

These items are available in the File menu:

New. Choose **New** to display a new menu screen, where you may create a new Gopher menu.

Open. Choose **Open** to open an existing Gopher menu file. A standard Windows File Open screen is presented, with a default listing of all .GMN files in the C:\BWTCP directory.

Close. Choose **Close** to close the current Gopher menu file. If you have modified the file, you will be prompted to save it.

Save. Choose **Save** to save the current Gopher menu file.

Save As. Choose **Save As** to save a new or modified file. A standard Windows File Save As screen will be displayed. Files are saved with the default extension .GMN.

Recent File. This item is shown only until you have saved at least one menu file. After menu files are saved, the four most recent files are displayed. Select the file you want to open.

Exit. Choose Exit to exit the Gopher Menu Builder program.

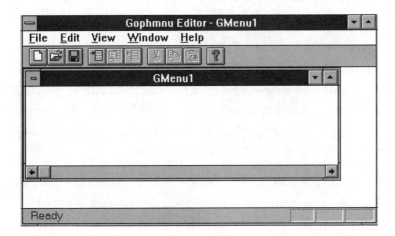

Figure 5.10 Beame & Whiteside GOPHMNU.

Edit Options Gopher Menu Editor

These items are available in the Edit menu:

Insert. Choose **Insert** to display the Edit Menu Item screen, which you can use to enter a new line in the Gopher menu file.

Edit. Choose **Edit** to invoke the Edit Menu Item screen, which carries the information for the selected line. You can use this screen to modify the information for the selected line in the Gopher menu file.

Delete. Choose **Delete** to delete the selected line from the current Gopher menu.

Cut. Choose **Cut** to cut the selected line from the Gopher menu and place it on the Windows Clipboard.

Copy. Choose **Copy** to copy the selected line from the Gopher menu and place it on the Windows Clipboard.

Paste. Choose **Paste** to paste the contents of the Windows Clipboard at the current cursor location.

View Options Gopher Menu Editor

These items are available in the View menu:

Toolbar. Select this item to show the Toolbar buttons at the top of the menu window.

Status Bar. Select this item to show the Status Bar at the bottom of the menu window.

Gopher Menus

Gopher menus are a series of options organized into a hierarchical menu. Using the Menu Builder, you can create a new menu or add to or edit an existing menu. To create a new menu or add a new menu item, select the **Edit** menu and choose **Insert** (or use the **Insert** toolbar button). The Edit Menu Item dialog box will appear as shown in Figure 5.11. The fields available are:

Menu Type This option describes the type of menu item you are creating. Each choice has a corresponding letter or number associated with it, to identify the menu typeand icon type. You can specify text files, Telnet resources,

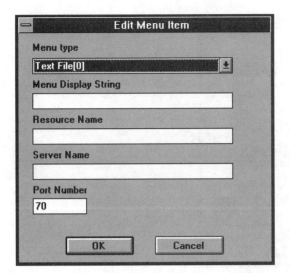

Figure 5.11 Beame & Whiteside GOPHMNU Edit Menu.

directories, images, and many other file types. Click on the arrow at the right side of the field to display a list of menu types. Select the appropriate type from this list. The list of menu types can be found in Chapter 3.

Menu Display String Enter the character string you want the user to see on a menu line for this item. For example, if you were setting up a text file with information about your Gopher, you might call this item: About This Gopher.

Resource Name The Resource Name is the path that tells the Gopher server which information or file to obtain when the user double-clicks on a menu choice. This information could be the path and name of a file, the name of a directory, and so on.

Server Name Enter either IP address or host name of the server where the information is located.

Port Number The port number that the menu item is to use. The default Gopher port number 70 is used for files, directories, and the like. Telnet sessions use port 23. If the resource uses a different port number to connect, enter the number here. A sample Edit Menu Item screen is shown in Figure 5.12.

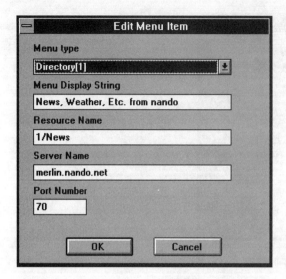

Figure 5.12 Beame & Whiteside GOPHMNU Edit Menu Item.

When you have completed all the fields, click on **OK** to accept the entries and return to the Main Menu screen. To add items, click on **Insert** from the Edit menu and repeat the procedure detailed above. When you have finished adding your menu items, click on **Save As** in the File menu. Type the name for the menu you wish to save, and click on **OK**.

Windows NT Gopher Server

The European Microsoft Windows NT Academic Centre (EMWAC) is a project based at the University of Edinburgh and sponsored by Datalink Computers, Digital Equipment Corporation, Microsoft, Research Machines, Sequent, and the University of Edinburgh. One of their first endeavors was to release a freeware Gopher server based on the Microsoft Windows NT operating system. The Gopher program was written by Chris Adie. The EMWAC NT Gopher implementation has these features:

- Runs as a Windows NT service with executables available for Intel, MIPS, or Digital Alpha systems.

- Offers UNIX Compatibility Mode, which allows easy conversion of Gopher files and directories from a UNIX platform to Microsoft NT.

- Is multithreaded.

- WAIS database searching capability is supported and a WAISTOOL tool kit is also available.

- Has a caching option and uses memory-mapped file I/O, both for improved performance.

- Utilizes NT system-management functions, such as logging errors to the Event Logger, configuration through the Control Panel, and optionally logs HTTP transactions to a server log.

NT Gopher Installation

The server software is included on the accompanying CD or may be retrieved from:

`ftp://emwac.ed.ac.uk/pub/gophers`

The software includes two zipped files, one for Intel-based hardware and one for DEC Alpha. The Intel version is distributed in the GSI386.ZIP file.

If you are implementing the server on the Intel platform, a Windows NT system with a network connection and 16 MB of memory should suffice.

In summary, the installation steps are:

1. Use PKUNZIP to unzip the software distribution files into a directory of your choosing, which you should create now (e.g., D:\GOPHER). Later, you will want to plan a directory structure that makes sense for your installation, moving files to be served to the data directory, and the software distribution files to another directory. But for now, for simplicity, we'll commingle the files in one directory.

    The files that will be unzipped include:

GOPHERS.EXE	Server executable
GOPHERS.CPL	Control Panel applet
GOPHERS.HLP	Control Panel applet help file
GOPHERS.PS	Gopher Manual Postscript

GOPHERS.DOC	Gopher Manual MS Word
GOPHERS.WRI	Gopher Manual Windows Write
COPYRITE.TXT	Copyright statement
READ.ME	Version features, etc.

Additional files in this book to be used for installation are included on the CD in the \EMGOPHER\ directory:

ABOUT.TXT	Gopher text file
GOPHER.GFR	Gopher links file
ABOUT.TXT	Alias file in a subdirectory called \EMGOPHER\ALIAS.GFR\A

2. Sign on to an Administrator's account on the NT system.

3. Copy the file GOPHERS.EXE to the \WINNT35\SYSTEM32 directory. Go to the Security/Permissions menu item in the File Manager, and verify that the System user has read permission on GOPHERS.EXE.

4. Copy the GOPHERS.CPL file and GOPHERS.HLP to the WINNT35\SYSTEM32 directory. Select the Control Panel from the Program Manager to verify that the Gopher Server icon is in the Control Panel.

5 Set up a subdirectory off the main Gopher directory (e.g., D:\GOPHER\ALIAS.GFR). Copy the file ABOUT.TXT from the \EMGO-PHER\ALIAS.GFR directory on the CD. This is the alias information file and should not be confused with the other ABOUT.TXT file, which carries the welcome message for your server. Copy the files ABOUT.TXT and GOPHER.GFR from the CD to the main Gopher directory (e.g., D:\GOPHER).

6. From Windows, click on the **MS DOS** icon to go to the MS DOS command line. Type in: **gophers -install**. This will install Gopher as a service and also register it with the Event Logger.

7. Start the NT Control Panel and double-click on the **Services** icon (Figure 5.13). The Gopher Server should be shown as a service, as in Figure 5.14.

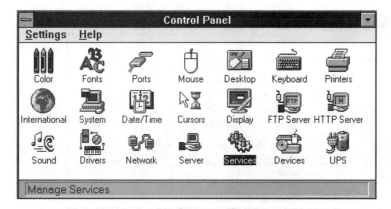

Figure 5.13 NT Control Panel services.

8. Select the Control Panel and click on the Gopher Server applet (Figure 5.15). The Configuration window will appear as in Figure 5.16.

9. Set the Data Directory for the server. This is the directory where the Gopher files you want to make available will be stored. The default is D:\GOPHER. You can put this directory on a file server if you wish, but with some reservations.

   For testing, leave the directory set to the default. One consideration to understand is about establishing directories on a file server versus a local computer. On a local system, directories are mapped to individual users and when the user logs off, the mappings go away. If your gopher server

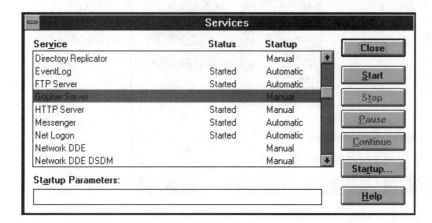

Figure 5.14 NT Services Gopher.

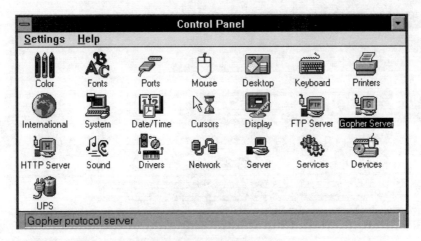

Figure 5.15 NT Control Panel Gopher Server.

starts up when the operating system loads, specify the Data Directory,
using a UNC form of directory name. For example, on the server GUMBY
with the data directory (or sharename) of DOCS, your Data Directory
specification will be:

```
\\GUMBY\DOCS
```

Gopher Server

Data directory: d:\Gopher

TCP/IP port: 70

File extension to Gopher type mapping:

[Default]	0	Text
ARC	5	PC binary
AU	s	Sound
BMP	I	Image
DLL	9	Binary
EXE	9	Binary
GIF	g	GIF Image
HTM	h	HTML
HTML	h	HTML
SRC	7	WAIS index

New mapping
Change mapping
Delete mapping

☐ Unix compatibility mode

☐ Enable caching with timeout: 5 minutes

☒ Log transactions in directory: D:\WINNT35

OK Cancel Defaults Help

GOPHERS version 0.92

Figure 5.16 NT Gopher Server configuration.

10. Next, indicate the TCP/IP port on which the Gopher Server will receive incoming connections. The default is port 70.

11. Review the file extension to Gopher type mapping. Leave the defaults as they appear for the initial installation.

12. Leave the UNIX compatibility mode box unchecked at this time.

13. Caching may be enabled for the Gopher server by clicking on the checkbox. You can also indicate the time-out interval, in minutes, specifying how often the cache files will be re-created. The default is 5 minutes. For now, leave the box unchecked, which is the default.

    You can improve performance by utilizing caching. When a client is served a menu, the menu is stored in a cache file in the directory CACHE.GFR. When the menu is next requested, the cache file is used. Because contents of directories change, the cache needs to be re-created periodically. If the server detects that the cache file is older than the time-out period configured through the Control Panel applet, it re-creates it.

14. Gopher transactions can be logged to the Windows NT Event Log. The default location is D:\WINNT35. Check the Log transactions in directory box so that we can log these items from each request to the log file:

    • Time and date of the request.

    • IP address of the Gopher server and client.

    • The file or directory the client requested (selector string).

    A new log file is created daily. The file-name format is GSyymmdd.LOG.

15. Once you have finished with the configuration parameters, click on **OK**.

16. Go to the Control Panel and click on the **Services** applet. Start the Gopher Server by clicking on the **Start** button (Figure 5.14). Later, you may want to have the server start automatically when the system boots: Click on the **Startup** button to configure this option.

Testing the NT Gopher Server

To test the server you can use the files from the CD (ABOUT.TXT, etc.) or you can create a few files using your favorite editor.

When you installed the software you should have copied the file ABOUT.TXT from the CD and placed it in the D:\GOPHER directory. This file that resides on the Server is a typical top-level text file that you will find on most Gophers, welcoming visitors and describing the server.

The file GOPHER.GFR, also in the D:\GOPHER directory, is an example of a Gopher link file. The server recognizes any file with the .GFR extension as a link file. It is within such files that you define links to other Gopher servers. Open the file with Windows Notepad to get an idea about how you will construct links. As you can see from the file, several keys can be assigned values to construct a link, including:

Name. This string is displayed on the client menu to describe the menu item (e.g., About the University Gopher).

Host. The name of the computer on which the information resides.

Port. The TCP/IP port number where the remote Gopher server is running.

Numb. A number indicating in what order this item should appear on the menu.

Path. Gopher selector for the linked directory or file. The format of the selector is:

- The first character is the Gopher type.

- Next is a backslash (\).

- Path name of the file, relative to the Gopher data directory.

Type. Gopher type character for the remote object that overrides the type assigned from the file extension to Gopher type-mapping table.

Notice that each link in the .GFR files is separated by a hash symbol (#).

Unless you use the alias capability of the Server, the Gopher client will use the file and directory names when constructing the menu display. Therefore, we'll use Gopher's alias to display a user-friendly name. The alias information is

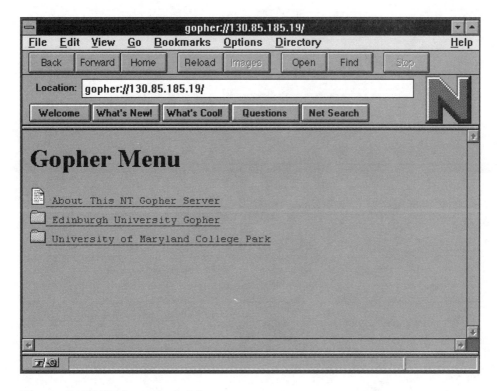

Figure 5.17 NT Sample Gopher menu.

stored in the ALIAS.GFR directory that you created. In our example, we'll use the alias file for the file ABOUT.TXT. This file is included on the CD and should have been placed in the D:\GOPHER\ALIAS.GFR directory during installation.

Once you have created these test files, start up your Gopher client, preferably on another machine (the example shows the Netscape browser) and point your Gopher to the IP address (or domain name) of your NT server. For example, open a URL to:

```
gopher://yoursite.domain.com/
```

The Gopher menu in Figure 5.17 should appear.

World Wide Web Servers

The Windows and Windows NT environments certainly have no shortage of software for implementing a World Wide Web server. These products run the gamut from freeware offerings developed experimentally (and they work) to robust, fully featured commercial products that, feature for feature, meet and beat their Unix counterparts on many, perhaps most counts. And many Web servers in this chapter fall somewhere between. Which server is right for you? To answer that question you will have to match each server against your requirements. Ask yourself these questions, and measure the server's features against your answers: Do you require a server that provides elementary or advanced capabilities in:

- performance?
- security?
- image mapping?
- CGI programming?

- full-text indexing?

- flexibility and tools for systems administration?

- on-board utilities (e.g., analysis of log files)?

- prepackaged mail forms, database interfaces, and so on?

- documentation?

When you've analyzed your requirements and evaluated and tested the offerings in this chapter, you'll be able to implement a server well suited to your needs.

SerWeb: An HTTP Server for Win 3.1 and NT

SerWeb is a freeware World Wide Web (WWW) server that runs under Microsoft Windows 3.1 or Microsoft Windows NT. The server was written in Visual C++ by Gustavo Estrella and the source code is available as part of the software distribution. This is a barebones implementation of HTTP version 0.9. Some of the features that may be important to you were not implemented, including logging to a file, security, and CGI. This is in no way a criticism. But the program's author undertook it as a part-time project, and, as such, it is very good. Let us not look a gift horse in the mouth.

Why then would one want to use the program? Well, if you want to begin to understand how HTTP works and also see how Winsock programming works, this is probably a great place to start. You can examine the source code and test the server's features and get a chance to look under the hood. If you are interested in writing your own Web server under Windows, this is an excellent introduction.

Installing the SerWeb HTTP Server
To install the SerWeb HTTP Server:

1. Retrieve the server software:

   ftp://sunsite.unc.edu/pub/micro/pc-stuff/ms-windows/winsock/apps
   and the file name is serweb03.zip.

2. Create a directory on your PC for the server software (e.g., C:\SERWEB). Unzip the files with PKUNZIP and place them in the SERWEB directory.

3. Use your favorite editor to edit the SERWEB.INI file (Figure 6.1). We list the parameters found in this file:

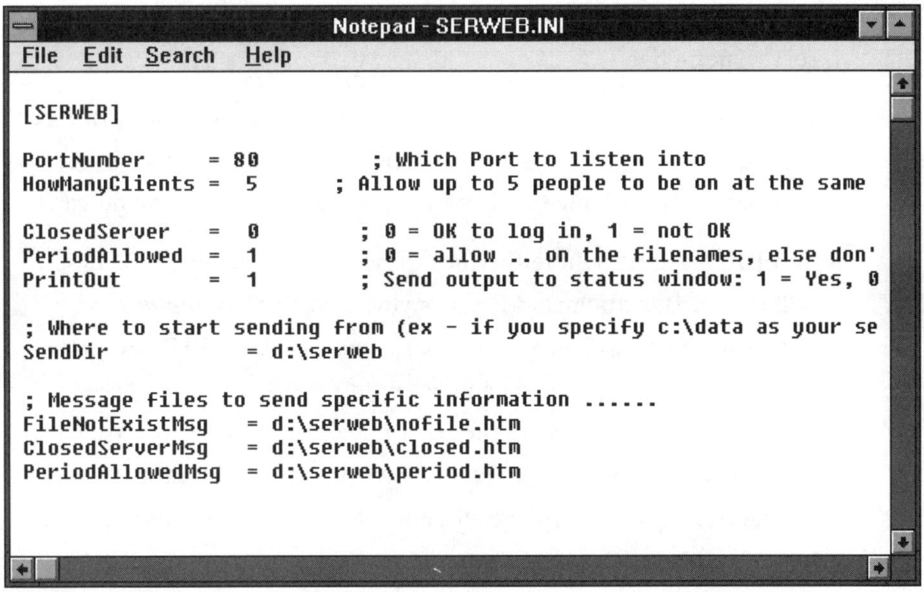

```
┌─────────────────────────────────────────────────────────────────┐
│ ─              Notepad - SERWEB.INI                        ▼ ▲   │
├─────────────────────────────────────────────────────────────────┤
│ File  Edit  Search  Help                                          │
├─────────────────────────────────────────────────────────────────┤
│ [SERWEB]                                                          │
│                                                                   │
│ PortNumber    = 80         ; Which Port to listen into            │
│ HowManyClients = 5        ; Allow up to 5 people to be on at the same │
│                                                                   │
│ ClosedServer   =  0        ; 0 = OK to log in, 1 = not OK         │
│ PeriodAllowed  =  1        ; 0 = allow .. on the filenames, else don' │
│ PrintOut       =  1        ; Send output to status window: 1 = Yes, 0 │
│                                                                   │
│ ; Where to start sending from (ex - if you specify c:\data as your se │
│ SendDir          = d:\serweb                                      │
│                                                                   │
│ ; Message files to send specific information ......               │
│ FileNotExistMsg   = d:\serweb\nofile.htm                          │
│ ClosedServerMsg   = d:\serweb\closed.htm                          │
│ PeriodAllowedMsg  = d:\serweb\period.htm                          │
│                                                                   │
└─────────────────────────────────────────────────────────────────┘
```

Figure 6.1 Editing the SERVEB.INI file.

- **PortNumber**. The port number where the server will listen for connections. The default is 80.

- **HowManyClients**. Identifies the maximum number of clients who can access the server at any one time. The default is 5, which should be tweaked upward or downward, depending on the size of your machine and the performance your clients are experiencing.

- **ClosedServer**. If set to 0 (zero), the default, the server will communicate with the client. If set to 1 (one), the server will send the ClosedServer Msg detailed below. This setting is useful if you want to update files on the server, or if you have other house-keeping that may warrant denying access. This parameter can be toggled from the server menu bar.

- **PeriodAllowed**. If set to 0 (zero), the server will allow requests for file names with a .. on the path (for example C:..\MYDOC\RESUME.TXT). This command can be used to get files outside of the SendDir (explained below). The default is 1 (one), which won't

allow period requests. This parameter can be toggled from the
server menu bar.

- **PrintOut**. If set to 1 (one), the default, status messages are printed.
If set to 0 (zero), no messages are printed and the system will run a
little faster. This parameter can be toggled from the server menu bar.

- **SendDir**. Defines where the files to be made available to clients
will reside. This command is synonymous with *Document Root*,
which we have explained. For testing, set to C:\SERWEB and place
your test HTML documents and so on in that directory. Later, you
can create a directory structure that makes sense for your installation. For example, you may want to set up a DOC directory (e.g.,
C:\SERWEB\DOC) and place all your HTML documents in it. If you
leave SendDir at C:, the default, users will have access to all your
files (this choice, of course, is NOT recommended!). When you
have set to C:\SERWEB, if someone opens a URL to
http://yourhost.site.com they will be requesting documents from
the C:\SERWEB directory.

- **FileNotExistMsg**. If a client requests a file that doesn't exist, the
file pointed to by this parameter will be sent to the client. The
default is C:\SERWEB\NOFILE.HTM. For our testing, leave at the
default. After testing, you'll want to modify this file and replace the
message that comes with the distribution. You may want to change
to the name of your home page file, which we will define as
INDEX.HTM.

- **ClosedServerMsg**. The default file is C:\SERWEB\CLOSED.HTM,
which will be sent to the client when ClosedServer = 1. After
testing, you'll want to modify this file and replace the message that
comes with the distribution.

- **PeriodAllowedMsg**. The default file is C:\SERWEB\PERIOD.HTM.
This file will be sent if the client requests a .. in the path and the
PeriodAllowed = 1. After testing, you'll want to modify this file and
replace the message that comes with the distribution.

4. Use your editor to modify the NOFILE.HTM, CLOSED.HTM, and PERIOD.HTM if you wish to change them now.

5. Copy your modified SERWEB.INI file to the C:\WINDOWS directory.

6. Start your TCP/IP connection if it is not already running. For example, with Trumpet, Run TCPMAN.EXE and Dial your service provider.

7. The CD supplies a sample home page template called \SERWEB\INDEX.HTM. Place the file in the C:\SERWEB directory. Two other files accompany the home page, REDBALL.GIF and HOME.GIF. Copy these too from the CD to C:\SERWEB. Refer to Chapter 7 for advice on HTML authoring and editing if you are new to HTML and you would like to customize your home page. With this sample, you can fashion a quick home page for testing and eventual production.

8. From The Windows File menu, select **Run** and start the Serweb server by executing the SERWEB.EXE program. A Serweb window should open and display logging information as in Figure 6.2.

9. Start up your favorite Web client (e.g., Netscape or Mosaic) and select Open URL. Key in your server's URL (i.e., IP address and home page name). For example:

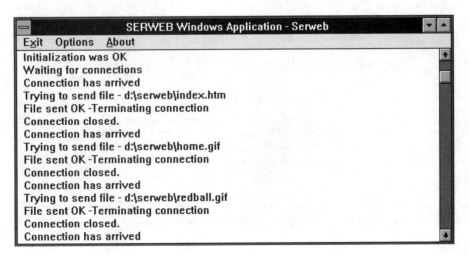

Figure 6.2 SERWEB logging.

```
http://198.69.33.75/INDEX.HTM
```

10. The Home Page should appear as in Figure 6.3.

Web4HAM: A Web Server for Windows

Web4HAM is a WWW server developed by Gunter Hille at the University of
Hamburg, Germany. The product is in its early development (version 0.17r1)
and offers an easy-to-install Web server with these features:

- The server can handle up to five client sessions.

- It produces a log file of sessions in SDF format.

- It supports private directories for special hosts or domains.

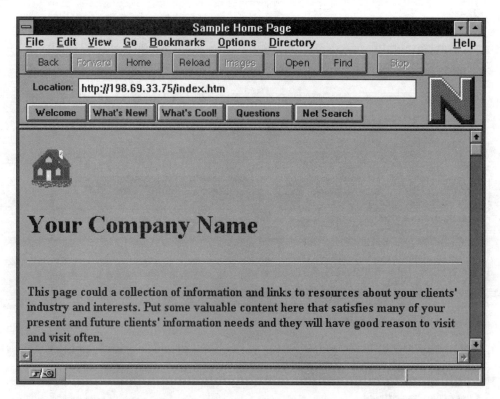

Figure 6.3 SERWEB home page.

- It supports the GET, HEAD, and SPACEJUMP (Imagemap) methods.

- It includes an interface to Paradox 4.0 files.

- The server has been tested with the Trumpet Winsock and NetManage's Chameleon.

Installing Web4HAM

The necessary zipped files, WEB4HAM.ZIP and WEB4HAM.DOC, are included on the CD or can be retrieved from:

```
ftp://ftp.informatik.uni-hamburg.de/pub/net/winsock
```

To install Web4HAM:

1. Create the directories C:\WEB4HAM and C:\WEB4DOC.

2. Unzip the WEB4HAM.ZIP file into the C:\WEB4HAM directory and the WEB4DOC.ZIP file into the C:\WEB4DOC directory.

3. Run your browser and access the documentation files. From your browser's File menu open the local file:

   ```
   C:\WEB4DOC\HOME.HTM.
   ```

   Notice that many of the demonstrable features will not work until later, when we start the server.

4. Create a data directory where your accessible HTML files will reside. Name this directory C:\WWW (you can restructure your directories later, but for now we'll use some directories for illustration). Additionally, add a subdirectory of OTHERS to C:\WWW (i.e., C:\WWW\OTHERS).

5. Modify the configuration file, WEB4HAM.INI, through Windows Notepad or your favorite editor to include the changes listed in the example below (the Web4HAM.INI File). This file should be kept in the same directory as the WEB4HAM server program (C:\WEB4HAM). All necessary initialization is done in this file.

The Web4HAM.INI File

The Web4HAM.INI file contains the necessary configuration information for your server. You can modify the location of your log file, document directory, and other parameters to administer the features of your Web4HAM server.

The [INIT] Section

```
[INIT]
DataDir    = C:\WWW\OTHERS
LogFile    = C:\WEB4HAM\WEB4HAM.LOG
ErrFiles   = C:\WEB4HAM\WEBER
HTTPort    = 80
Debug      = 0
Iconic     = 0
Logall     = 0
RxTimeout  = 30
```

- **DataDir**. This is the default data directory if no match is found in the host lists (see the [255...] section below). Place your HTML documents in this directory (and in the subdirectories of this directory). This is the equivalent of a *DocumentRoot* directory.

- **LogFile**. This is the file name of the server log file, where detail from client requests is written. This file is in SDF format and so is easily portable to various Windows programs (e.g., import to databases for reporting), but because it is not in common log format, Web statistics utilities from other sources will not be readily usable with these logs.

- **ErrFiles**. Specify the path to the error files (and the prefix of the error message files). You may change the name to any name with fewer than six characters. The server relies on a complete set of HTML files holding the error messages (e.g., WEBER200.HTM, WEBER201.HTM,...). You should eventually examine each of these error message files and make sure that the error messages that are returned to the client browser are phrased in the way you wish them to be. If not, use an HTML editor and modify them as you deem necessary.

- **HTTPort**. The Port number the server will listen on (default: 80).

- **Debug**. Should be set to zero. Currently used by the software author for debugging.

- **Iconic**. Set to 1 if the server will start without opening a window. Set to 0 to display client requests in a window.

- **Logall**. Set to 0 to show only the first line of client requests in the log file (i.e., WEB4HAM.LOG). Set to 1 to show all lines sent by client in the log file.

- **RxTimeout**. The next packet from the client must arrive within xx seconds.

The [PROGRAMS] Section

```
;
;left hand side must be a valid filename (8 + 3 characters)
;
[PROGRAMS]
PDXDEMO.SH=C:\WEB4HAM\WEB2PDX.EXE DEMO
```

At the left side of the equal (=) sign is the name of a specific search engine. The extension .SH is mandatory for a search engine. At the right side of the equal sign is the path to the program that will be executed by the server and an optional argument (DEMO in our example).

The [255...] Section

You will need to modify the IP addresses in this file to control access to your files. For testing, replace the occurrences of 198.69.33.75 (and associated mask values—e.g., 198.69) with your IP address.

```
; keep this order: special hosts first!
[255.255.255.255]
; dedicated hosts with full ip address
127.0.0.1 = c:\www
198.69.33.75          = c:\www
[255.255.255.0]
;dedicated class C subnets
198.69.33   = c:\www\others
[255.255.0.0]
;other class B domains
198.69      = c:\www\others
[255.0.0.0]
44.0        = c:\www\others
; hosts not in this section will have access to the default directory
specified by the variable "DataDir"
```

All directories are considered root directories for the listed hosts. In other words, a host who has access to the directory C:\WWW can also access files in all the C:\WWW subdirectories, but cannot access a file in C:\ or C:\FTP.

Entries will always be scanned in the order listed above. The first matching entry will be allowed, and so the server makes the directory associations in this way: local host and trusted hosts (in your domain) have access to the root DataDir, next come the hosts of specific class B domains, last are the hosts of specific class A domains. Hosts not listed will have access only to the default directory specified in the [INIT] section as DATADIR, which in our example is C:\WWW\OTHERS.

Do not use host names or domain names because the server does not use DNS calls. Therefore you will find IP numbers only in this file and in the LogFile.

Be aware that the way in which root directories are handled may not conform to the HTTP protocol. The same URL will point to different locations for different hosts. If we consider this URL:

```
http://my.domain./home.htm
```

in our sample configuration, it might be converted to these local directories, depending on your entries in the [255...] section of the WEB4HAM.INI file:

```
C:/WWW/HOME.HTM or to C:/WWW/OTHERS/HOME.HTM
```

Therefore, duly consider your placement of files, the security required (which addresses have access to them), and how the operational-management activities required to support your directory configuration will be affected.

The [SUFFIXES] Section

```
 [SUFFIXES]
HTM=text/html
PS =text/postscript
TXT=text/plain
DOC=text/msword
RTF=text/rtf
GIF=image/gif
JPG=image/jpeg
MPG=video/mpeg
WAV=audio/wav
AU =audio/ulaw
MID=audio/x-midi
ARC=file/arc
HQX=file/hqx
LHA=file/lharc
EXE=file/pcexe
TAR=file/tar
UUE=file/uuencode
ZIP=file/zip
ZOO=file/zoo
Z =file/tar.z
```

When a query comes from a client, the MIME content type will be returned. The content type is based on the suffix of the file (left of the equal sign) and the MIME type (right of the equal sign) in the [SUFFIXES] section.

6. Next, copy the files from the WEB4HAM directory to the C:\WWW directory so that you'll have sample HTML pages to access. Because the links from the home page (HOME.HTM) will not work unless you copy all the necessary files, the easiest way is to copy all the files, even the executables. Also copy the files INDEX.HTM, REDBALL.GIF, and HOME.GIF from the WEB4HAM directory on the CD to the C:\WWW\OTHERS directory so that you can test access from "outsiders," as specified in the WEB4HAM.INI file. Once you've completed testing, you will want to clear out these directories and populate them with your HTML files.

7. Through the Windows Program Manager Properties menu, set up an icon for the WEB4HAM.EXE file.

8. Make sure your Winsock is running. For example, run the Trumpet Winsock program, TCPMAN.EXE from the program manager in Windows.

9. To start the server, click on the icon for Web4ham.

10. Start Mosaic or Netscape and, through the File menu, select Open URL. Enter your server's address in the URL box in the form:

    `http://198.69.33.75/home.htm`

    You should see the barebones home page (HOME.HTM) that comes with the WEB4HAM distribution provided on the accompanying CD (Figure 6.4). If you have access to a machine that is considered "outside" (as defined in the INI file and by reference to the OTHERS directory), you can test those restrictions and access the C:\WWW\OTHERS\INDEX.HTM file (Figure 6.5) by typing in this URL:

    `http://98.69.33.75/others/index.htm`

The Web4HAM Log File

Client requests are recorded in the file WEB4HAM.LOG. The first line in each request is written to the log file unless you set the **Logall** variable to 1 in the WEB4HAM.INI file.

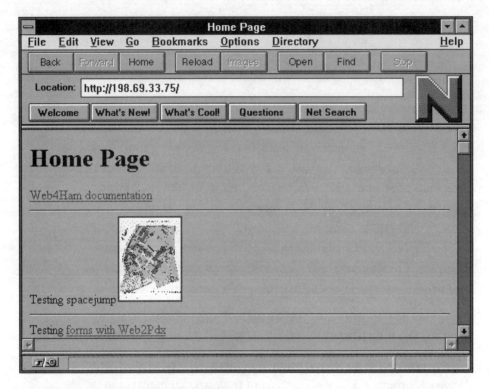

Figure 6.4 Web4HAM home page.

The log-file format is: Each line consists of four fields. The first is the date, in the format YYYYMMDD, followed by the time, in the format HHMMSS. The third item is the IP address of the client, and the fourth is the first line of the client browser's request. Server start and stop messages are also included in the file. Occasionally you may also see error messages from the Winsock in this file.

The log file is written in SDF format, which can be handled by many PC database and spreadsheet programs. You can therefore create reports showing server usage and statistics. Here is an excerpt from a sample log file:

```
19940320,194953,"rigel","Web4Ham/0.14 started"
19940320,195020,"127.0.0.1","GET /maxmor.htm HTTP/1.0"
19940320,195020,"127.0.0.1","HTTP/1.0 200 ok"
19940320,195028,"127.0.0.1","c:\serweb/maxmor.htm 17274 bytes sent"
19940320,195140,"rigel","Web4Ham/0.14 stopped"
```

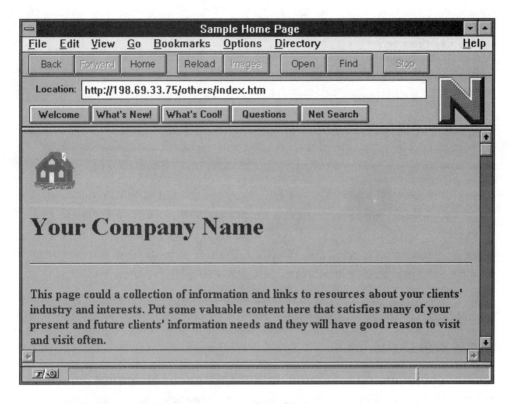

Figure 6.5 Web4HAM home page—Outsiders.

Spacejump (ISMAP) Method for the Web4HAM System

With a spacejump method, a map or a picture can be sent to the client and the user can click on a location on the map to let the server react, depending on the coordinates.

With the Web4HAM server, this is called the *Spacejump Method*. A map or picture must be marked with the ISMAP attribute to react to the spacejump method. A script holds the URLs that will be sent to the user who has clicked on a defined region. Each region has specified coordinates and a specified URL of a document.

Creating a Form

To create a document with a map using the spacejump method, these steps are required on the server's side: A document with a map having an ISMAP attribute, the map image file, and a script file with coordinates in the \SPACEJMP directory.

Here is the part of the document holding the link to the picture:

```
<A HREF="SPACEJMP/SCRIPT.JMP"><IMG SRC="INFOSMA.GIF" ISMAP>
100 100 SPACEJMP\DOC01.HTM
500 500 SPACEJMP\DOC02.HTM
```

If the root directory for a client is C:\WWW\ and the client clicks near to point (100,100), then the file C:\WWW\SPACEJMP\DOC01.HTM will be sent.

Notice, however, that you have to prefix the path with SPACEJMP\, because this is a command to the server (having no idea about the client's actual path). In the requested documents you have to specify relative paths. The best is to put all references inside the \SPACEJMP directory. If the document DOC01.HTM has an anchor <IMG SRC="MYPIC.GIF">, then the client requests the picture with a GET /SPACEJMP/MYPIC.GIF command.

Windows httpd

Windows httpd, originally based on the NCSA Unix httpd Server, was written by Bob Denny. The operation and configuration of the Windows server closely parallels those of the Unix server. Here are some of the features supported:

- Speaks both HTTP/1.0 and HTTP/0.9 protocols.

- Is designed to be a small, fast, and efficient server.

- Can deliver about 16 requests per second on a 486DX/66 with 8 Mb memory.

- Parallels features of Unix servers with CGI interface, Image-map support, access controls, log file and log-file analysis, and more.

The information provided here will give you a quick start. Extensive HTML documentation is included with the package, as well as demonstration pages illustrating basic server functions, forms, image maps, access controls, and other important features. The information provided here is especially useful because these concepts, features, and some configuration files apply not only to the Windows httpd server, but to the WebSite, the Beame & Whiteside WWW server, and other products that were either ported from Unix or written by Bob Denny.

The software is available from:

```
http://www.city.net/win-httpd/whttpd14.zip
```

Windows httpd Installation

The software distribution can be unzipped, the necessary directories created, and the server run with no configuration-file editing. Documentation can be viewed through your Netscape or Mosaic browser.

To install the software:

1. Create a directory named HTTPD on your hard drive (C:\HTTPD). The directory must be given the name HTTPD.

2. Place the retrieved zip file into the C:\HTTPD directory.

3. Run PKUNZIP with the -d switch to create the required directory structure on your machine. PKUNZIP must be version 2.04g or later.

4. Edit your AUTOEXEC.BAT file and add the line SET TZ=EST4EDT or the appropriate setting for your time zone. The 4 in this example means four hours west of Greenwich Mean Time (GMT). If you don't use daylight time in your area, omit the second three-letter time-zone abbreviation. Reboot your system to have this time take effect.

5. Start the Trumpet Winsock (TCPMAN.EXE) by selecting **Run** from the File menu in the Windows Program Manager, if you don't already have it running. Alternatively, if you're using Chameleon, click on the **Custom** icon to start the Chameleon Winsock.

6. Start Netscape or Mosaic and use the Open Local File option and point to the local file: C:/HTTPD/HTDOCS/INDEX.HTM. This choice will allow you to browse the online documentation (Figure 6.6). That documentation includes a demonstration and survey of Windows httpd as well as instructions for installing the software.

Running Windows httpd

To start up the httpd server, simply **Run** httpd.exe from the Windows File menu (eventually you'll want to set up a program icon for the Windows desktop). The minimized httpd idle icon will appear. Once started, you can use Netscape or

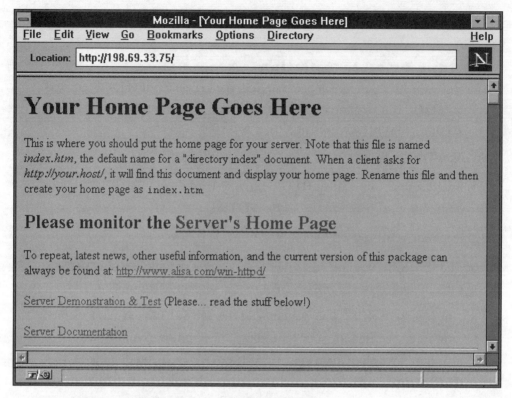

Figure 6.6 Windows httpd home page.

Mosaic and from the file menu **Open** URL and insert the IP address of your machine. For example, the URL might be:

```
http://198.69.33.75/
```

By default, the page INDEX.HTM will be accessed. Once you've acquired basic skills in HTML authoring you can revise the index.htm page and create your own home page. Various features, some quite complex, are incorporated in the httpd server for Windows. Spend some time reviewing the documentation on subjects such as CGI scripts, forms, and access control. Also refer to the reference material cited in the httpd software distribution for tutorials on these subjects. This is an excellent and comprehensive implementation of http and will require some work and study.

Advanced Server Configuration

You've seen that the Windows httpd server installs very quickly and easily. Now you'll need to administer several configuration files to assure proper settings for your "production" environment.

Windows HTTPd Configuration Files

The four configuration files in the httpd distribution are:

- Server Configuration File

- Server Resource Map

- Global Access Configuration File

- MIME Types Configuration File

If you run the server right out of the box, you need change none of these configuration files. As you progress in developing the server's features, though, you'll probably want to change some of the settings (called *directives*) in these files. A directive is, for example, the server administrator's address (**ServerAdmin**). When changing the directives in the configuration files, it is best to keep in mind a few rules and guidelines. These rules apply to all the Windows HTTPd server's configuration files:

- All the configuration files are stored in the C:\HTTPD\CONF directory, by default.

- Before making changes, back up each of the files. Copy HTTPD.CNF, SRM.CNF, ACCESS.CNF, and MIME.TYP to some backup directory. Then, if things start to fail or act unruly, you can restore your original files.

- The directives in these files are case-insensitive; therefore, you may use uppercase and lowercase as you see fit.

- Comment lines begin with #. Lines that should be ignored begin with #, the hash sign, which must be the first character on the line. Comments must be on a line by themselves.

- One directive per line. Each line in these files consists of *directive* data. *Directive* is a keyword that httpd recognizes, followed by one space; *data* is specific to the directive.

- Extra white space is ignored: You can put extra spaces or tabs between directive and data. To embed a space in data without separating it from any subsequent arguments, use a (\) character before the space.

The Server Configuration File—HTTPD.CNF

This is the server configuration file. The printout below is the sample—HTTPD.CNF file that is included with the Windows HTTPd software distribution. The bold items are the headings of the sections that hold the individual directives for the configuration file. All lines are commented out (#) in this file because if a directive is not specified, the server provides a default. The default is mentioned in the comments for each section. Each directive in the file (and some that are not included) is explained in the section following the printout.

```
#─────────────────────────────
# HTTPD.CNF
#
# Main server configuration for NCSA WinHttpd V1.3 (Windows)
#
# This is the main server configuration file. It is best to
# leave the directives in this file in the order they are in, or
# things may not go the way you'd like.
#
# Do NOT simply read the instructions in here without understanding
# what they do; if you are unsure, consult the online docs. You have
# been warned.
#
# NOTE: path defaults are relative to the server's installation
# directory (ServerRoot). Paths should be given in Unix
# format (using '/').
#
# Bob Denny <rdenny@netcom.com> 13-Aug-94
#─────────────────────────────
# ServerRoot: The directory the server's config, error, and log files
# are kept in. This directory should be specified on the startup command line.
#
# Format: ServerRoot <path>
#
# ServerRoot c:/httpd/
#
# Port: The port the standalone listens to. 80 is the network standard.
#
# Port 80
#
```

```
# Timeout: The timeout applied to all network operations. If you are on
# a slow network, or are using a SLIP or PPP connection, you might try
# increasing this setting to 60 sec.
#
# Format: Timeout nn (seconds)
#
# Timeout 30
#
# ServerAdmin: Your address, where problems with the server should be
# e-mailed.
#
# Format: ServerAdmin <email addr>
#
# ServerAdmin www-admin
#
# ErrorLog: The location of the error log file. If this setting does not start
# with / or a drive spec (recommended!), ServerRoot is prepended to it.
#
# Format: ErrorLog <path/file>
#
# ErrorLog logs/error.log
#
# TransferLog: The location of the transfer log file. If this setting does not
# start with / or a drive spec (recommended!), ServerRoot is prepended to it.
#
# Format: TransferLog <path/file>
#
# TransferLog logs/access.log
#
# ServerName allows you to set a host name which is sent back to clients for
# your server if it's different from the one the program would get (i.e., use
# "www" instead of the host's real name). Make sure your DNS is set up to
# alias the name to your system!
#
# Format: ServerName <domain name>
#
# no default
```

Server Configuration File Directives

The following sections detail the directives that this file recognizes.

ServerRoot

The ServerRoot directive sets the directory in which httpd lives. Upon startup, httpd expects to find the Server Configuration File as /conf/httpd.cnf in the ServerRoot directory. Other Server Configuration directives may use this directory to give relative paths for locations of files.

Directive Format: *ServerRoot dir*

Where *dir* is an absolute path of a directory on your server machine. Only one ServerRoot directive is allowed in the server configuration file.

Default: If you do not specify a ServerRoot, httpd assumes:

ServerRoot C:/httpd/

Example: *ServerRoot D:/httpd/*

This command would set ServerRoot to the directory D:/httpd.

Port   The Port directive sets which port httpd listens to for clients.

Directive Format: *Port num*

num is a number from 0-65536. Most ports below 1024 are reserved. The normal port for an HTTP daemon is 80, and this is the default for URLs that specify http:// service. Only one Port directive is allowed in the configuration file.

Default: If you do not specify a Port, httpd assumes:

Port 80.

Example: *Port 8080*

The server would listen on Port 8080.

TimeOut   The TimeOut directive sets the maximum time the server will wait for any network Read or Write operation. This setting includes the time the server will wait for a client to initiate a transaction after connecting. Network writes are 4 K, and each is individually timed. Normally, 30 seconds is adequate; however, if the server or any clients are on an extremely slow SLIP or PPP link, you may need to increase this time. If the server and clients are on a private high-speed net, you can reduce the time out so that the server will quickly drop a connection that was canceled in midstream by a client. This reduction will slightly increase the server's capacity.

Directive Format: *TimeOut time*

Where *time* is the time in seconds the server should wait. Only one TimeOut directive is allowed in the configuration file.

Default: If you do not specify a TimeOut, httpd assumes:

TimeOut 30

This is a time out of thirty seconds.

Example: *TimeOut 60*

You might set the TimeOut to 60 if you use a slow link.

ServerAdmin   The ServerAdmin directive gives the server your e-mail address so that the server can give people your address for reporting error conditions.

Directive Format: *ServerAdmin address*

Where *address* is an e-mail address. Only one ServerAdmin directive is allowed in the server configuration file. If you do not specify a ServerAdmin, httpd assumes nothing and prints no address for reporting errors.

Example: *ServerAdmin webmaster@ajax.com*

Errors will have the address **webmaster@ajax.com** as the person to contact.

ErrorLog   The ErrorLog directive sets the file to the httpd that will log errors it encounters. It currently logs these error conditions:

- Clients who time out.

- Scripts that produce no output.

- #haccess.ctl files that attempt to override things they do not have permission to override.

- Server bugs that produce a segmentation violation or bus error.

- Problems in configuring User Authentication.

Directive Format: *ErrorLog file*

file is the name of the file to which errors will be logged. It is either a full path name or a partial path name relative to ServerRoot. Only one ErrorLog directive is allowed in the configuration file.

Default: *ErrorLog logs/error.log*

Examples: *ErrorLog logs/httpderr.log*

Logs errors to the file logs/httpderr.log.

ErrorLog NUL : Effectively turns off error logging and is not recommended.

TransferLog　The TransferLog directive tells httpd where to record client accesses.

Here is the log-file format. Each line consists of:

remote-host [date] request

- *remote-host* is the host name (or IP address) of the client.

- *date* is the current date.

- *request* is the HTTP request sent by the client.

You can determine the name of the file accessed through *request field*.

Directive Format: *TransferLog file*

file is the name of the file to which transfers will be logged. It is either a full path name or a partial path name relative to ServerRoot. Only one TransferLog directive is allowed in the configuration file.

Default: If you do not specify a TransferLog, httpd assumes: *TransferLog logs/access.log*

Example: *TransferLog logs/download.log*

 Logs transfers to the file logs/download.log in the ServerRoot directory.

TransferLog NUL: Effectively turns off transfer logging.

ServerName　The ServerName directive sets the host name that httpd should return when creating redirection URLs. This directive should be used on systems where gethostbyname may not work on the local host, or where the host name returned should be a DNS alias such as www.ajax.com.

Directive Format: *ServerName FQDN*

Where FQDN is the full host name (Fully Qualified Domain Name) to be returned as the server address. Only one ServerName directive is allowed in the server configuration file.

Default: If you do not specify a ServerName, httpd retrieves it through system calls.

Example: *ServerName www.ajax.com*

This command would set the server's host name as www.ajax.com, as opposed to bert.ajax.com, which would be returned from the gethostname system call.

Note: The following directives are not included in the printout above, and therefore their defaults are assumed.

AccessConfig   The AccessConfig directive gives httpd the location of the global-access configuration file.

Directive Format: *AccessConfig file*

file is the name of the global-access configuration file. It is either a full path name or a partial path name relative to ServerRoot. Only one AccessConfig directive is allowed in the configuration file.

Default: If you do not specify an AccessConfig, httpd assumes:

AccessConfig conf/access.cnf

Example: *AccessConfig /httpd/admin/access.cnf*

httpd looks for access configuration in the file /httpd/admin/access.cnf.

ResourceConfig   The ResourceConfig directive gives httpd the location of the resource configuration file.

Directive Format: *ResourceConfig file*

file is the name of the resource configuration file. It is either a full path name, or a partial path name relative to ServerRoot. Only one ResourceConfig directive is allowed in the configuration file.

Default: If you do not specify a ResourceConfig, httpd assumes:

ResourceConfig conf/srm.cnf

Example: *ResourceConfig conf/resource.cnf*

httpd looks for the resource configuration in the conf/resource.cnf file in the ServerRoot directory.

TypesConfig   The TypesConfig directive gives httpd the location of the typing configuration file. This is the file with which httpd maps file-name extensions to MIME types to return to HTTP/1.0 clients. You should not need to edit the MIME.TYP file. Instead, use the AddType directive, which instead. can be found in the Server Resource Map file, SRM.CNF.

Syntax: *TypesConfig file*

file is the name of the types file. It is either a full path name or a partial path name relative to ServerRoot. Only one TypesConfig directive is allowed in the configuration file.

Default: If you do not specify a TypesConfig, httpd assumes:

TypesConfig conf/mime.typ

Examples: *TypesConfig conf/mimetype.typ*

The server looks for types configuration in the file conf/mimetype.typ in the ServerRoot directory.

The Server Resource Map File: SRM.CNF

This is the Server Resource Map file. Its directives control layout of documents and the name specifications that the server makes visible to users. The printout below is the sample SRM.CNF file that is included with the Windows HTTPd software distribution. The bold items are the headings for the sections including individual directives for the configuration file. If directive lines are commented out (#) in this file, a default is provided by the server. The default is mentioned in the comments for each section. Each directive in the file (and some that are not included) is explained in the section following the printout.

```
#————————————————————————
# SRM.CNF
#
# Server resource configuration for NCSA WinHttpd V1.3 (Windows)
```

```
#
# The settings in this file control the document layout and name specs
# that your server makes visible to users. The values in the comments
# are the defaults built into the server.
#
# NOTE: Path defaults are relative to the server's installation
# directory (ServerRoot). Paths should be given in Unix
# format (using '/').
#
# Bob Denny <rdenny@netcom.com> 13-Aug-94
#
#─────────────────────────────────
# DocumentRoot: The directory out of which you will serve your
# documents. By default, all requests are taken from this directory, but
# aliases may be used to point to other locations.
#
# DocumentRoot c:/httpd/htdocs
#
# DirectoryIndex: Name of the file to use as a prewritten HTML
# directory index. This document, if present, will be opened when the
# server receives a request incorporating a URL for the directory, instead
# of generating a directory index.
#
# DirectoryIndex index.htm
#
# AccessFileName: The name of the file to look for in each directory
# for access control information. This file should have a name that is
# blocked from appearing in server-generated indexes!
#
# AccessFileName #haccess.ctl
#
# =========================
# Aliasing and Redirection
# =========================
#
# Redirect allows you to tell clients about documents which used to exist in
# your server's namespace, but do no longer. This command allows you to tell the
# clients where to look for the relocated document.
#
# Format: Redirect fakename url
#
# Aliases: Add here as many aliases as you need, up to 20. One useful
# alias to have is for the path to the icons used for the server-
# generated directory indexes. The paths given below in the AddIcon
# statements are relative.
#
# Format: Alias fakename realname
#
```

```
Alias /icons/ c:/httpd/icons/
# ScriptAlias: This command controls which directories include DOS server
# scripts.
#
# Format: ScriptAlias fakename realname
#
ScriptAlias /cgi-dos/ c:/httpd/cgi-dos/
ScriptAlias /cgi-bin/ c:/httpd/cgi-dos/
#
# WinScriptAlias: This command controls which directories include Windows
# server scripts.
#
# Format: WinScriptAlias fakename realname
#
WinScriptAlias /cgi-win/ c:/httpd/cgi-win/
#
# ==========================
# MIME Content Type Control
# ==========================
#
# DefaultType is the default MIME type for documents for which the server
# cannot find the type from file-name extensions.
#
# DefaultType text/html
DefaultType text/plain
#
# AddType allows you to tweak MIME.TYP without actually editing it, or to
# make specific files be specific types.
#
# Format: AddType type/subtype ext1
#
# ReadmeName is the name of the README file the server will look for by
# default. The server will first look for name.htm, include it if found,
# and then for name.txt and include it as plaintext if found.
# NOTE: Do not include an explicit extension; it is an error.
#
# Format: ReadmeName name
#
ReadmeName #readme
#
# ==========================
# AUTOMATIC DIRECTORY INDEXING
# ==========================
#
# The server generates a directory index if no file is in the
# directory the name of which matches DirectoryIndex.
#
```

```
# FancyIndexing: Whether you want fancy directory indexing or standard.
#
# FancyIndexing on
#
# IconsAreLinks: Whether the icons as well as the file names in a fancy index are links.
#
#
# IconsAreLinks off
#
# AddIcon tells the server which icon to show for different files or file-name
# extensions. In preparation for the upcoming Chicago version, you should
# include explicit 3-character truncations for 4-character endings. Don't
# rely on the DOS underpinnings to silently truncate for you.
#
AddIcon /icons/text.gif .html .htm .txt .ini
AddIcon /icons/image.gif .gif .jpg .jpe .jpeg .xbm .tiff .tif .pic .pict .bmp
AddIcon /icons/sound.gif .au .wav .snd
AddIcon /icons/movie.gif .mpg .mpe .mpeg
AddIcon /icons/binary.gif .bin .exe .bat .dll
AddIcon /icons/back.gif ..
AddIcon /icons/menu.gif ^^DIRECTORY^^
AddIcon /icons/dblank.gif    ^^BLANKICON^^
#
# DefaultIcon is the icon to show for files that do not have an icon
# explicitly set.
#
DefaultIcon /icons/unknown.gif
#
# AddDescription allows you to place a short description after a file in
# server-generated indexes. A better place for these is in individual
# "#haccess.ctl" files in individual directories.
#
# Format: AddDescription "description" file name
#
# IndexIgnore is a set of file names that directory indexing should ignore
# Here, I've disabled display of our readme and access-control files,
# plus anything that starts with a "~", which I use for annotating HTML
# documents. I have also disabled some common editor backup file names.
# Match is on file NAME.EXT only, and the usual * and ? metachars apply.
#
# WARNING: Be sure to set an ignore for your access control file(s)!!
#
# Format: IndexIgnore name1 name2...
#
IndexIgnore ~* *.bak *.{* #readme.htm #haccess.ctl
#
## END ##
```

Server Resource Map File Directives

The next sections list the directives that this file recognizes.

DocumentRoot The DocumentRoot directive sets the directory from which httpd will serve files. If you need to serve files outside this directory, you can use the Alias directive.

Directive Format: *DocumentRoot dir*

Where *dir* is an absolute path of the directory from which you want documents to be served. Only one DocumentRoot directive is allowed in the server configuration file.

Default: If you do not specify a DocumentRoot, httpd assumes:

DocumentRoot C:/httpd/htdocs

Example: *DocumentRoot C:/httpd/web*

This command would set DocumentRoot to the directory C:/httpd/web.

DirectoryIndex When a client requests a directory, the server can return a prewritten index or generate one from the file system. The DirectoryIndex directive sets the file the server should look for as a prewritten index to a given directory. Only one DirectoryIndex directive is allowed in the server configuration file.

Directive Format: *DirectoryIndex file*

Where *file* is a file name.

Default: If you do not specify a DirectoryIndex, the server assumes:

DirectoryIndex index.htm

Example: *DirectoryIndex index.htm*

This command would set DirectoryIndex to index.htm. A request for a given directory (e.g., http://198.69.33.75/) would cause the server to look for the file

DocumentRoot index.html. If found, the server would send it back to the client. Otherwise it would create and return an index from the file system, which would appear much like a Gopher or FTP menu.

AccessFileName When returning a document to a client, the server looks for access control files in the document's directory as well as its parent directories. This directive sets the name of the file the server should look for to find access control files. Only one AccessFileName directive is allowed in the server configuration file.

Directive Format: *AccessFileName file*

Where *file* is a file name.

Default: If you do not specify an AccessFileName, the server assumes: *AccessFileName #haccess.ctl*

Example: *AccessFileName #access.ctl*

This command would set AccessFileName to #access.ctl.

Redirect The Redirect directive creates a virtual document on your server, and any accesses to it will be redirected to a new URL. Several Redirect directives may appear in the configuration file.

Directive Format: *Redirect virtual URL*

virtual is the translated location that should trigger a redirect.

URL is the URL of the new document.

Example: *Redirect /dir1* http://newserver.widget.com/dir1

This command would cause requests for /dir1 to be redirected to the new location, **http://newserver.widget.com/dir1**.

Alias The Alias directive creates a virtual document (or directory) on your server. Any accesses to it will be satisfied by a different file or directory. Several Alias directives may appear in the configuration file.

Directive Format: *Alias virtual path*

virtual is the translated location of the file/directory.

path is the full path name of the file or directory that should be used to fulfill the request.

Example: *Alias /icons/ C:/httpd/icons/*

This command would cause requests for /icons to be satisfied from the directory C:/httpd/icons. Thus, if someone requested /icons/redball.gif, the server would return C:/httpd/icons/redball.gif.

ScriptAlias   The ScriptAlias directive creates a virtual directory on your server. Any accesses to that directory will be satisfied by returning the output of a CGI server script in that directory. Several ScriptAlias directives may appear in the configuration file.

Directive Format: *ScriptAlias virtual path*

virtual is the translated location of the script directory.

path is the full path name of the directory holding server scripts that fulfill the request.

Note: Always place a trailing (/) after ScriptAlias directives that refer to directories, to prevent similar entries from conflicting with each other.

Example: *ScriptAlias /cgi-dos/ C:/httpd/cgi-dos/*

This command would cause requests such as /cgi-bin/foo to be satisfied by running the script C:/httpd/cgi-dos/foo.exe. Thus, if someone requested /cgi-dos/foo.exe, the server would run C:/httpd/cgi-dos/foo.exe and send its output to the client.

WinScriptAlias   The WinScriptAlias directive creates a virtual directory on your server. Any accesses to that virtual directory will be satisfied by returning the output of a Windows CGI script in that directory. Several WinScriptAlias directives may appear in the configuration file.

Directive Format: *WinScriptAlias virtual path*

virtual is the translated location of the script directory.

path is the full path name of the directory including server scripts that fulfill the request.

Example: WinScriptAlias /cgi-win c:/httpd/cgi-win/

This command would cause requests such as /cgi-win/foo.exe to be satisfied by running the Windows program c:/httpd/cgi-win/foo.exe.

DefaultType   If the server can't type a file by normal means, it will type it as DefaultType. Only one DefaultType directive should appear in the configuration file.

Directive Format: *DefaultType type/subtype*

type/subtype is the MIME-like type.

Default: If no DefaultType is present, the server assumes:
DefaultType text/html

Example: *DefaultType text/plain*

This command would cause a file with an unknown extension to be returned as type text/plain.

AddType   Allows you to add entries to the server's default typing information and cause an extension to be of a specified type. These directives override any conflicting entries in the MIME.TYP file.

Directive Format: *AddType type/subtype extension*

type/subtype is the MIME-like type for the document.

Extension is the file-name extension to map to this type. This command can be a file-name extension, a full path name, or a file name. You may use as many AddType directives as you wish.

Default: The default types are in the types configuration file, MIME.TYP.

Example: AddType text/plain doc

This command would cause any file ending in .doc to be served as type text/plain.

ReadmeName This directive specifies the file name the server should look for when indexing a directory, in order to add a paragraph of description to the end of the index it automatically generates. Generally, these paragraphs are used to give a general survey of what's in a directory. Only one ReadmeName directive should appear in the configuration file.

Syntax: *ReadmeName name*

name is the name of the file the server should look for when trying to find a description file. The server will first look for name.htm, and if it is found, will display the HTML inlined with its own index. If it finds *name*, it will include the file as plain text.

Default: If no ReadmeName is present, the server assumes nothing.

Example: ReadmeName #readme

When generating an index for a directory, the server will look for #readme.htm, and will insert it if found. It will then look for #readme and insert it if found. If it finds nothing, it will include nothing.

FancyIndexing The FancyIndexing directive specifies whether you want fancy directory indexing (with icons and file sizes) or standard directory indexing. Only one FancyIndexing directive should appear in the configuration file.

Directive Format: *FancyIndexing setting*

setting is either *on* or *off*.

Default: If no FancyIndexing directive is present, the server assumes: *FancyIndexing on*

Example: *FancyIndexing off*

Turns fancy indexing off.

IconsAreLinks This directive specifies whether you want fancy directory indexing to have the icons be links as well as the displayed file names. Only one IconsAreLinks directive should appear in the configuration file.

Syntax: *IconsAreLinks setting*

setting is either *on* or *off.*

Default: If no IconsAreLinks directive is present, the server assumes: *IconsAreLinks off*

Example: *IconsAreLinks on*

Turns icon links on.

AddIcon   Tells the server the kind of icon to show for a given file type in a directory index. You may use as many AddDescription directives as you wish.

Directive Syntax: *AddIcon icon name1 name2...*

icon is a virtual path to an image file that should be shown for files that match the pattern of names.

name is a file extension (like .htm), a partial file name, or a complete physical path name.

 Two special "names" are used for the directory index display. The name "^^DIRECTORY^^" identifies the icon that is to be used to indicate a subdirectory in the list. The name "^^BLANKICON^^" identifies the icon that is used in the title header of the directory display as a placeholder to provide correct alignment for the column labels. This icon should be of the same width as the other icons.

Default: No default icons.

Example: AddIcon /icons/sound.gif .au .wav .snd

When the server is indexing and finds a file with the extension .au, .wav, or .snd it will refer to /icons/sound.gif as an image to show beside the file name.

DefaultIcon   This directive specifies which icon should be shown in an automatically generated directory listing for a file that has no icon information. Only one DefaultIcon directive should appear in the configuration file.

Directive Syntax: *DefaultIcon location*

location is the virtual path to the icon on your server.

Default: If no DefaultIcon is present, the server assumes nothing.

Example: *DefaultIcon /icons/unknown.gif*

This command would cause a file with no icon to be given the icon /icons/unknown.gif.

AddDescription   Tells the server how to describe a file or a file type while generating a directory index. You may use as many AddDescription directives as you wish.

Directive Syntax: *AddDescription "whatever" fileid*

fileid is either a file-name extension (like .htm), a file name, or a full real path name to a file on your system. *Whatever* must be surrounded by quotation marks and is a short (preferably < 1 line) description of the file.

Default: No default descriptions.

Example: AddDescription junk.txt ("just a junk file"). A portion of the server's index for junk.txt's directory will look something like this:

```
junk.txt : just a junk file (5000 bytes)
```

IndexIgnore   Tells the server which files to ignore when generating an index for a directory.

Directive Syntax: *IndexIgnore pat1 pat2...*

pat (pattern) is a file extension or file name that should be ignored. When the server is looking in a directory, it will try to match each of these strings to the right-hand side of the entry's string, and if it matches will ignore that entry in its directory index.

Default: The only entry ignored by default is '.'.

Example: *IndexIgnore #haccess.ctl #readme.htm*

The server will ignore files named *#haccess.ctl* and *#readme.htm* when indexing a directory.

AddEncoding   Allows you to specify an encoding type for a document with a given file-name extension. To serve encoded documents to clients, the client must support the given encoding method, as well as the HTTP encoding extension. You may use as many AddEncoding directives as you wish.

Document Format: *AddEncoding type extension*

type is the encoding type for the document.

extension is the file-name extension to map to this encoding.

Default: No default encodings.

Example: *AddEncoding x-gzip gz*

This command would cause any file ending in .gz to be marked encoded using the x-gzip encoding method.

The Global Access Configuration File: ACCESS.CNF

This is the Global Access Configuration file. The directives in this file control access and security for your server. The printout below is the sample ACCESS.CNF file that is included with the Windows HTTPd software distribution. Each directive in the file (and some that are not included) is explained in the section following the printout.

```
#———————————————————————————
# ACCESS.CNF
#
# Global access configuration for NCSA WinHttpd V1.3 (Windows)
#
# This is server global-access configuration file. It is best to
# leave the directives in this file in the order they are in, or
# things may not go the way you'd like.
#
# Do NOT simply read the instructions in here without understanding
# what they do; if you are unsure consult the online docs. You have
# been warned.
#
# Bob Denny <rdenny@netcom.com> 13-Aug-94
#
```

```
#-------------------------------------------------
#
# The following access configuration establishes unrestricted access
# to the server's document tree. There is no default access config, and so
# _something_ must be present and correct for the server to operate.
#
# This setting should be changed to whatever you set ServerRoot to.
#
<Directory c:/httpd>
Options Indexes
</Directory>
#
# This setting should be changed to whatever you set DocumentRoot to.
#
<Directory c:/httpd/htdocs>
#
# This setting may also be "None", "All", or "Indexes"
#
Options Indexes
#
# This setting controls which options the #HACCESS.CTL files in directories can
# override. Can also be "None", or any combination of "Options", "FileInfo",
# "AuthConfig", and "Limit"
#
AllowOverride All
#
# Controls who can get stuff from this server.
#
<Limit GET>
order allow,deny
allow from all
</Limit>
#
</Directory>
#
# You may place any other directories for which you wish to have access
# information after this one.
```

Global-Access Configuration File Directives

When creating a document or directory tree, the server allows you to control some aspects of that tree's branches (directories). You can restrict access to a branch to "allowed" hosts or authenticated users. Directories considered unsafe can be made more secure by disabling specific server functions in those directories.

The two methods for controlling access to directories are the Global-Access Configuration File and Per-directory Access Configuration Files.

Global-Access Configuration File (ACF)

A document in your server's conf directory, specified by the Server Configuration file (HTTPD.CNF) directive AccessConfig, controls access to any directory in your tree. The httpd server requires that you set up the Global ACF (ACCESS.CNF).

Per-directory Access Configuration Files: Within your document tree, files with the name (normally #haccess.ctl) specified by the AccessFileName directive in the Resource Configuration File (SRM.CNF), control access to the directory they are in as well as any subdirectories. Per-directory ACFs are optional. They can be restricted or completely forbidden by the Global ACF.

Beyond the general information that applies to all the server configuration files, the access control files support the notion of sectioning directives. Some access control directives require that specific information apply to all directives in a given section; these are called *sectioning directives*.

These directives are formatted in much the same way as HTML tags. For each sectioning directive, two components are needed: an opening directive and a closing directive. For instance, for the sectioning directive Foo, with one argument datum, the opening directive would be:

```
<Foo datum>
```

The closing argument would be:

```
/Foo>
```

The information given in the opening directive will affect all other directives between the opening and closing sectioning directive.

Example: <Directory C:/admin/Web>   The opening directive

        require group physics

        </Directory>   The closing directive

Directory is the sectioning directive. Therefore, the information given by the opening directive, C:/admin/Web, applies to the *require* directive within.

This is a list of the directives and sectioning directives used when writing an ACF. Each directive specifies where it can be used, and gives examples of usage.

Directory   Directory is a sectioning directive that controls the directory to which access control directives apply. This directive applies only to the Global ACF. All directives in the Global ACF must be contained in a Directory section.

Directive Syntax: Opening Directive: *<Directory dir> dir* is the absolute path name of the directory you are protecting.

Closing directive: *</Directory>*
Example: *<Directory C:/admin/Web>*
Options None
</Directory>

The directives within the Directory section above would apply only to the server directory *C:/admin/Web*.

Options   The Options directive controls which server features are available in a given directory. The Windows version supports only one discrete option, and so *all* is redundant. This arrangement will change in the future. This directive applies to both the Global ACF and per-directory ACFs.

Directive Syntax: *Options opt1 opt2 ... optn*

Each *opt* is one of these:

> *None*—No features are enabled for in directory.

> *All*—All features are enabled for in directory.

> *Indexes*—The server allows users to request indexes in this directory.

Disabling this option disables ONLY the server-generated indexes. It does not stop the server from sending any precompiled index file it may find in there (the name of which depends on DirectoryIndex).

Default: If no Options directives are given for this directory or any of its parents, the server assumes: *Options All*

Example: *Options Indexes*

The server would allow users to index this directory and its subdirectories.

AllowOverride   The AllowOverride directive controls which access control directives can be overruled by a per-directory ACF. The global ACF cannot be restricted by this directive. This directive may appear only in the global ACF.

Directive Syntax: *AllowOverride or1 or 2 ... or n*

Each *or* is one of these:

> *None*—ACFs are not allowed in this directory.
>
> *All*—ACFs are unrestricted in this directory.
>
> *Options*—Allow use of the Options directive.
>
> *FileInfo*—Allow use of the AddType and AddEncoding directives.
>
> *AuthConfig*—Allow use of these directives:
>
>> AuthName
>>
>> AuthType
>>
>> AuthUserFile
>>
>> AuthGroupFile
>
> *Limit*—Allow use of the Limit sectioning directive.

Default: If no AllowOverride directives are given for this directory or any of its parents, the server assumes:

AllowOverride All

Example: *AllowOverride Limit FileInfo*

ACFs in this directory are allowed to use *Limit, AddType, and AddEncoding*.

AddType   The AddType directive acts exactly as it does in the resource configuration file. This directive applies to both the Global ACF and per-directory ACFs.

Directive Syntax: See the description in the resource configuration section.

AddEncoding The AddEncoding directive acts exactly as it does in the resource configuration file. This directive applies to both the Global ACF and per-directory ACFs.

Directive Syntax: See the description in the resource configuration section.

AddDescription The AddDescription directive acts exactly as it does in the resource configuration file. This directive applies to the per-directory ACFs only.

Directive Syntax: See the description in the resource configuration section.

AddIcon The AddIcon directive acts exactly as it does in the resource configuration file. This directive applies to both the Global ACF and per-directory ACFs.

Directive Syntax: See the description in the resource configuration section.

IndexIgnore The IndexIgnore directive acts exactly as it does in the resource configuration file. This directive applies to both the Global ACF and per-directory ACFs.

Directive Syntax: See the description in the resource configuration section.

DefaultIcon The DefaultIcon directive acts exactly as it does in the resource configuration file. This directive applies to both the Global ACF and per-directory ACFs.

Directive Syntax: See the description in the resource configuration section.

ReadmeName The ReadmeName directive acts exactly as it does in the resource configuration file. This directive applies to both the Global ACF and per-directory ACFs.

Directive Syntax: See the description in the resource configuration section.

AuthName The AuthName directive sets the name of the authorization realm for this directory. This realm is a name given to users so that they know which user name and password to send. This directive applies to both global and per-directory ACFs and must be accompanied by AuthType, AuthUserFile, and AuthGroupFile directives for user authentication to work properly.

Directive Syntax: *AuthName name*

Where name is a short name describing this authorization realm. Can include spaces.

Default: No default.

Example: *AuthName CorpHQ*

Sets the authorization name of this directory to CorpHQ.

AuthType   The AuthType directive sets the type of authorization used in this directory; it applies to both global and per-directory ACFs. This directive must be accompanied by AuthName, AuthUserFile, and AuthGroupFile directives for user authentication to work properly.

Directive Syntax: *AuthType type*

type is the authentication type to use for this directory. Only *Basic* is currently implemented.

Default: No default.

Example: *AuthType Basic*

Sets the authorization type of this directory to *Basic*.

AuthUserFile   The AuthUserFile directive sets the file to use as a list of users and passwords for user authentication. This directive applies to both global and per-directory ACFs. This directive must be accompanied by AuthName, AuthType, and AuthGroupFile directives for user authentication to work properly.

Directive Syntax: *AuthUserFile path*

path is the absolute path of a user file created with the htpasswd support program.

Default: No default.

Example: *AuthUserFile C:/httpd/conf/htpasswd.ctl*

Sets the authorization user file for this directory to *C:/httpd/conf/htpasswd.ctl.*

AuthGroupFile   The AuthGroupFile directive sets the file to use as a list of user groups for user authentication. This directive applies to both global and per-directory ACFs. This directive must be accompanied by AuthName, AuthType, and AuthUserFile directives for user authentication to work properly.

Directive Syntax: *AuthGroupFile path*

path is the absolute path of group file to use in this directory.

Default: No default.

Example: *AuthGroupFile C:/httpd/conf/htgroup.ctl*

Sets the authorization group file for this directory to C:/httpd/conf/htgroup.ctl.

Limit   A sectioning directive controlling which clients can access a directory. This directive applies to both the global and per-directory ACFs.

Directive Syntax: Opening Directive: *<Limit meth1 meth2...methn>*

Each *meth* is one of these methods:

   GET —Allows clients to retrieve documents and execute scripts.

   PUT —Not Implemented.

   POST —Allows clients to submit data using Mosaic forms and any other POST-based operations.

Closing directive: *</Limit>*

Only these directives are allowed inside Limit sections:

      order

      deny

allow

require

Example: `<Limit GET>`

```
order deny, allow
deny from all
allow from .ncsa.uiuc.edu
require group sdg
</Limit>
```

The only clients alloweed to use the GET method in this directory must be from ncsa.uiuc.edu, and authenticate to group sdg.

Order The order directive affects the order in which *deny* and *allow* directives are evaluated within a Limit section. This directive is available only within Limit sections.

Directive Syntax: *order ord*

ord is one of these:

deny,allow—In this case, the *deny* directives are evaluated before the *allow* directives.

allow,deny—In this case, the *allow* directives are evaluated before the *deny* directives.

Default: If no order is given, the server assumes: *order deny,allow*

Example: `<Limit C:/admin/Web>`
```
order deny, allow
deny from all
allow from .ncsa.uiuc.edu
</Limit>
```

In the /admin/Web directory, the server evaluates the *deny* directive first. Thus, everyone is denied. It then evaluates the *allow* directive, and decides to allow clients from .ncsa.uiuc.edu.

Deny The *deny* directive affects which hosts can access a given directory with a given method. This directive is available only within Limit sections.

Directive Syntax: *deny from host 1 host 2 ... host n*

host is one of these:

> A domain name, like .ncsa.uiuc.edu (notice the leading dot!), in which host names must end to be allowed.
>
> A fully qualified host name.
>
> A full IP address of a host.
>
> The keyword *all* means that all hosts will be denied.
>
> Default: No default applies.

Example: `<Limit C:/admin/Web>`
```
order deny, allow
deny from all
allow from .ncsa.uiuc.edu
</Limit>
```

In the /admin/Web directory, the server evaluates the *deny* directive first. Thus, everyone is denied. It then evaluates the *allow* directive, and decides to allow clients from .ncsa.uiuc.edu.

Allow   The *allow* directive affects which hosts can access a given directory with a given method. This directive is available only within Limit sections.

Directive Syntax: *allow from host 1 host 2 ... host n*

host is one of these:

> A domain name.
>
> A domain name, like .ncsa.uiuc.edu, in which host names must end to be allowed.
>
> A host name. A full host name.
>
> A full IP address.
>
> An IP address of a host.
>
> A partial IP address.
>
> The first 1–3 bytes of an IP address, for subnet restriction.
>
> The keyword *all* means that all hosts will be allowed.

Example: `<Limit C:/admin/Web>`

```
arder deny, allow
deny from all
allow from .ncsauiuc.edu
</Limit>
```

In the /admin/Web directory, the server evaluates the *deny* directive first. Thus, everyone is denied. It then evaluates the *allow* directive, and decides to allow clients from .ncsa.uiuc.edu.

Require The *require* directive affects which authenticated users can access a given directory with a given method. This directive is available only within Limit sections.

Directive Syntax: *require entity en1 en 2 ... en n*

en are entity names, separated by spaces.

entity is one of these:

> *user*—only the named users can access this directory with the given methods.

> *group*—only users in the named groups can access this directory with the given methods.

> *valid-user*—all the users defined in the AuthUserFile are allowed access upon providing a valid password.

> Default: No default applies.

Example: `<Limit GET PUT>`
```
order deny, allow
deny from all
allow from .ncsa.uiuc.edu
require user ls
require group sdg
</Limit>
```

In this directory, the server evaluates the *deny* directive first. Thus, everyone is denied. It then evaluates the *allow* directive, and decides to allow clients from .ncsa.uiuc.edu. Now, it uses user authentication and allows only users who are named ls or are in the group sdg.

Access Control and Security

You will also want to know how to manage users for user authentication. To use user authentication, you'll need to edit and manage user files and group files. To deal with user files, the support directory of the distribution has a DOS program called HTPASSWD.EXE. Usage: *htpasswd [-c] file user.*

The -c, if present, tells htpasswd to create a new passwd file of the specified name instead of editing an old one. *file* is the path name of the user file you wish to edit. The user parameter is the name of the user you wish to add or edit. If htpasswd finds the user you specified, it will ask you to change the user's password. Type the new password (it will ask twice). The server will then update the file. If htpasswd doesn't find the specified user, it will ask you to give the user an initial password.

Group Files

Here is the format of the group file:

```
groupname: member1 member2 ...
```

Or, each line includes the name of a group, and a list of members separated by spaces.

Mosaic 2.0 (Windows and Unix) and NCSA httpd 1.1 (Windows and Unix) allow access restriction based on several criteria:

Username/password-level access authorization.

Rejection or acceptance of connections based on Internet address of client.

A combination of these two methods.

The two levels at which access control can work are: per-server and per-directory. The information below primarily covers per-directory access control. See information above on the Access Configuration File for more detail on setting up server-wide access control.

Per-directory access control means that users with Write access to part of the file system that is being served can control access to their files as they wish. They need not have root access on the system or Write access to the server's primary configuration files.

Access control for a given directory is controlled by a file (normally named #haccess.ctl) residing in that directory. The server reads this file on each access to a document in that directory (or documents in subdirectories). There is no correspondence between user names and passwords on specific server systems (e.g., in a Windows sharing password file, or the NT security system) and user names and passwords in the access control schemes we're discussing for use in the Web. As illustrated in the examples, Web-based access control uses wholly distinct password files; a user need never have an actual account on a given server system to be validated for access to files being served from that system and protected with HTTP-based access control.

By-Password Access Control Example

The example below assumes you want to restrict files in a directory called *stuff* to user name *John* and password *Quirk*. Here's what you would need to do to set up access control on a directory:

Create a file called #haccess.ctl in directory stuff that looks like this:

```
AuthUserFile c:/httpd/conf/authusr.pwd
AuthGroupFile c:/httpd/conf/empty.pwd
AuthName ByPassword
AuthType Basic
<Limit GET>
require user John
</Limit>
```

The user and group password files may be located in any directory. The Windows version of httpd requires a valid filespec for both the user and group password files. The distribution kit has a file called empty.pwd that can be used as a placeholder when password files aren't needed.

AuthName can be anything you want. AuthType should always currently be Basic.

Create the password file c:/httpd/conf/authusr.pwd. Use the htpasswd program distributed with httpd as follows:

```
htpasswd -c c:\httpd\conf\authusr.pwd John
```

Type the password—Quirk—twice, as instructed. Check the authusr.pwd file and you will see something like:

```
John:e7ggHFt5de45
```

That's all. Now try to access a file in directory stuff. Mosaic should ask for a user name and password, and not give you access to the file if you don't enter *John* and *Quirk*. If you are using a browser that doesn't handle access control, you will not be able to access the document at all.

Protection by Password with Multiple Users

This example illustrates a document that is accessible to user *John* with password *Quirk* and user *Mary* with password *Tacky*.

The #haccess.ctl file used in this example is:

```
AuthUserFile c:/httpd/conf/authusr.pwd
AuthGroupFile c:/httpd/conf/empty.pwd
AuthName Example
AuthType Basic
<Limit GET>
require user John
require user Mary
</Limit>
```

Use the **htpasswd** command without the -c flag to add users—for example:

```
htpasswd c:\httpd\conf\authusr.pwd John
htpasswd c:\httpd\conf\authusr.pwd Mary
```

Creating a Group File

If you want to give access to a directory to more than one user-name/password pair, follow the same steps as for a single user name/password with these additions:

Add users to the directory's #haccess.ctl file.

Use the htpasswd command without the -c flag to additional users—for example:

```
htpasswd c:\httpd\conf\authusr.pwd John
htpasswd c:\httpd\conf\authusr.pwd Mary
```

Create a group file. Call it C:\httpd\conf\authgrp.pwd and have it look something like this:

```
my-users: John Mary
```

where *John* and *Mary* are the user names.

Then modify the #haccess.ctl file in the directory stuff to look like this:

```
AuthUserFile C:/httpd/conf/authusr.pwd
AuthGroupFile C:/httpd/conf/authgrp.pwd
AuthName ByPassword
AuthType Basic
```

```
<Limit GET>
require group my-users
</Limit>
```

Notice that AuthGroupFile now points to your group file and that group my-users (rather than individual user *John*) is now required for access.

Any user in group my-users can use his or her individual user name and password to gain access to directory stuff.

Protection by Network Domain—Allow

This example illustrates a document that is accessible only to clients running on machines inside domain

sowebo.charm.net.

The #haccess.ctl file used in this example is:

```
AuthUserFile c:/httpd/conf/empty.pwd
AuthGroupFile c:/httpd/conf/empty.pwd
AuthName Example
AuthType Basic
<Limit GET>
order deny,allow
deny from all
allow from .sowebo.charm.net
</Limit>
```

Protection by Network Domain—Deny

This example illustrates a document that is accessible to clients running on machines anywhere but inside domain sowebo.charm.net.

The #haccess.ctl file used in this example is:

```
AuthUserFile c:/httpd/conf/empty.pwd
AuthGroupFile c:/httpd/conf/empty.pwd
AuthName Example
AuthType Basic
<Limit GET>
order allow,deny
allow from all
deny from .sowebo.charm.net
</Limit>
```

MIME Types Configuration File

You may want to add MIME types to your server for local use. It is recommended that you use the AddTypes directive instead of modifying the

MIME.TYP file. Nonetheless, here is the format for the types configuration file: Each line includes information for one http type. These types resemble MIME types. If you plan to add new ones, you should use subtypes beginning with x-, such as *application/x-myprogram*. Lines beginning with # are comment lines, and suitably ignored. Each line consists of: *type/subtype ext1 ext 2 ... ext n.*

type/subtype is the MIME-like type of the document.

ext* is any number of space-separated file-name extensions that should be returned to the client if a file with the given extension is referenced.

Beame & Whiteside World Wide Web Server

The Beame and Whiteside World Wide Web Server is one of Beame & Whiteside's "personal publishing initiatives." Such a package is intended to bring Web publishing opportunities to the masses at the desktop level. If you have worked with the Windows httpd server by Bob Denny, you'll see striking similarities between the two. Essentially, three files handle configuration: HTTPD.CNF, ACCESS.CNF, and SRM.CNF. Refer to information detailing these files in the section above on Windows httpd. The similarities appear to result from the server's origins—both are ports from the Unix NCSA httpd server (although the Windows httpd server by Bob Denny has subsequently been rewritten). Because the Beame & Whiteside package was in its early stages of development at press time, the features were rather limited. Nonetheless, you can experiment with it and serve documents, which is what it's all about.

The Beame & Whiteside WWW server is part of an entire suite of client and server products available for Windows 3.1. Installation of the Beame & Whiteside client and server product suite, including their TCP/IP implementation, is covered in detail in Chapter 4 and is required reading for installation and support of their WWW server.

The accompanying CD has modified configuration files that you can use to get started.

Follow these steps to make your server operational:

1. Create the directory C:\BWTCP\LOGS.

2. Copy these files that were installed with the Beame & Whiteside software installation to another directory, so that you can return to them later:

HTTPD.CNF

ACCESS.CNF

SRM.CNF

3. Copy the files listed here from the directory \BWTCP on the CD to the appropriate directories:

File	Copy to
HTTPD.CNF	C:\BWTCP\CONF\HTTPD.CNF
ACCESS.CNF	C:\BWTCP\CONF\ACCESS.CNF
SRM.CNF	C:\BWTCP\CONF\SRM.CNF
MIME.TYP	C:\BWTCP\CONF\MIME.TYP
INDEX.HTM	C:\BWTCP\CONF\INDEX.HTM
HOME.GIF	C:\BWTCP\CONF\HOME.GIF
REDBALL.GIF	C:\BWTCP\CONF\REDBALL.GIF
ACCESS.LOG	C:\BWTCP\LOGS\ACCESS.LOG
ERROR.LOG	C:\BWTCP\LOGS\ERROR.LOG

4. Next, edit the file HTTPD.CNF with Notepad or your favorite editor and include your server's name on the line ServerName.

5. Save the file.

Because the Server is a stand-alone program, rather than a daemon running under inetd, all you need do is click on the Web Server icon to start the program once you've set up the configuration files and appropriate server directories (e.g., \logs). Go to a nearby browser and type in a url such as:

```
http://your.server.name
```

and the screen in Figure 6.7 should appear.

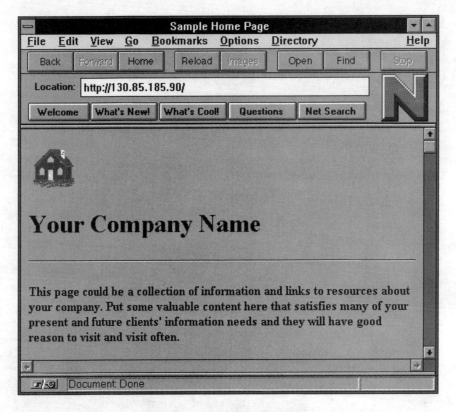

Figure 6.7 Beame & Whiteside Web Server.

EMWAC Windows NT World Wide Web Server

The European Microsoft Windows NT Academic Centre (EMWAC) has produced a number of excellent products for Microsoft NT. In addition to their Gopher server for NT, they have created a freeware HTTP server based on the Microsoft Windows NT operating system. This WWW implementation, written by Chris Adie and known as HTTPS, has these features:

- Runs as a Windows NT service with executables available for Intel, MIPS, or Digital Alpha-based systems.

- Is implemented as an HTTP/1.0 server that understands HEAD, GET, and POST methods.

- Supports CGI scripts and HTML forms. Example scripts in C are included.

- Supports clickable images (ISMAP).

- Is multithreaded.

- Utilizes NT system-management functions, such as logging errors to the Event Logger, configuration through the Control Panel, and optionally logging HTTP transactions in the server log file.

HTTPS Installation

The server software is included on the accompanying CD or may be retrieved from: ftp://emwac.ed.ac.uk/pub/https.

There are zipped files for the various supported platforms; the one for Intel-based hardware is HSI386.ZIP.

If you are implementing the server on the Intel platform, a Windows NT system with a network connection and 16 Mb of memory should suffice.

To install the HTTPS software, follow these installation steps:

1. Use PKUNZIP to unzip the software-distribution files to a directory of your choosing, which you should create now (e.g., C:\HTTP).

   Later, you will want to plan a directory structure that makes sense for your installation, moving files to be served to the data directory, and the software-distribution files to another directory. But for now, for simplicity, we'll commingle the files in one directory.

   The files that will be unzipped include:

HTTPS.EXE	Server executable.
HTTPS.CPL	Control Panel applet.
HTTPS.HLP	Control Panel applet help file.
HTTPS.PS	HTTPS Manual—Postscript.
HTTPS.DOC	HTTPS Manual—MS Word.
HTTPS.WRI	HTTPS Manual—Windows Write.
EGSCRIPT.ZIP	Sample CGI programs.
COPYRITE.TXT	Copyright statement.
READ.ME	Version features, etc.

2. Sign on to an administrator's account on the NT server.

3. Copy the file HTTPS.EXE and HTTPS.HLP to the \WINNT35\SYSTEM32 directory. Go to the Security/Permissions menu item in File Manager, and verify that the System user has read permission on HTTPS.EXE.

4. Copy the HTTPS.CPL file to the \WINNT35\SYSTEM32 directory. Select the Control Panel from the Program Manager to verify that the HTTP Server icon is in the Control Panel (Figure 6.8).

5. Set up a subdirectory, \FILES, off the main HTTP directory (e.g., C:\HTTP\FILES). Copy the files FYI*.* from the \EMHTTPS\FILES directory on the CD to the \FILES directory on your machine. These are text files that we will use to test the forms interface to WAIS databases. Also copy the necessary index files, MYINDEX*.*, from the CD to the main HTTPS directory (e.g., C:\HTTP), as well as the files DEFAULT.HTM, HOME.GIF, and REDBALL.GIF, which will be used for server testing.

6. From the Program Manager, Main program group, click on the MS DOS icon and go to the MS DOS command line. Type in: **https -install**.

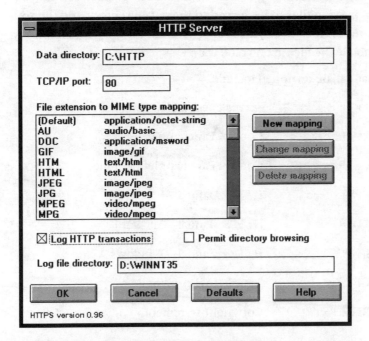

Figure 6.8 NT Control Panel HTTP Server.

This command will install HTTPS as a service and also register it with the Event Logger.

7. Start the NT Control Panel and double-click on the Services icon. The HTTP Server should be shown as a service, as in Figure 6.9.

8. Select the Control Panel and click on the HTTP Server applet. The Configuration window will appear as in Figure 6.8.

9. Define the Data Directory of your HTTP Server. The default is D:\HTTP. This is where your files will be located and it is the topmost directory that HTTP clients will be able to access. This directory may be on a disk using the FAT or the NTFS file system.

For testing, leave the directory set to the default. One consideration to understand is about establishing directories on a file server versus a local computer. On a local system, directories are mapped to individual users, and when the user logs off, the mappings go away. Thus, if your http server starts up when the operating system loads, specify the Data Directory, using a UNC form of directory name. For example, on the server GUMBY with the data directory (or sharename) of DOCS, your Data Directory specification would be:

`\\GUMBY\DOCS`.

10. Specify the TCP/IP port to be used for incoming connections. The default is port 80.

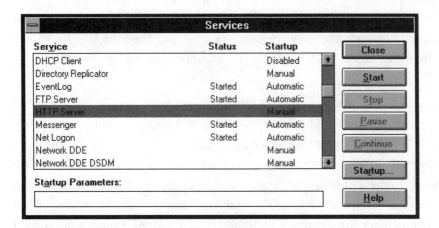

Figure 6.9 NT Control Panel Services.

11. Indicate the file extension to MIME type mapping. The server uses a mapping table to equate a file extension to a specific MIME type. For example, a file with the extension TXT equates to a MIME type/subtype of text/plain. Leave the defaults for initial installation.

12. HTTP transactions can be logged to the Windows NT Event Log. Check the Log HTTP transactions box so that we can log these items to the log file:

    Time and date of request.

    IP address or domain name of the server.

    IP address of the client.

    HTTP command.

    URL the client requested.

    Version of HTTP used (no version means HTTP 0.9).

13. Once you have finished with the configuration options, click on **OK**.

14. Go to the Control Panel and click on the Services applet. Start the HTTP Server by clicking on the **Start** button (Figure 6.9).

You default home page (DEFAULT.HTM) was installed in step 5 above when you transferred files from the CD to the server's data directory (e.g., D:\HTTP). The data directory is the "document root," where you make files available to HTTP clients. URLs are relative to this data directory. Start up your Mosaic or Netscape client, preferably on another machine, and Load the URL necessary to point to the server and Home page. For example, open a URL to:

`http://yoursite.domain.com/`

The server will send the document DEFAULT.HTM if it is in the data directory (Figure 6.10). If the file didn't exist, the server will send a list of files and subdirectories and the list will look much like a gopher or FTP listing. In this case, and by default, you are "browsing" a directory. You can enable directory browsing in the data directory and all subdirectories by checking the Permit directory browsing checkbox on the Control Panel configuration applet. If you still wish to mark some directories nonbrowsable, simply create a file named NOBROWSE and copy it into those nonbrowsable directories.

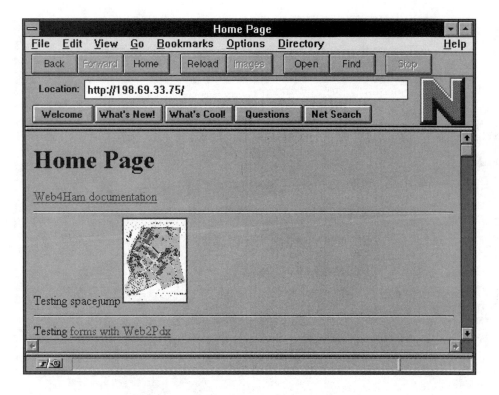

Figure 6.10 NT HTTP Server DEFAULT.HTM.

Searching WAIS Databases

The EMWACS HTTP SERVER can search your local WAIS databases. Refer to the section in the WAIS Toolkit for detailed information on the Toolkit. If your server receives an HTTP GET command for a URL that denotes an HTML file and includes a search term, the server passes the file name and search term to the WAISLOOK program. And correspondingly, the WAISLOOK program passes output back to the client as an HTML file with the search results.

The files you installed in step 5 above demonstrate how to use WAIS to index a large number of text files (although we have only a few in the example) that you wish to make available to Web browsers for searching. The file MYINDEX.HTM is an HTML file that prompts the user for search terms to search a series of FYI (For Your Information) files stored in the \FILES directory you created. To test this capability, enter this URL:

```
http://your.site.here/myindex.htm
```

A form will displayed asking for your search term(s) input (Figure 6.11). Key in a search term and the files where that term occurs will be listed for

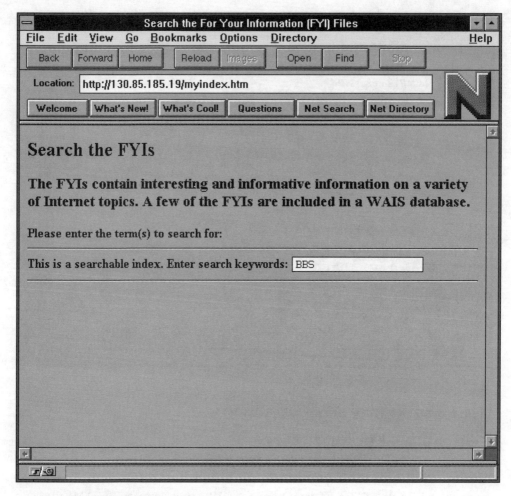

Figure 6.11 NT WAIS search form.

your selection, as in Figure 6.12. If you select one of the files, it will be displayed for your perusal (Figure 6.13).

HTTPS Forms

Included in the EMWCS software distribution is a zipped file named EGI386.ZIP that provides examples of forms.

Purveyor

Process Software Corporation, by an agreement with EMWAC, has enhanced the EMWACS Web server and is offering it as a commercial product called

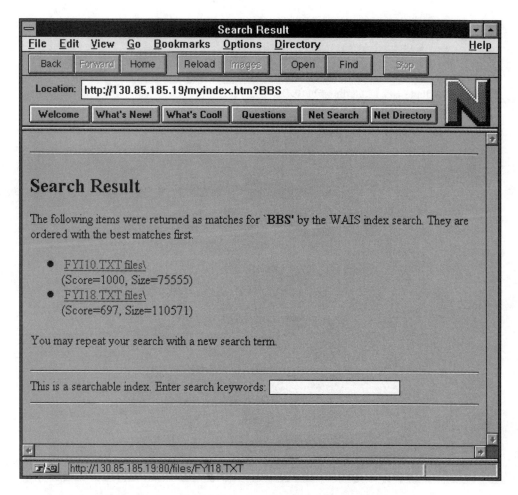

Figure 6.12 NT WAIS search files.

Purveyor. The product includes easily configurable security and system administration, full logging capabilities, and HTML development support.

Further information and ordering instructions can be obtained from **http://www.process.com**.

Installing the Purveyor Server

Once you have acquired the software, follow these steps to set up the server:

1. Move the distribution file, PRVI386.EXE, to a directory (e.g., \PROCESS). Run the program to unarchive the software.

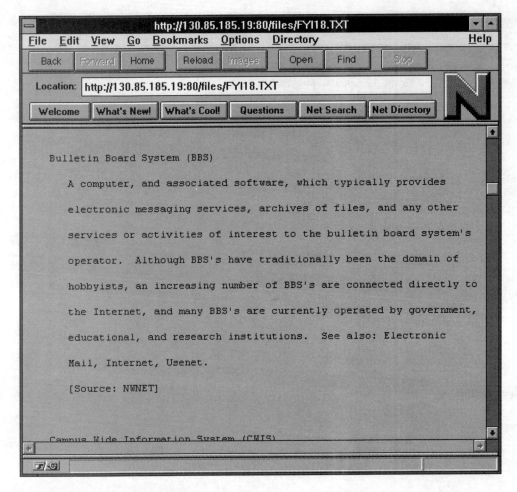

Figure 6.13 NT WAIS file.

2. The Setup program requires that you have Administrators Privileges under NT. Also, be sure to exit the File Manager because the setup procedure modifies the File Manager configuration. A setup screen will appear, as shown in Figure 6.14. Click on **Continue** to proceed with the installation, or you may want to view the ReadMe file.

Next, a screen will appear (Figure 6.15) that asks for installation information, including your name, company, and the product serial number. Key in each value and click on **Continue**.

The setup routine will now ask for a directory where the files can be installed (Figure 6.16). Key in the appropriate drive letter for your installation and the path: \WIN32APP\PSC\PURVEYOR and click on **Continue.**

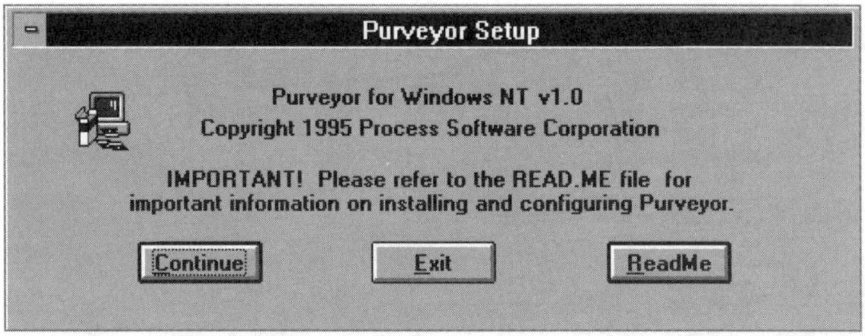

Figure 6.14 Purveyor Setup screen.

Once the files are copied to the appropriate directory, you will receive a screen, as shown in Figure 6.17, which says that the installation was successful. You can now click on **Start** to proceed to the Control Panel so that you can configure Purveyor.

Now configure the following items on the screen shown in Figure 6.18.

Data Directory

This is the directory that will house your documents (it is often referred to as the *Document Root*). By default, the directory is \WIN32APP\PSC\PURVEYOR. The directory you specify must be accessible by the user account under which the Web server runs. For testing, leave the directory set to the default. One

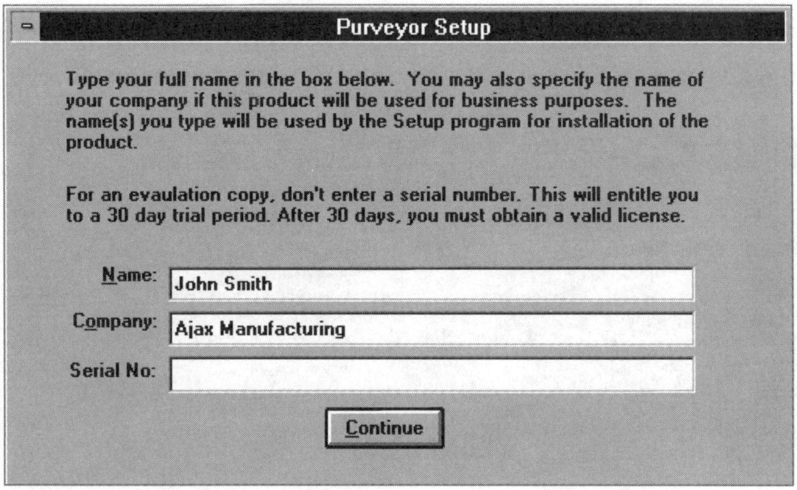

Figure 6.15 Purveyor installation information.

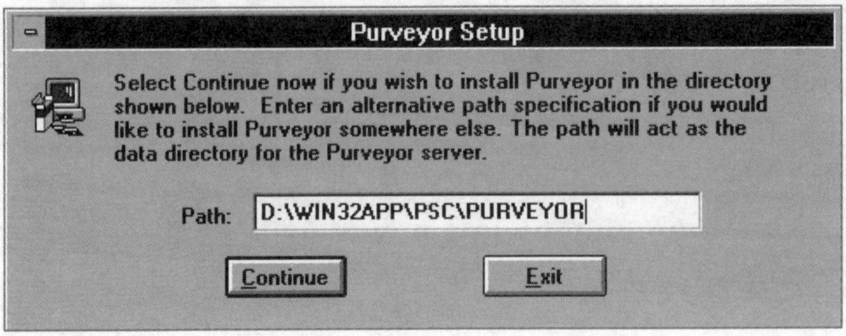

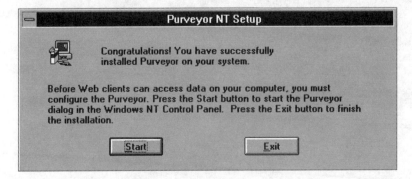

Figure 6.16 Purveyor path information.

consideration to understand is about establishing directories on a file server versus a local computer. On a local system, directories are mapped to individual users, and when the user logs off, the mappings go away. Thus, if your Web server starts up when the operating system loads, specify the Data Directory using a UNC form of directory name. For example, on the server GUMBY with the data directory (or sharename) DOCS, your Data Directory specification would be:

```
\\GUMBY\DOCS
```

TCP/IP Port

This is the port at which the server listens for incoming connections. The default is port 80. If you wish to change it, use a port number greater than 1024.

Default File Name

The Default file name, DEFAULT.HTM, is shown as the page that will be served to clients when no file name is specified in a URL. If you change the name of the

Figure 6.17 Purveyor installation successful.

Figure 6.18 Purveyor configuration.

default home page, you must also change files by that name in any subdirectories included.

Permit Directory Browsing

If you wish to allow users to browse through directories as they would on a Gopher or FTP server, you can Permit Directory Browsing. For testing, leave the box unchecked to disable browsing. If you permit directory browsing and the file DEFAULT.HTM exists in a directory, the server will send the file to the client. Otherwise, the server will send a list of files. **Note**: If you don't want a directory to be browsable, just create a file named NOBROWSE in that directory. Clients will be able to access DEFAULT.HTM, but will no longer be able to receive a list of directory contents.

Log HTTP Transactions Check the Log HTTP transactions box to enable logging of each request to a log file. Each day a log file will be created with the file-name format: Hsyymmdd.log. These log files will be stored, by default, in the \WINNT35 directory. The following information is recorded in the log file:

- Time and date of the request.

- IP address or domain name of the server.

- IP address of the client.

- HTTP command that was executed.

- URL requested by the client.

- Version of the HTTP protocol used.

Enabling DNS Lookup If you select the Enable DNS Lookup checkbox, the client's IP address will be resolved to a domain name and written to

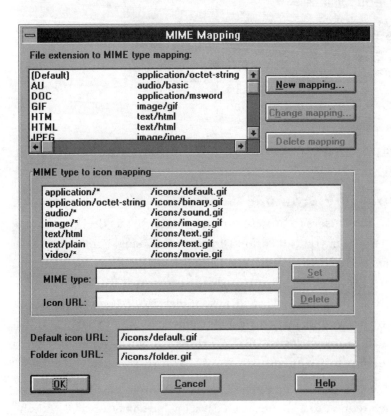

Figure 6.19 Purveyor MIME type table.

the transaction log. One word of caution: this choice may adversely affect the server's performance somewhat.

License If you have an evaluation copy of Purveyor you won't need a serial number. However, if you register the software and receive a license number, you can enter it by clicking on the **License** button.

Mime Mapping The server determines a file's MIME type by referring to the MIME type table displayed through the Control Panel applet (Figure 6.19). You can modify this table by selecting the New Mapping, Change Mapping, or Delete Mapping buttons.

Virtual Paths A virtual path is essentially an alias for an NT directory path (Figure 6.20). For example, your virtual path may be defined as ~smith, with the corresponding NT path of

C:\WIN32APP\PSC\PURVEYOR\STUFF\MYSTUFF.HTML

You would then announce the URL of http://system.domain.com/~smith /mystuff.htm to have people access the file. When the server sees a URL that includes a tilde (~), it checks to see if a virtual path has been set up with that name. If it finds a virtual path by that name, it replaces the path with the corresponding NT path and processes the requested file. Remember, virtual path names always start with a tilde.

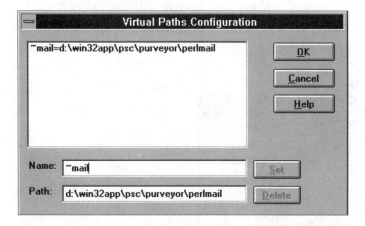

Figure 6.20 Purveyor virtual path.

Users and Groups

You can control which users and groups have access to your server by configuring them in the user database. Access Control Lists (ACL) are created and control this level of security. The client browser will be asked to authenticate the individual user with user name and password (Figure 6.21), and the browser will transmit the user input to the server, which checks the input against the user database. It is important to keep users and groups, discussed in this context, from having any association with the NT operating system's users and groups.

To add new users:

1. From the Control Panel applet, click on the **Users** button. The users configuration dialog box will appear as in Figure 6.22.

2. Enter the new user name *Brian* in the user-name field and enter a password in the password field.

3. Click on the **Set** button to clear the user-name field and click on **OK** to save the information.

To add a new group:

1. Click on the **Groups** button and the Groups Configuration dialog box will appear (Figure 6.23).

2. Enter a group name *Accounting* in the New field of the dialog box. The Group Membership dialog box (Figure 6.24) will appear with the names of all members of the selected group on the right and all users who are not members on the left.

Figure 6.21 Client authentication.

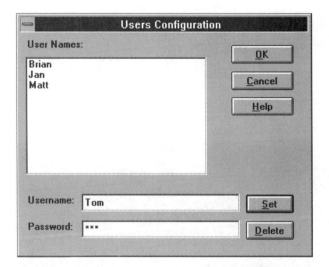

Figure 6.22 Purveyor user configuration.

3. Add the user *Brian* by selecting the user name from the left side and clicking on **Add**. Once you've finished adding users, click on the **OK** button to save changes.

URL Masks

A URL mask has the format of a URL and can use an asterisk (*) as a wild card to replace any of the URL parts. For example: *//host.site.com/* indicates access

Figure 6.23 Purveyor groups configuration.

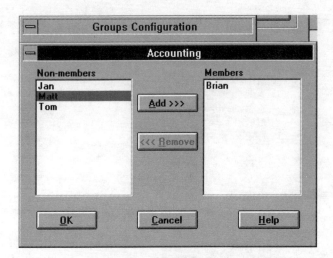

Figure 6.24 Purveyor group membership.

to all documents, by any type (e.g., Gopher, HTTP) to all files at the location **host.site.com**. A mask of gopher://host.site.com/*.txt indicates gopher access to all .txt files at host.site.com. It is important that masking is done purely on a text basis; port numbers and IP addresses may interfere with matching.

Proxy Server
To configure the proxy server:

1 Click on the **Proxy Server** button and the Proxy Server dialog box will appear (Figure 6.25). You can enable the proxy server feature by checking the box titled Enable proxy server.

2. You can restrict use of the proxy server to clients within your organization by entering an IP address mask in any or all of these:

   HTTP services

   Gopher services

   FTP services

   The format is 130.85.*

3. Indicate the URLs or URL masks of locations that you don't want the server to serve to clients in the Don't serve URLs text box.

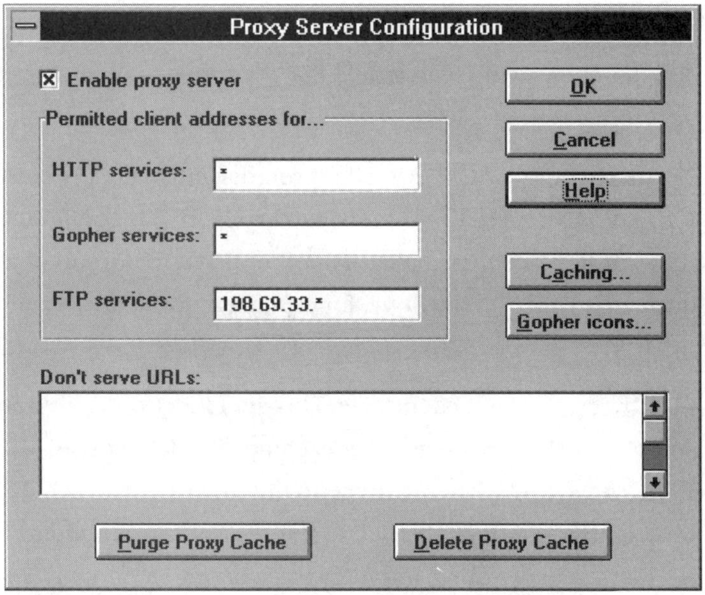

Figure 6.25 Purveyor Proxy Server dialog box.

4. Click on the **Caching** button if you would like to enable, disable, or configure proxy caching (Figure 6.26).

5. Click on the **Gopher** icons button to define icons the server will use to display Gopher menus (Figure 6.27).

6. Click on **OK** to save the changes.

Proxy Caching

When the proxy server retrieves data from a remote server for a client, it can store a copy of the data in a cache. The next time the client requests that URL, the proxy server checks the cache for the data. The benefit to you is better performance, because the server can retrieve the data from local disk rather than a remote server. You can enable proxy caching from the Proxy Caching dialog box.

To enable caching:

1. From the Control Panel applet, click on the **Proxy Server** button.

2. Next, check the box titled Enable proxy caching.

3. Enter the following values to configure proxy caching:

Indicate the disk directory where you would like the cache to be stored in the field *Cache directory*.

The default for the cache is C:\CACHE. The directory must already exist and must be located on an NTFS drive. Thus, if your C: drive is configured as FAT, you will want to place the cache on another drive. Make sure that you have adequate disk space on the drive, for caching tends to use a significant amount of disk.

Indicate, in megabytes, the Max cache size. This specification is used to limit the amount of disk that can be used for caching. The default is 10 Mb. The server will allow the cache to grow beyond this amount, but each day it will purge the cache and reduce the size to the value you've configured here. A rule of thumb is to set this parameter to be about 25 percent less than the actual maximum you'd allow.

The *Purge cache at* field is the time of day that the cache purging should take place. The default is 180 minutes past midnight, or 3:00 A.M.

The *Lifetime of unread cache files* field holds the period of time for which the server keeps unused files. The default is four days. In the edit box (Figure 6.26) you can type a list of URL masks and corresponding times. Separate each line by a CTRL+Enter.

In the *Maximum lifetime of cache files* field, indicate the maximum file lifetime since it was retrieved. Specify URL masks and corresponding times, as well as a default time (usually seven days). The server determines cache lifetime at the time the file is cached; changing the maximum lifetime affects only new additions to the cache, not files already cached. In HTTP/1.0, the original document may indicate an Expires: header indicating a date when the data are no longer valid. If this expires value is indicated, then it, rather than the value set in this dialog box, determines the lifetime of the file.

In the *Don't cache URLs* list box, specify the URLs and URL masks that you would like the server *not* to cache. Enter URLs separated by spaces or new lines (CTRL + Enter).

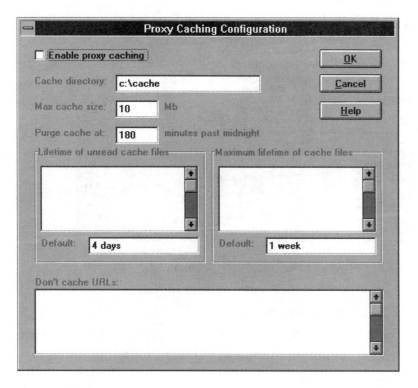

Figure 6.26 Purveyor proxy caching configuration.

Gopher Menu Icons

When a client accesses a Gopher server through the Purveyor proxy server, the server translates Gopher file types to MIME types. You can configure file types as well as the icons that represent the different Gopher file types when served to the client browser.

To configure the Gopher icon mapping:

1. From the Control Panel Applet, click on the **Proxy Server** button.

2. From the Proxy Server dialog box, click on the **Gopher** icons button.

    A list box will be displayed showing the current mapping. The left column is the Gopher type, followed by the HTTP MIME type and finally the URL or the icon to be used. You may add, change, or delete entries.

3. When you've finished reviewing or changing the entries, click on **OK** or **Cancel** to exit.

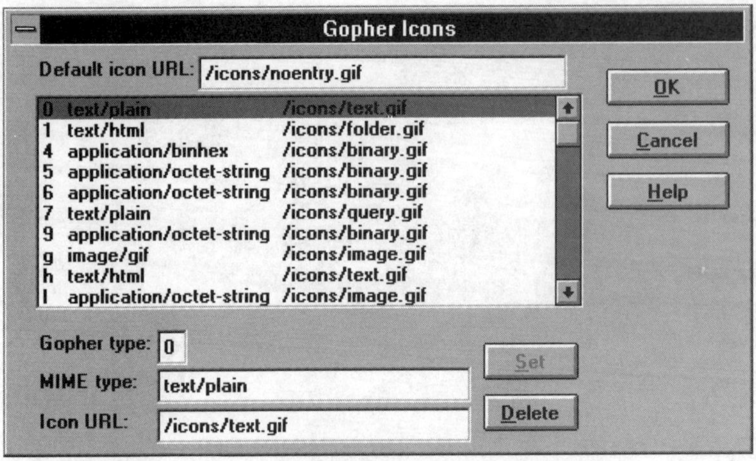

Figure 6.27 Purveyor Gopher Icons dialog box.

Access Control Lists

Access Control Lists take the format of <header name>: <method>, <name>, <ip address>. An example of how these values are entered is shown in Figure 6.28.

<header name> must be one of these:

- Allow-user
- Allow-group
- Reject-user
- Reject-group

<method> must be one of these:

- GET
- HEAD
- POST
- the asterisk character (*)

<name> must be a user name or group name that you have configured through the user and group dialog boxes or the asterisk character (*).

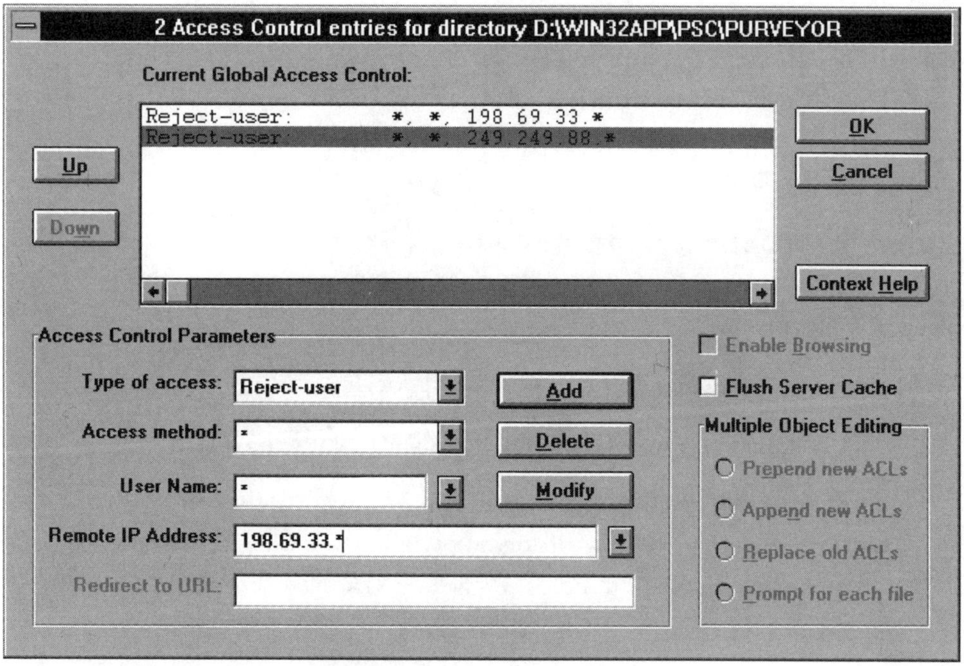

Figure 6.28 Purveyor access control entries.

<ipaddress> must be a valid IP address that may include wild cards (*).

Note: If you have directory browsing enabled through the Control Panel applet, hide the ACL files by using the File/Properties menu in the File Manager.

Access Control

You can restrict access to files and directories based on client user names, IP addresses, and the HTTP methods used by the client requests. The server permits three types of access control: Global, Virtual Path, and File and Directory control. When a client requests access to a particular file, the server verifies and enforces access control in this order:

- Global

- Virtual Path

- File and Directory

Thus, a client who tries to access a particular file must have access at the Global, Virtual Path, Directory and File level if any restrictions are in effect at these levels. The client who is "rejected" at any level receives a message that the requested file doesn't exist, even though it does, or a prompt for user name and password, if applicable.

Summary: Configuring Access Controls

To configure access control at the Global, Virtual Path, or File and Directory level:

1. Open the NT File Manager and select a file or directory.

2. Select Edit Access Control from the Purveyor pull-down menu.

3. If more than one level of access control is available for the object, the Choose Access Control Type dialog box will appear. Check the type of access control you want to edit and click on **OK**. Next, the Edit ACL box will appear.

4. Now you can change the location of the Access Control Entry within the file by using the **UP** or **Down** button. You can add, change, or delete entries. And you can enable directory browsing.

5. Last, click on the **OK** or **Cancel** button to exit.

Testing Access Control

A very significant feature of the server is ability to test access controls.

To test individual access control:

1. Select an object you would like to test through the File Manager.

2. From the Purveyor menu item, choose Test Access Control and the Test Access Control dialog box will appear.

3. Enter the access parameters in the Access Parameters text boxes (you may use the * wild card to indicate all). If you want to test virtual paths, check the Use Virtual Path if Applicable box.

4. You can examine the results of your test in the Test Results box by clicking the **Test Access** button. If you want to edit the ACLs in the

selected files, click on the **Edit Access** button. This choice will open the Edit ACL dialog box for every file and directory you have chosen. If you want to edit the entries for one of the files or directories you have chosen, double-click on one of the entries in the Test Results box.

5. If you want to clear the results, press the **Clear Results** button.

6. Click on the **Close** button to exit.

Finding Objects with Access Control

To find objects with a specific type of access control:

1. From the File Manager, select a directory and choose Find Access Control from the Purveyor pull-down menu.

2. Check the appropriate box (or boxes) to indicate the type of access control you want to check for (Figure 6.29). If you would like to search subdirectories as well, check the Search subdirectories box. If you want to check for file access control, check the File Access Control box.

3. Click on the **OK** button to start the search, and results will be displayed as in Figure 6.30, or click on the **Cancel** button to return to the File Manager.

Adding Access Control Entries

To add access control for a directory or file:

1. Select the directory or file from the File Manager and choose Edit Access Control from the HTTPS pull-down menu. If more than one level of

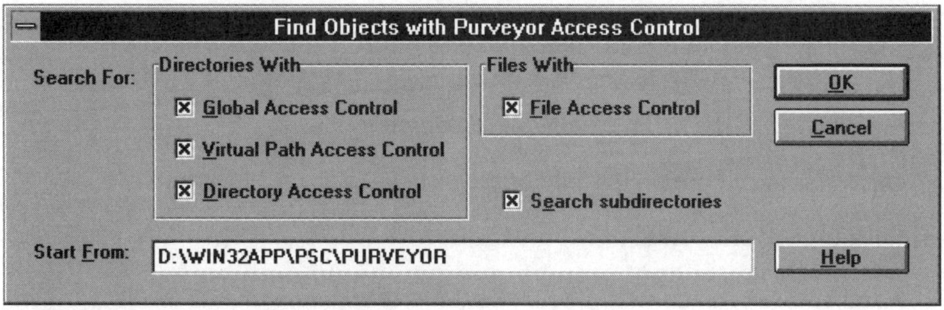

Figure 6.29 Purveyor Find Objects.

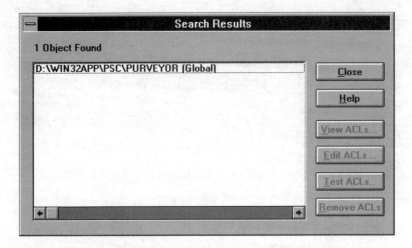

Figure 6.30 Purveyor Find Objects search results.

control is allowed for the object, the Choose Access Control Type dialog box appears. Check the type of access control you want to edit and click on **OK**. The Edit ACL dialog box will then appear. If only one type of control is possible, only the Edit ACL dialog box will appear.

2. You may now configure these parameters:

   • Choose an option from the Type of access list box.

   • Choose an Access Method (* indicates all methods).

   • Indicate a user or group from the User Name/Group Name list box (* is valid for users, but not for groups).

   • Indicate a valid IP address or host name of clients you wish to restrict in the Remote IP Address list box (* indicates all addresses).

   • Enter the path where you would like to redirect requests in the Redirect to URL list box. This field applies only if *redirect* to access is selected in the Type of access drop-down menu.

3. Once you have entered the parameters, click on the **Add** button.

4. Click on **OK** or **Cancel** to exit.

   Note: You can select multiple files or directories and add access-control entries for more than one file or directory at a time. Simply select multiple files or directories through the File Manager and use the same Edit Access Control procedure as with individual files (above). The difference will be that you will be presented with multiple radio boxes in the Multiple Object Editing dialog box.

Access Control Examples

Adequate access control is required on your server if you wish to ensure any degree of security. You have several levels of access control:

- users

- groups

- virtual path

The examples provided here give you a good introduction to the various methods for controlling access.

Basic authentication of clients can be accomplished by establishing users and groups on your server. Users are the individuals who access your server with a browser. Each user can have a user name and password that will provide basic capability for authentication. Users can also be placed in groups and the group can be assigned some control over access. As mentioned previously, the user name and associated password are not to be confused with users on the NT system. Users on the Purveyor server need not be established users with accounts on the NT system. User names, passwords, and groups are set up using the Control Panel applet. In the Advanced Server Configuration box, click on **Users**... to add or remove users and their associated passwords, or **Groups**... to add or remove groups and group members. You will need to exit the Control Panel applet (and restart the server when prompted) for the new users or groups to take effect. The Purveyor File Manager Extension will display all the users and groups in the Edit Access Control dialog .

Virtual Paths can be defined in the Control Panel applet (Figure 6.31). A Virtual Path is one that points to another directory and always starts with a tilde (~). Some benefits of a Virtual Path are:

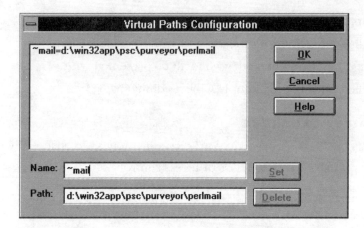

Figure 6.31 Purveyor virtual paths configuration.

Being able to provide access to different drives. For example, ~ddrive could be defined as d:\.

Rather lengthy paths can be abbreviated and simplified with a Virtual Path. For example,~sales could be defined as C: \WIN32APP\PSC\PURVEYOR\ STATISTICS\SALES.

Then you would use the Virtual Path as part of the URL. http://host.site .com/~sales/quarter1.html would (as defined above) point to C:\WIN32APP\ PSC\PURVEYOR\STATISTICS\SALES\QUARTER1.HTML.

Each access control entry (ACE) consists of four parts (excluding redirect-to ACEs, which are discussed later); they are the Type of access control entry, Access Method, User or Group, and IP address. The four types of access control entries are: accept-user, accept-group, reject-user, and reject group. The four types of Access Methods are: *, GET, POST, and HEAD. Users and Groups were discussed above. The IP address can have wild cards so that you could restrict access to a file from hosts 192.42.95.* or 192.42.9?.* , for example. With Access Control Lists (ACLs) you must remember that they have a reject-user, *, *, * implicitly applied. If you place an ACL on a file or directory, the implied reject-user will, by default, reject everyone. If no ACL is set up, then everyone has access.

The sequence of entries is important, too. Access control entries are processed in sequence, and once a match is found, processing stops. For example, if a reject-user entry is applied for a particular user, the request is rejected, even if an accept-user or accept-group comes later in the sequence of entries.

For illustration, let's discuss some simple entries:

Users: Brian, Matt, Jan, Tom.

Groups: Accounting (Users Brian and Matt), Sales (Users Jan and Tom).

Virtual Paths: ~sales = C:\WIN32APP\PSC\PURVEYOR.

A file such as

C:\WIN32APP\PSC\PURVEYOR\STATISTICS\SALES\QUARTER1.HTML has this ACL:

```
reject-user: *, Jan, *
allow-group: *, Sales, 198.69.33.*
```

Another file (say)

C:\WIN32APP\PSC\PURVEYOR\STATISTICS\SALES\BUDGET.HTML has this ACL:

```
reject-user: *, Tom, *
allow-group: *, Accounting, 198.69.33.*
```

Thus, only members of the group Sales can access ~sales/quarter1.html, and only from hosts 198.69.33.*. User Jan is explicitly rejected even though she is in the Sales group. All others are rejected because of the implicit reject-user: *,*,*. The second example rejects user Tom and allows anyone in the Accounting group from hosts in the 198.69.33.* mask. All other users are implicitly rejected.

We find also a hierarchy of Access Control Lists. It includes:

- **Global ACL**—Every request to the server is checked against this ACL. It is set just like a directory ACL on the Default Directory for the server (see Figure 6.32 and Figure 6.28). In our sample configuration you would set the ACL on C:\WIN32APP\PSC\PURVEYOR.

- **Virtual Path ACL**—If the user specified a virtual path, this ACL is checked. If the user uses the full URL path to the file, rather than the URL with a Virtual Path in it, the Virtual Path URL will *not* be checked.

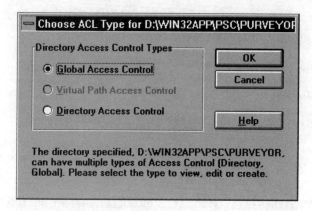

Figure 6.32 Purveyor Global Access Control.

- **Directory ACL**—If the user specifies a directory rather than a file for directory browsing, this ACL is checked; it can be used to control client access to an FTP area.

- **File ACL**—Controls access to a particular file.

Using the File Manager Extension

After you have set up some users and some groups, you can use the File Manager Extension (Figure 6.33) to easily set up ACLs on files and directories. Simply select the files and/or directories you want to control and use the Purveyor menu to go to Edit Access Control. If a directory is selected that can have more than one type of access control, you will be prompted for which type to edit or create. Examples would be Global and directory or Virtual Path and directory.

Next, use the Edit dialog box to specify which types of access control and which users or groups you want to control. You can type either a node name or an IP Address in the IP Address box. Use the **Add/Modify/Delete** buttons to insert, change, and remove individual access control entries. Use the **Up** and **Down** buttons to position each ACE. Always remember that order is important: The first entry that applies will be used. Context help is available for the fields in this dialog box.

Figure 6.33 Purveyor File Manager extension.

If you are editing multiple files, by specifying multiple files in the File Manager before clicking on **Edit Access Control**, you have the option of specifying how the new ACLs you are entering are merged with the existing access control for an object. By default, you will be prompted for each file, but you can force the new ACLs to be placed at the beginning or the end, or you can replace the old ACLs entirely. If prompting is selected, a dialog box will be displayed to let you merge in the new ACLs or skip that file.

Verifying or testing access is simple and straightforward. Use the Test Access Control menu item and select the object you want to test, fill in the necessary fields, and click the **Test Access** button. The results will be displayed in the list box. Check the Use Virtual Path checkbox if you want the Virtual Path access tested. If the results aren't what you expected, click the **Edit Access** button to edit access for all the selected objects. Double-click on a line in the list box to edit the access for just that object. Continue to edit and test the access until it is correct.

The Find Objects menu item (Figure 6.29) is used to find objects that have any access control configured. The results are displayed in a list box (Figure 6.30) with files indented two spaces and listed below their parent directories. Directories have the type of access control found listed next to the name. You can select any file or directory and use the buttons to view, edit, test, or remove its associated access control.

The Remove Access Control works like the File Manager Delete function. You will have to confirm the removal of the various types of access control.

View Access Control allows you to see what access control entries are in the various ACL files (Figure 6.34). Select the objects you want to view, click on **View Access Control**, and the ACL will be displayed. Next you can Edit, Test, or Remove the ACL. You can use the **Next Object** and **Previous Object** buttons to move between the selected objects.

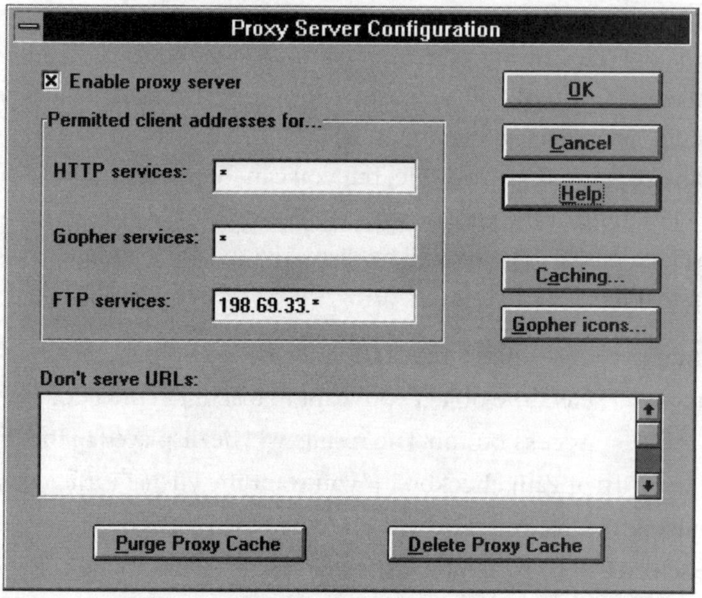

Figure 6.34 Purveyor viewing access control.

In summary, the steps necessary to add access control are:

1. Create a user and group using the Control Panel applet.

2. If the object will be accessed via a Virtual Path, create the Virtual Path using the Control Panel applet.

3. From the File Manager, select the object and click on **Edit Access Control** in the Purveyor menu.

4. If prompted, specify the type of access control you want to edit or create.

5. Using the **Add**, **Modify**, **Delete**, and **Up** and **Down** buttons, enter the access control entries into the list box. The User/Group combo box will have all the users and groups you created in step 1.

6. Click **OK** to save your changes or **Cancel** otherwise. If multiple objects were selected and Prompt for each file is set, use the Merge ACLs dialog box to specify how you want the new ACEs merged into the existing access control.

7. Use the Test Access menu item (or toolbar button) to verify that the proper people now have access to the object.

General Information about ACL Files

Access Control Lists (ACLs) control which users and groups have access to particular directories and files and from which IP addresses. As you'll see below, these files have names starting with $HTTPS$ or are stored in directories starting with $HTTPS$ and cannot be accessed because the server does not allow access to files or directories with the $HTTPS$ sequence.

The server examines the request in light of the sequence of entries within an ACL. The server will allow or reject a request based on the first entry it finds in the ACL corresponding to the client request. Thus remember that if you allow a client access to a file, but an entry above it in the ACL causes the request to be rejected, the client request will not be allowed.

Global Access Control

You can control access to the entire server by using Global Access Control. The Global Access Control file, $HTTPS$.GAC, located in the HTTP Data Directory, is created through the Global Access Control dialog box. If access is permitted in this file, the server will proceed to the next level of access control, Virtual Path access control. If the $HTTPS$.GAC file is either not present, or inaccessible for some reason, the server assumes access is allowed.

Virtual Path Access Control

The file $HTTPS$.VAC controls access to files and directories in a virtual path and the .VAC file is created via the Virtual Path Access Control dialog box. If access is allowed by the .VAC file, the server proceeds to the File and Directory Access Control restrictions. If the .VAC file is either not present, or inaccessible for some reason, the server assumes access is allowed.

Directory Access Control

If directory browsing is permitted through the server's Control Panel applet, and you wish to place restrictions on who can access a directory, you can set up an ACL for that directory. The directory access control file is called $HTTPS$.DAC and must be located in the directory it protects. If the .DAC file is either not present or inaccessible for some reason, the server assumes access is allowed unless the directory includes a NOBROWSE file, in which case browsing will never be allowed whether the .DAC file is present or not.

File Access Control

You can restrict access at the file level by creating an ACL for each file you wish to protect. These ACLs have the same name as the file they protect and must be located in a subdirectory called $HTTPS$.ACL. This subdirectory must be located at the same directory level as the file it is intended to protect.

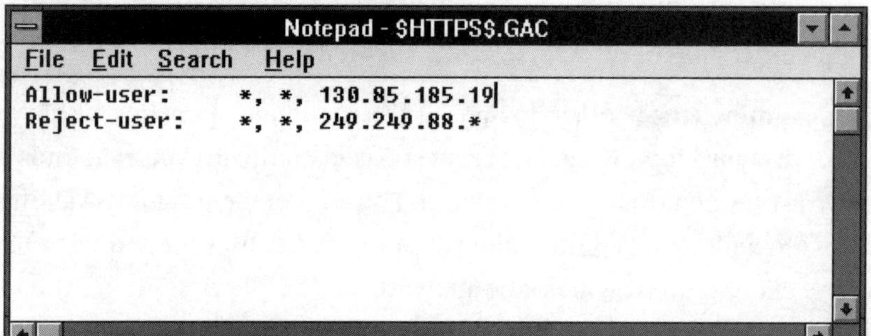

```
Notepad - $HTTPS$.GAC
File   Edit   Search   Help
Allow-user:    *, *, 130.85.185.19
Reject-user:   *, *, 249.249.88.*
```

Figure 6.35 File structure of Purveyor Access Control.

In all access control files (.GAC, .VAC, .DAC, .ACL), hide the files by using the File/Properties menu in the File Manager. An example of the structure of these files is shown in Figure 6.35.

Purveyor Utilities

The Purveyor software distribution comes with a number of very important utilities and sample CGI programs. These utilities include:

- Comment, a program to solicit feedback via forms.

- A mail form.

- Forms that take input and return it to the browser and/or write to a file.

- A log-file analysis/server statistics program.

COMMENT.EXE

The Comment program allows client users to fill in an HTML form to generate e-mail and also saves messages to disk files. The program can effectively handle mailing as delivered, or you can modify it to add capabilities, because the source code is included (in "C").

The HTML form in the distribution (Figure 6.36) includes six fields:

sendto *sendto* is a name that COMMENT uses to look up mail addresses and log file locations. **yourname**, **companyname**, **telephone**, and **email** are simple ASCII string fields. **comment** is a text-area variable.

COMMENT.HTM is a form that collects and submits the data listed above. The *sendto* field must be one of a specific limited set of options, and so a select field is the appropriate type. When the submit request passes the field data to COMMENT.EXE, one additional file is needed for execution. The file COMMENT.CNF (modify the COMMENT.CNF file with the necessary values for your site) is a text file that includes the name of the file to be served to the user in response. In the sample provided, that file is COMMENT1.HTM, which thanks the user for the message. That name must be the first line of the file. Each additional line has five entries in the format listed below. Modify the COMMENT.CNF file with the necessary values for your site (Figure 6.37).

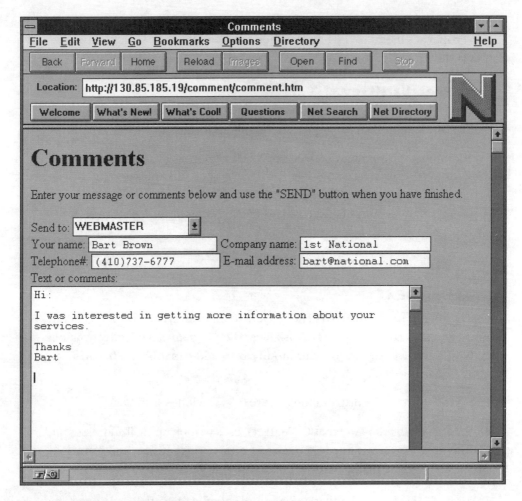

Figure 6.36 Purveyor Comment form.

Each field in this code line is explained below.

```
sendtodata   logfile mailfrom mailto mailserver
```

sendtodata   sendtodata is the exact value passed in the sendto field. The reason for using a select field in this form is that there must be an exact match with the contents of the sendto field and the first item on one of the lines in the COMMENT.CNF file to ensure proper operation of COMMENT.EXE. This field may include blank spaces.

logfile   logfile is the name of a file in which each message is saved in ASCII form. This may be either an absolute path name (beginning with a drive designation or a backslash) or a relative path name (beginning with anything else). Do not use a forward slash (/), even though it is standard for URL addresses. This is a file name, not a URL.

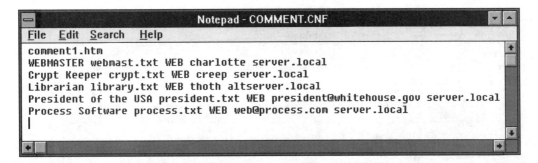

```
Notepad - COMMENT.CNF
File   Edit   Search   Help
comment1.htm
WEBMASTER webmast.txt WEB charlotte server.local
Crypt Keeper crypt.txt WEB creep server.local
Librarian library.txt WEB thoth altserver.local
President of the USA president.txt WEB president@whitehouse.gov server.local
Process Software process.txt WEB web@process.com server.local
|
```

Figure 6.37 Purveyor COMMENT.CNF file.

mailfrom   mailfrom is an address name used in the FROM field of a mail message. Ordinarily this is the name of a special user account set up for this-purpose. It must be a local account that is "known" by the server defined in mailserver (see below).

mailto   mailto is an address name for the account that is the message's actual target, and translates the "alias" in sendto into an actual e-mail address. It can be any legitimate mail address reachable by the server defined in mailserver (see below).

mailserver   mailserver is the name of an SMTP mail server. The server must be able to handle the mail to and from the defined addresses. Both must be legitimate mail accounts and mailfrom must be local to the server.

The mail-handling program BLAT.EXE must be in the same directory as COMMENT.EXE to prevent confusion in path names. BLAT.EXE also uses GENSOCK.DLL, which must also be installed and running, but can reside in any directory listed in the PATH environment variable (or in the same directory as BLAT.EXE). You can access the form by using Netscape or Mosaic and opening a URL to:

`http://yourhost.site.com/comment/comment.htm`

EGSCRPT1.EXE

The EGSCRIPT1 program allows users to fill in an HTML form (Figure 6.38) and returns a text file describing all the data that were entered. This program is a useful example for CGI programmers. EGSCRIPT1 accepts form input and serves a returning text file that describes all the system data and form data (Figure 6.39). It is a useful tool for debugging HTML forms.

The sample HTML file EG1FORM.HTM includes an example of every type of field you can have in an HTML form. It requires both EGSCRPT1.EXE and ANDROMED.GIF in the same directory. The source file EGSCRPT1.C is

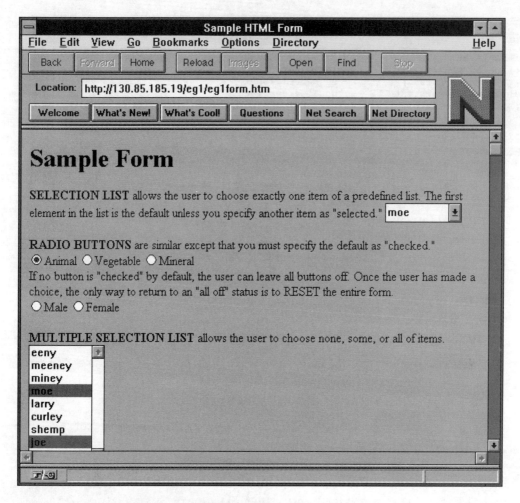

Figure 6.38 Purveyor EGSCRIPT1 form.

included to allow you to make modifications and examine the source example. It is not required for operating EGSCRPT1.EXE. You can access the form by using Netscape or Mosaic and opening a URL to:

```
http://yourhost.site.com/eg1/eg1form.htm
```

EGSCRPT2.EXE

EGSCRIPT2 allows users to fill in an HTML form (Figure 6.38) and writes a description of all the data to a text file. It is similar to EGSCRPT1.EXE except that it writes the information to a file rather than serving this text back to the browser. The output file must have the extension .HFO and it must be an

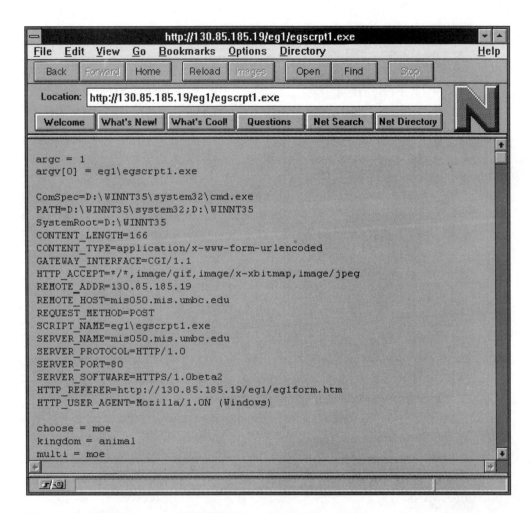

Figure 6.39 Purveyor EDSCRIPT1 return data.

existing file, properly addressed, in a directory where the server has Write access (also be sure to check the Properties of the .HFO file to ensure that it is not marked *read only*). The new information is appended to the current content of the file. The sample HTML file EG2FORM.HTM includes an example of every type of field you can have in an HTML form. It requires both EGSCRPT2.EXE and ANDROMED.GIF in the same directory. The source file EGSCRPT2.C is included to allow you to make modifications and examine the source example. It is not required for operating EGSCRPT1.EXE. The executable EGSCRPT2.EXE is invoked with a path relative to the directory in which the HTML form resides. The file that EGSCRPT2.EXE invokes, however, must be named with a path relative to the server's default data directory. For example, if the required files all reside in a subdirectory of the default data directory named EG2, then the executable SUB\EGSCRPT2.EXE is simply EGSCRPT2.EXE, but the data file FORM.HFO must be specified as EG2\FORM.HFO. The resulting HTML FORM definition would be:

```
<Form method=POST action="egscrpt2.exe/eg2/form.hfo">
```

This definition may seem strange, because both EGSCRPT2.EXE and FORM.HFO reside in the same subdirectory, but it is simply because EGSCRPT2.EXE is invoked by the form with a path relative to the form, and FORM.HFO is invoked by EGSCRPT2.EXE with a path relative to the default data directory.

You can access the form by using Netscape or Mosaic and opening a URL to:

```
http://yourhost.site.com/eg2/eg2form.htm
```

MAILDEMO.PL

MAILDEMO.PL allows users to fill in an HTML form (Figure 6.40) to generate e-mail. PERLMAIL.PL is a PERL script that handles input from an HTML form and e-mails the field values in a structured form. Unlike the COMMENT.EXE example, which is intended for use with no modification of the source code, this sample is intended to serve as the starting point for a PERL programmer who needs to create an application that uses e-mail as part of the system. The form of the sample mail is intended to show the PERL programmer how tags and values are used in a structured message. This technique is especially useful for applications in which the generated e-mail message needs to be parsed by another application.

You must modify MAILDEMO.PL for your local installation:

1. The initial *require* statement must address your local path to the file CGI-LIB.PL.

2. The default data for communications and line testing must be changed if you use it.

You must modify MAILDEMO.HTM for your local installation:

1. The value of the hidden-field mail hub must be a valid local mail server.

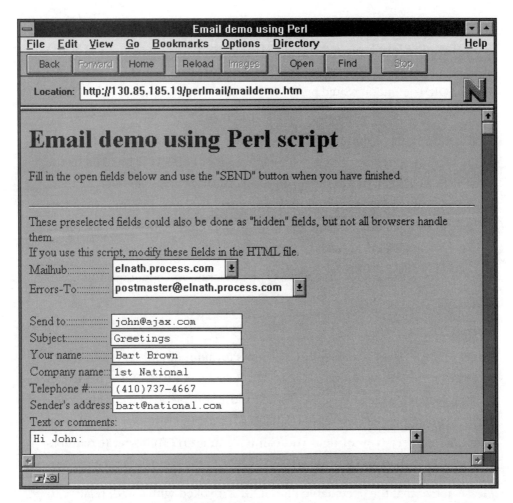

Figure 6.40 Purveyor MAILDEMO form.

2. The value of the hidden field errorsto must be a valid e-mail account.

3. The paths to PERL.EXE and MAILDEMO.PL in the FORM command must be correct for your local installation, with differences as listed below.

Please notice that the executable PERL.EXE is invoked with a path relative to the directory in which the HTML form resides. The scripts that PERL.EXE invokes, however, must be named with a path relative to the server's default data directory. For example, if the required files all reside in a subdirectory of the default data directory named PERLMAIL, then the executable PERLMAIL\PERL.EXE is simply PERL.EXE, but the script PERLMAIL\ MAILDEMO.PL must be specified as PERLMAIL\MAILDEMO.PL. The resulting HTML FORM definition would be:

```
<Form method=POST action="perl.exe?perlmail/maildemo.pl">
```

This definition may seem strange, for both PERL.EXE and MAILDEMO.PL reside in the same subdirectory, but it is simply because PERL.EXE is invoked by the form with a path relative to the form, and MAILDEMO.PL is invoked by PERL with a path relative to the default data directory. Also, it is very important that no check for a valid mail originator appears in the e-mail field. This lack can lead to mail-handling errors or "faked" messages.

You can access the form by using Netscape or Mosaic and opening a URL to:

```
http://yourhost.site.com/perlmail/maildemo.htm
```

SHOWTAGS.PL

SHOWTAGS.PL is a PERL script that accepts form input and serves an HTML page that describes all the variable-tag data. Like EGSCRPT1.EXE, it is a useful tool for debugging HTML forms, especially those you intend to use with a PERL script. The sample HTML file FORMTEST.HTM (Figure 6.38) includes an example of every type of field you can have in an HTML form. It requires ANDROMED.GIF, PERL.EXE, and SHOWTAGS.PL in the same directory.

Please notice that the executable PERL.EXE is invoked with a path relative to the directory in which the HTML form resides. The scripts that PERL.EXE invokes, however, must be named with a path relative to the server's default data directory. For example, if the required files all reside in a subdirectory of the default data directory named SHOWTAGS, then the executable SHOWTAGS\PERL.EXE is simply PERL.EXE, but the script SHOWTAGS\SHOW-TAGS.PL must be specified as SHOWTAGS\SHOWTAGS.PL. The resulting HTML FORM definition would be:

```
<Form method=POST action="perl.exe?showtags/showtags.pl">
```

This definition may seem strange, because both PERL.EXE and SHOWTAGS.PL reside in the same subdirectory, but it is simply because PERL.EXE is invoked by the form with a path relative to the form, and SHOWTAGS.PL is invoked by PERL with a path relative to the default data directory.

WWWSTAT.CMD

WWWSTAT.CMD reads the server log files and creates an HTML formatted summary of server statistics. WWWSTAT.CMD is an adaptation of the program developed by Roy Fielding as part of the Arcadia project at the University of California, Irvine. The author maintains a WWW server with updated information at **http://www.ics.uci.edu/WebSoft/wwwstat/** and requests e-mail from anyone using the program regularly to **fielding@ics.uci.edu**. Please notice that this version is a specific adaptation and the original given on the author's home page will not work in the NT environment without similar adaptation.

WWWSTAT.CMD acts as a command-line program with this form:

```
wwwstat      [-helLoOuUrvx]
             [-i pathname]
             [-a IP_address] [-A IP_address]
             [-c code] [-C code]
             [-d date] [-D date]
             [-n archive_name] [-N archive_name]
             [-t hour] [-T hour]
             [logfile ...] [logfile.gz ...] [logfile.Z ...]
```

Display Options:

-h   Help—just display this message and quit.

-e   Display all invalid log entries on STDERR.

-l   Do display full IP address of clients in my domain.

-L   Don't (i.e., strip the machine name from local addresses).

-o   Do display full IP address of clients from other domains.

-O   Don't (i.e., strip the machine name from nonlocal addresses).

-u   Do display IP address from unresolved domain names.

-U   Don't (i.e., group all unresolved addresses under that name).

-r   Display table of requests by each remote ident or authuser.

-v   Verbose display (to STDERR) of each log entry processed.

-x   Display all requests of nonexistent files to STDERR.

Input Options:

-i   Include the following file. The given file should be either a prior wwwstat output or an archive of prior wwwstat output files (compressed with the extension gz, Z, or z). If the given file name is an archive (identified by one of the extensions) then each file in the archive is extracted and included in the result.

Search Options (include in summary only those log entries) can use perl regular expressions as an argument (regep), with a few exceptions, listed here:

-a   Containing a host name/IP address matching the given regexp (except + and .).

-A   Not containing a host name/IP address matching the regexp (except + and .).

-c   Containing a server response code matching the given regexp.

-C   Not containing a server response code matching the given regexp.

-d   Containing a date (e.g., "Feb 2 1994") matching the given regexp.

-D   Not containing a date (e.g., "Feb 2 1994") matching the given regexp.

-t   Containing an hour ("00"—"23") matching the given perl regexp.

-T   Not containing an hour ("00" — "23") matching the given perl regexp.

-n   Containing an archive (URL) name matching perl regexp (except + and .).

-N   Not containing an archive (URL) name matching perl regexp (except + and .).

If no log file is specified, the default is the most recent log file.

The conversion from a .PL to a .CMD file created the restriction of allowing no more than nine command-line arguments. If you need more, you can invoke PERL directly:

```
perl wwwstat.cmd arguments
```

This version ignores a standard option switch (-s srmfile), which is used to designate a log-file directory. For the NT environment, this program uses the NT registry to locate the log files. Log files must use daily logs with the standard naming convention HSyymmdd.LOG, where yymmdd is the date of the logged events.

Examples of Use: If you want to concatenate the data from several logs, specify all on the command line (no wild cards), or use a script like this:

```
perl wwwstat.cmd HS950101.log >jan.htm
perl wwwstat.cmd -i jan.htm HS950102.log >tmp.htm
rename tmp.htm jan.htm
perl wwwstat.cmd -i jan.htm HS950103.log >tmp.htm
rename tmp.htm jan.htm
....etc....
```

Using this daily script maintains an up-to-date summary page:

```
perl wwwstat.cmd -i current.htm >tmp.htm
rename tmp.htm current.htm
```

CSMHTTPD

The CSMHTTPD server is developed by the Computer Software Manufaktur (CSM) company of Vienna, Austria. Its name at the time of product release will probably be "Alibaba," but that has not been determined at the time of this writing.

The server is packed in one self-extracting archive, ALIBETA3.EXE, available from the CSM server at:

```
ftp://ftp.eunet.co.at/pub/vendor/csm/alibaba/ALIBETA3.exe
```

Features of CSMHTTPD include:

- A multithreaded WWW server.

- Implemented as a NT system service.

- Utilizes the HTTP 1.0 protocol.

- Provides CGI capability, including Windows CGI.

- Many configurable parameters (port, server root, document root, and so on.

- Logging.

- Image mapping.

- Access control by user, group, and/or site.

CSMHTTPD Installation

To install the software:

1. Move the archive file, ALIBETA3.EXE to a directory (e.g., D:\CSMHTTPD).

2. From the NT File Manager, Run the ALIBETA3.EXE program and the archive will be unpacked.

3. Once the files are unpacked, double-click on the SETUP.EXE file through the File Manager and a dialog box will be displayed, titled: "CSMHTTPD Setup" (Figure 6.41). The window will include a welcome message stating: "Welcome to CSMHTTPD a WWW Server from Austria. This program will actually set up CSMHTTPD". Click on **Continue**.

4. A dialog box titled: "Get Dest Path for CSMHTTPD" will be displayed next (Figure 6.42). Indicate the Path (in an NTFS partition) where you want the files located (e.g., D:\CSMHTTPD). Click on **Continue**.

5. A dialog box (Figure 6.43) with a check box will appear with the instructions: "Install also demofiles (including feature lists and so on).

Figure 6.41 CSMHTTPD Setup.

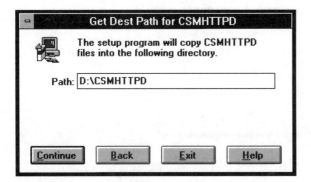

Figure 6.42 CSMHTTPD destination path.

For an initial setup it is strongly recommended that you include demo files." Leave the box checked and click on **OK**.

6. Next, a dialog box (Figure 6.44) asking "Allow directory browsing for clients" appears. Leave the checkbox checked and click on **OK**.

7. You will be asked to choose the map type for your server (Figure 6.45). Check "Use NCSA compatible map files." Your other choice (unchecked) is: "Use CERN compatible map files." An informational message is also displayed, advising you that "Depending on what you use, and if the demo files are installed, you have to go into the directory [INSTALL]\click and have to execute one of the batch jobs USECERN or USENCSA." Click on **OK**.

8. Next, indicate where the server INI file should be stored (Figure 6.46). Leave the default check on the box for "Create CSMHTTPD.INI in the

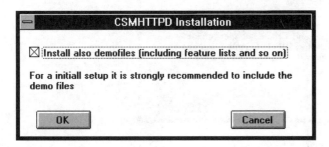

Figure 6.43 CSMHTTPD demo files installation.

Figure 6.44 CSMHTTPD directory browsing.

WINNT directory. Your other choice is "Create CSMHTTPD.INI in the installation directory." You will also see the informational message, which says: "If you create CSMHTTPD.INI in the installation directory, don't forget to copy it to the WINNT directory after setup is finished." But you can also use your old (currently configured) CSMHTTPD.INI file. Click on **Continue**.

9. You should now see a screen (Figure 6.47) that says "Setup succeeded." The setup of CSMHTTPD is now completed. You must now install CSMHTTPD as a system service with this command:

```
csmhttpd -install
```

If you have CSMHTTPD already installed, please enter:

```
csmhttpd -remove
```

before you enter csmhttpd -install.

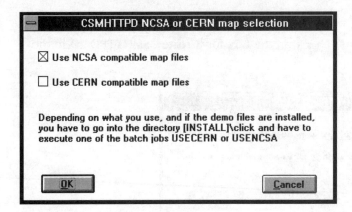

Figure 6.45 CSMHTTPD Map Type.

Figure 6.46 CSMHTTPD Path for INI file.

10. To install the server as a "service," type (from DOS) csmhttpd -install.

11. Go to the Control Panel and click on the **Services** icon. You should now see "CSMHTTPD a WWW-Server from Austria" listed as a service. Now, change the startup option to "automatic" so that the

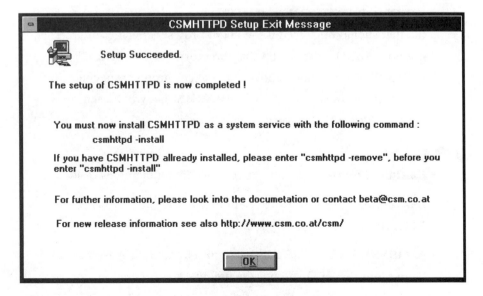

Figure 6.47 CSMHTTPD successful installation.

HTTP server will start on boot-up. You will need to stop and restart the server each time you make changes to the INI file.

12. Go to your favorite browser (e.g., Netscape or Mosaic) and "Open Location" http://your.server.name/and you should see the default home page.

CSMHTTPD.INI

Configuration of the server is done by changing the CSMHTTPD.INI file. With Windows Notebook, or your favorite editor, you may modify some server parameters that are listed within "Sections" (indicated within brackets; for example [NETINFO] of the INI file):

[NETINFO]

• **PORT=80**: You can change the default port number that the server listens on.

[SERVERROOT]

• **SERVERROOT=path**: Identifies the path where your documents will reside. The server will serve up documents only from this directory and associated subdirectories to client browsers.

• **DIRECTORYINDEX=filename**: This name identifies the default file that should be served if the client browser specifies a directory, but not a specific file within that directory. For example, if INDEX.HTM is specified above and a client browser specifies the URL, http://host.site.com/, the INDEX.HTM file will be sent from the SERVERROOT directory, if the file exists.

[IMAGES]

• **IMAPFILE=path**: Indicates the path where all map files reside.

• **IMAGEMAPTYPE=number**: Defines whether the map type is NCSA (type 1) or CERN (type 2).

• **ALIASNAME=alias**: The alias name for clickable images; it should be put into the HREF of your documents.

[ACCESS]

- **ACCESSFILENAME=filename**: Identifies a file with a list of user/group names and related passwords. If this file exists in a directory, the client browser will receive a command to prompt for user name and password.

```
ALLOWDIRECTORYINDEX=[0][1]
```

0 = Do not allow directory browsing (a 403 Forbidden message will be sent)

1 = Allow browsing

- **INDEXIGNORE=filename [filename...]**: A listing of files to be ignored when the server builds a directory index for the client browser. Up to 40 entries are allowed.

[ALIAS]

- ALIASNAME=VALUE:

[ICONS]

When files are displayed in a directory listing, every entry is prefixed with an icon. Which icon is used is determined by the extension/icon relationship that you define.

The format is ICONnn=iconname.extension description, where:

nn— is a number up to 99 (leave no unused numbers in the list).

.extension— is the file extension to be associated with the icon.

description— includes information that will be displayed in the listing.

Special extensions are:

DIRECTORY—Used to define an icon for a directory.

PARENTDIR—Used to define an icon for the parent. directory.

LOOKINTO—Used to define the contents of the HTML TITLE that will be displayed in the index.

[MIME]—Defines file types using MIME type/file-extension relationships.

[SCRIPTALIAS]—Works like the alias section.

[LOGFILES]

- **ERRORLOG=pathname**. Defines the path where the log file will reside. The file name is constructed as follows:

  ERYYMMDD.LOG, where YY is the year, MM is the month, and DD is the day.

- **USEERRORLOG=number**. Defines whether or not you will use the error log. 1 = errors will be written to the log file. 0 = no errors will be written to the log file.

- **LEVELERRORLOG=number**. There are three error levels.

- **ACCESSLOG=pathname**. Path and file name of the access log that conforms to the common log format.

- **USEACCESSLOG=number**. 1= write access information to the log file. 0 = no access information will be written to the log file.

[HTTPERRORMESSAGES]

- You may define HTTP messages here (e.g., 403 Forbidden).

WebSite

WebSite is a 32-bit server designed for Windows NT and Windows 95. WebSite is a product of O'Reilly & Associates, Inc., created in cooperation with Bob Denny and Enterprise Integration Technologies, Inc.

A significant advantage of this product is that Website's author was one of the pioneers in constructing servers for the Windows 3.1 platform, with the Windows httpd product. The Windows httpd product has seen significant improvement in its short life (actually long life, measured by the Web server market), and its features have been continually enhanced with the help of feedback from an installed user base. And so, Bob Denny has taken the best of the Windows httpd server, enhanced it, and added significant features that make the WebSite product an excellent solution for your Web server needs. If you have any experience with Windows httpd, the transition to WebSite should be painless.

WebSite includes important features, including:

- The WebSite server itself, which allows you to:

    Serve hypermedia documents.

    Selectively control access to your pages.

    Utilize a number of CGI options, including Perl, DOS, and Windows CGI interfaces.

    Administer options through the simple-to-use Windows interface.

    Run the program as a desktop application or as a Windows NT "service."

- The WebView program, which gives you a graphical representation of your Web server and its associated links, and also serves as an authoring tool.

- A full-featured browser, Enhanced Mosaic 2.0, is included with the distribution.

- The WebIndex and WebFind Programs, which let you organize and search documents by keyword.

- A MapEdit Program, which allows you to quickly and easily create clickable maps for your server.

- Documentation accompanies the distribution in hard-copy, "book" form, rather than in hypertext, as with Windows httpd.

WebSite Hardware and Software

There are a number of hardware and software requirements for installing and running the WebSite server. The server runs under both Windows NT and Windows 95, but for discussion (and because Windows 95 is late out of the blocks), we concentrate on NT here. You should have Windows NT 3.5, and you should have long file names enabled (which is the default). You'll probably want at least a 486 with 16 Mb of memory, and, of course, a network connection. To fully test and appreciate all the server's features you'll need the usual complement of helper applications, including: Lview for full-color images, Wham for audio files, and MPEGPlay for movies. You can download these from various locations, including:

`http://www.ncsa.uiuc.edu/SDG/Software/WinMosaic/viewers.html`

Depending upon your programming preferences, you can choose from a Visual Basic, Perl, or POSIX shell and tools CGI environment.

WebSite Installation

WebSite is distributed on two 3.5-inch disks and installs through a setup program. To install WebSite:

1. Insert Disk 1 into your 3.5-inch drive and through Program Manager, **Run** the program SETUP.EXE. As an alternative, you can locate the file through the File Manager and click on **SETUP.EXE** to run it. The WebSite Setup screen in Figure 6.48 will appear.

2. Click on **Install** on the WebSite Setup screen and Figure 6.49 will appear. This screen requires that you define a directory for installing the software distribution. The default directory is C:\WEBSITE. For testing, click on **Continue** to accept this as the default directory where the executables and supporting files will be stored.

Figure 6.48 WebSite Setup.

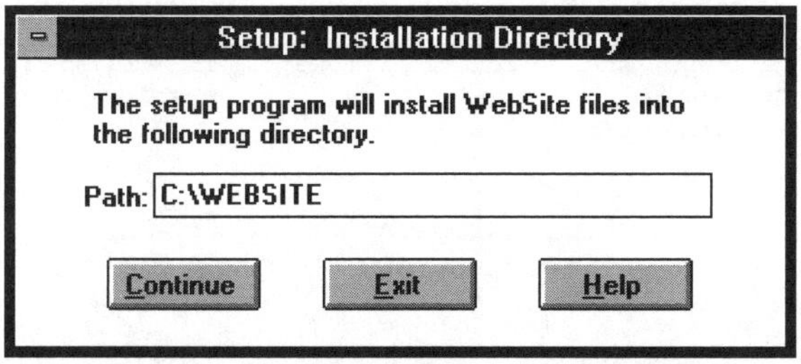

Figure 6.49 WebSite installation path.

3. Next, you will be prompted for the full name of your server and the e-mail address of the server administrator (Figure 6.50). Enter the full name of your server—for example: fido.ajax.com. For the e-mail address, enter the full e-mail address of the webmaster—for example: **john@ajax.com**. Once you've done this, click on **Continue**.

4. You will now be prompted for the path of your document or data directory and the name of your index document (Figure 6.51). If you have a directory with Web pages, you'll want to point to that in the Path field. If not, leave the default HTDOCS. The field name, Index document, refers to the file name of the file you want served up if the browser specifies a directory in a URL without a file name. WebSite will then serve the browser the file INDEX.HTML, if it exists.

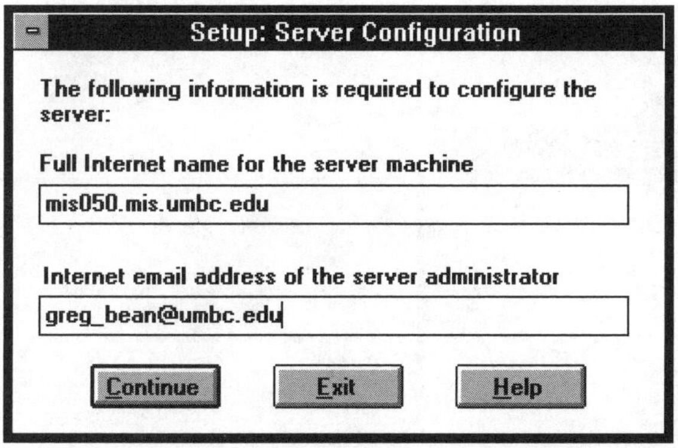

Figure 6.50 WebSite administrator information.

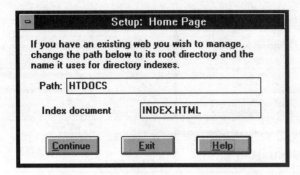

Figure 6.51 WebSite document directory information.

If you have documents being carried over from another Web server implementation where the file name was not INDEX.HTML, index the file name
here. Click on **Continue**.

5. Insert Disk 2 when you are prompted. Files will be copied (Figure 6.52)
to the necessary directories and a setup complete message will be
displayed as in Figure 6.53. Click on **OK** and a Windows Program
Manager group will be created (Figure 6.54).

6. WebSite will start up as a desktop application (with a minimized icon)
and you should work with it in that form until you decide whether you
wish to install it as an NT service.

7. Now you'll want to see if your server works. Go to your friendly
Netscape or Enhanced Mosaic browser and point to your server's home
page by opening a URL to:

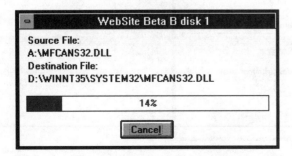

Figure 6.52 WebSite files copied.

Figure 6.53 WebSite successful installation.

```
http://your.server.name/
```

You should see the home page included with the software distribution as shown in Figure 6.55.

Exploring WebSite Features

ReadMe First

As you were instructed on the Setup Complete screen, click on the Read Me First icon in the WebSite Program Group and the Readme file will be displayed as in Figure 6.56. If you examine the URL you will notice that it references a "local file." This means that the browser did not use the WebSite server to access the document but rather used its local file browsing capabilities. You'll notice the asterisks on some of the links on the ReadMe page. Some links go to local files, and some run through the server.

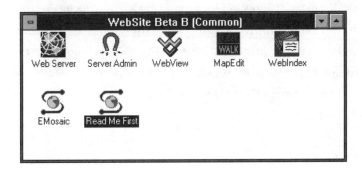

Figure 6.54 WebSite Program Manager group.

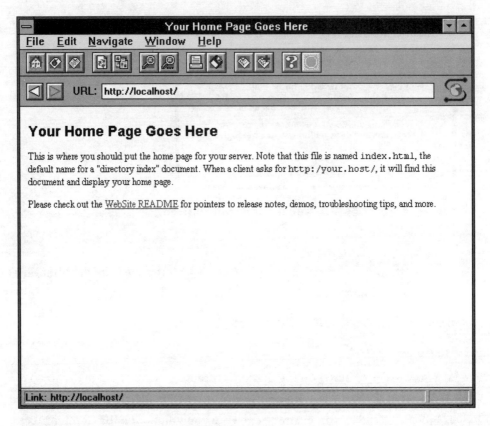

Figure 6.55 WebSite home page.

Server Self-Test

Next, you'll want to completely go through the server self-test, especially if you're new to Web servers. If you're familiar with Windows httpd, you will quickly recognize that many of the examples are from that server's documentation pages. We'll review especially important features and the significant enhancements not found in the Windows httpd implementation. I do strongly suggest, though, that you complete the WebSite Server Self-test checklist to ensure that your server is functioning properly, that you have the necessary auxiliary or helper software, and, most important, that you understand the server's capabilities.

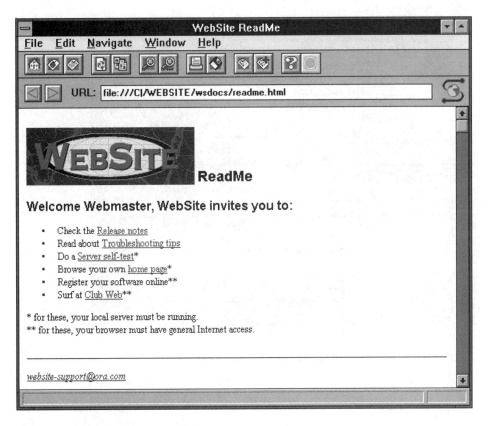

Figure 6.56 WebSite ReadMe.

WebSite Server Administration

One beauty about WebSite is that most, maybe all configurable parameters and options of the server can be maintained through the Windows interface. Opportunities for playing with Notepad and INI files are a thing of the past, and server administration is easily accomplished with a series of screens, which are presented through an application that offers a number of configurable information groupings. Figure 6.57 shows the WebSite Server Setup screen with the "tabs" at the top of the screen serving as menu buttons to take you into various facets of the application. The tabs or categories listed are:

- General

- Mapping

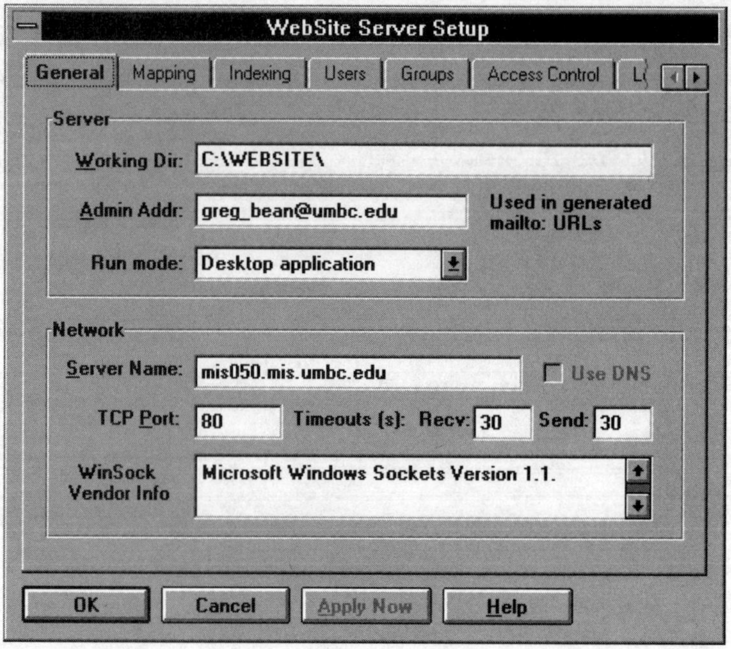

Figure 6.57 WebSite Server Setup screen.

- Indexing

- Users

- Groups

- Access Control

- Logging

- CGI

In this section I describe each of the screens behind the tabs and the various configurable options that are available.

General Setup

You'll immediately notice that you entered some of the information listed on this screen during the WebSite installation and setup procedure (Figure 6.57).

These fields are available for configuration:

Working Dir. This is the *server root* directory, not to be confused with the document root directory, where your Web documents are stored. The Working Dir: is where you installed the WebSite software.

Admin Addr. This is the fully qualified mail address of the server administrator. In any mail generated to URLs, this address will automatically be included.

Run mode. This setting indicates the mode under which WebSite is currently executing. You have three options:

• as an NT system "service" with an icon

• as an NT system "service" without an icon

• as a desktop Windows application

Server Name. The machine name assigned by your network administrator or Internet service provider.

Use DNS. Indicates whether the server should do a name lookup via DNS to include the fully qualified domain name of the client requester in the server log files.

TCP Port. The default port number for HTTP is 80 and you should leave this port set to the default.

Time outs—Recv and Send. The Time-out setting sets the maximum time the server will wait for any network Read or Write operation. This setting includes the time the server will wait for a client to initiate a transaction after connecting. Normally, 30 seconds is adequate, but if the server or any clients are on an extremely slow SLIP or PPP link, you may need to increase the time. If the server and clients are on a private high-speed net, you can reduce the time out so that the server will quickly drop a connection that was canceled in midstream by a client. This change will slightly increase the capacity of the server.

WinSock Vendor Info. This box lists your Winsock information.

Once you have reviewed or changed this information, you can click on **OK** to accept it. You will notice that within a few seconds of your click, you'll hear a beep indicating that your configuration has been updated.

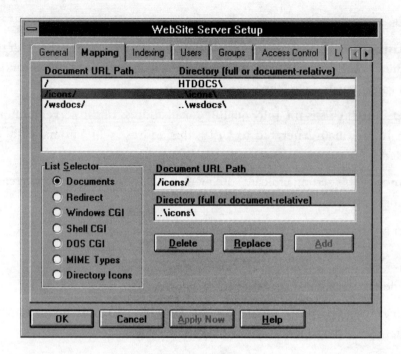

Figure 6.58 WebSite Mapping screen.

Mapping Setup

The Mapping screen gives you the opportunity to "map," or associate, Document URL Paths with NT directories, with either the full or document-relative directory specified. In other words, the example in Figure 6.58 shows the URL path of /icons/ (notice the normal URL slashes (/)) mapped to the NT directory ..\icons\ (and this is "document relative," meaning the \icons\ directory is directly beneath the document (HTDOCS) directory). Notice that if you didn't specify the directory in document- relative terms, you could have stated it as a full path, which would have been C:\WEBSITE\HTDOCS\ICONS\.

Indexing

Figure 6.59 shows an example of an Indexing setup screen. A number of configurable options are available that determine how your server handles Indexing. These are:

Figure 6.59 WebSite Indexing setup.

Features

Enable Indexing. If this box is checked, client browsers will be able to access directories on your server and receive listings of the directory contents, which appear much as they would in a Gopher or FTP listing (Figure 6.60).

Extended Indexing. This option will give the browser more detailed information.

Icons are Links. If you check this option the user will be able to click on the icons in the directory listing to access the related files.

Description from HTML. For any item in a listing you may add a link to an HTML file and users will be able to click on the link and view a description of the item.

Show MIME Types. If this command is enabled, users will be able to view the file's associated MIME type.

Ignore Patterns. If a user accesses a directory and you allow Indexing, a listing will be generated for the client showing each file in the directory. You can, however, omit or hide specified files from the list. The example in Figure 6.59 shows Ignore Patterns (meaning: don't list them) of any file that starts with a "#"

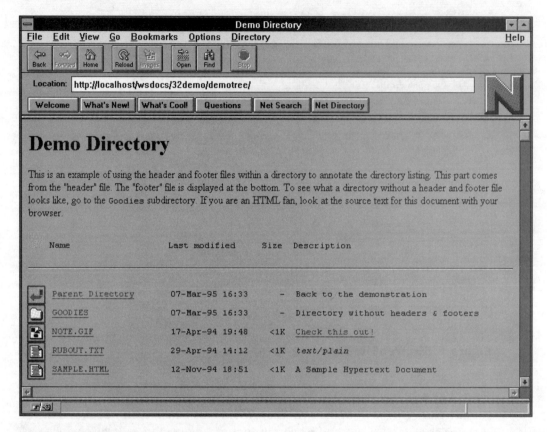

Figure 6.60 WebSite Indexing.

(for example, an access-control password file), ends in .bak (possibly backup files), or starts with a tilde (~).

If you wish to add patterns, simply add them in the box provided and click on **Add**. You can delete them by selecting the pattern from the window and clicking on **Delete**.

Special Documents

Index. This is the name of the file that should be served to the client who doesn't specify one in their URL. For example, if the browser points to http://your.server.name/, because no file is specified, the server will look for and serve up a file named index.html if it exists.

Header. When a directory list is generated you can add information at the front or top of the listing. That information would be carried in a file named #header in the example in Figure 6.59.

Footer. When a directory list is generated you can add information at the bottom of the listing. That information would be included in a file named #footer in the example in Figure 6.59.

Special Icons

- **Unkn**. **Type**. If a server lists a file and cannot recognize its file type, the unknown.gif file will be displayed in the listing.

- **Parent Dir**. This is the symbol to be displayed at the top of a directory listing to give an avenue for returning to a parent directory.

- **Sub Dir**. The icon to mark a subdirectory.

- **Spacer**. A placement marker.

Once you have modified these options, click on **OK** to proceed.

Users

Access to your server can be limited to selected users. Not only can access control be applied to the server as a whole, but it can be applied to selected directories and files. One way to control access to these resources is user authentication. Authentication is accomplished with a user name and password test. Figure 6.61 shows the Netscape browser in the authentication procedure.

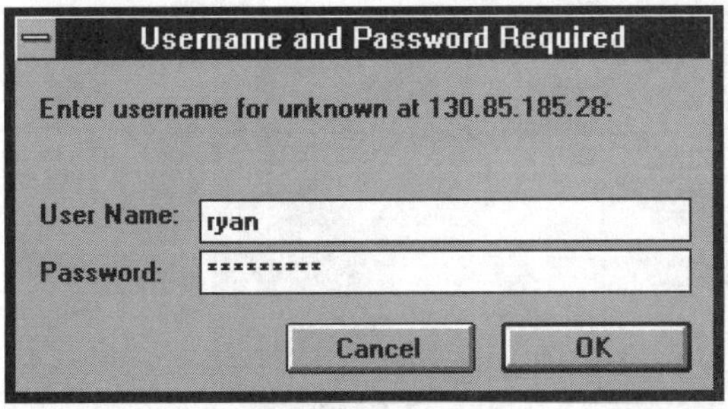

Figure 6.61 Netscape during authentication.

If the user provides the necessary user name and password, the server will allow the browser to access the resource (e.g., directory) in question. Figure 6.62 shows how you would set up a new user.

Logging

Figure 6.63 shows the options that are available for logging on the Website server. These are:

Logfile Names

- **Access**. The name of the log where all requests directed to your server are logged. The default is access.log.

- **Server**. The default is server.log.

- **Error**. The default is error.log.

Logging Directory

This is the location where the log files will reside. The default is a directory named *log*. A caption on the screen states, "If no leading drive spec or /, path is

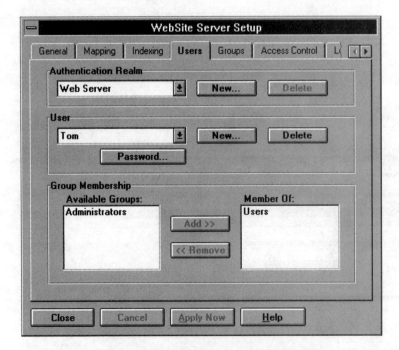

Figure 6.62 WebSite setting up new user.

Figure 6.63 WebSite logging options.

relative to server's working dir." This statement means that for the default the "logs" directory would be located in the NT directory of C:\HTDOCS\LOGS\ .

Client Hostname Lookup

- **Enable DNS Reverse Lookup**. If you check this box, the server will attempt to look up the domain name information for the requesting client so that it can be included in the server access log file. Enabling this action will, of course, cause your server to work a bit harder. If you leave it unchecked (the default), the DNS Reverse Lookup can be done through your log file analyzer application.

- **Tracing Options**. You can check some options from the series of checkboxes, and information will be written to the server log for troubleshooting. Once you have completed modifications on this screen, click on **Apply Now** and then click on **Close**.

- **CGI**. It is best to leave the CGI options screen as is, because these are for advanced CGI users.

WebView

Much as the Windows File Manager shows you the relationships between directories, subdirectories, and files, WebView shows you the relationships between links on your server. Also, documents may be edited and previewed from within WebView. Figure 6.64 shows a sample WebView screen. Reading from left to right on the screen, you have these objects:

Expansion Box

At the left of the line may appear a small box with a + or - . A plus (+) tells you that this item has at least one link and can be expanded.

File Type Icon

Next, you'll see an icon, such as the small, yellow document page that represents an HTML file. You'll also see icons representing such things as images and mailto items.

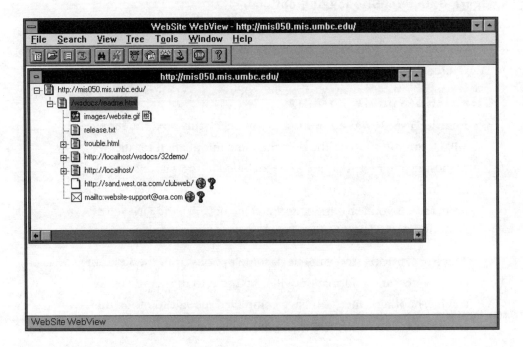

Figure 6.64 WebView.

Link Information

The actual link itself is listed. If you select View from the menu bar on the screen, you'll see that you can select from a number of WebView views. This choice essentially lets s you view your document trees from many perspectives. You may be curious about how the files are structured in NT directories, and so you would select the File Name view. Then, you may say: "Okay, I know how things look out on the C: drive, but what would be the URL references to those same files ?" Listed below is an example of one document and how it would be listed, depending on which view you selected from the menu:

View you select:	Link would appear as:
Hyperlink	/wsdocs/readme.html
File Name	C:\WEBSITE\WSDOCS\README.HTML
Title	WebSite ReadMe
Label	WebSite README
URL	http://mis050.mis.umbc.edu/wsdocs/readme.html

Properties

After you have selected a document you can choose the File Properties item from the menu bar to view characteristics or properties of the document. For each document selected you will see displayed four tabs on the screen as illustrated in Figure 6.65.

General

This screen is divided into two sections:

Link Properties. Link Properties describe the link to a document from its parent, including the hyperlink, label, and URL.

Document Properties. These fields describe the document itself, including title, file name, file type, size, and date last modified.

Access Properties

The Access Properties screen (Figure 6.66) allows you to display and change access controls for a document. You can define access control for any URL directory by selecting it and modifying the lists of user/groups and classes.

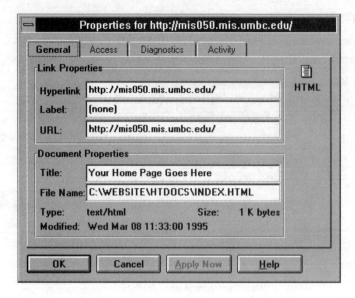

Figure 6.65 WebView Document Properties.

Diagnostic Properties

The Diagnostic Properties screen (Figure 6.67) shows you errors, warnings, and other information that WebView has identified about your HTML document. WebView validates your document against the HTML standard to generate any messages.

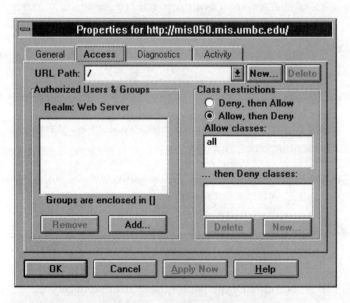

Figure 6.66 WebView Access Properties.

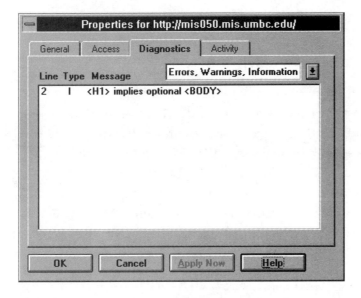

Figure 6.67 WebView Diagnostic Properties.

Activity

The Activity screen (Figure 6.68) will show activity for the specified document for the number of days indicated. This screen serves as a snapshot of the log file

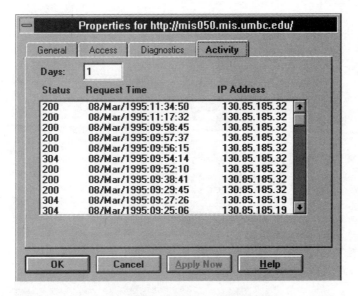

Figure 6.68 WebView Activity screen

for the document. Information displayed includes status of the request, date and time of the request, and IP address of the requesting browser.

Wizards

Wizards are tools that allow you to create and edit documents of a particular type. Two types included with WebView are the Home Page Wizard and the What's New Wizard. The Home Page Wizard (Figure 6.69) allows you to enter your organization's information through a form and have a Home Page automatically generated for you (Figure 6.70). You can also use the What's New Wizard to generate What's New pages for your server. For each What's New item or link, you enter the information shown in Figure 6.71. You **Add** each new item, and when you have entered all the items for a given date, you click on **Build It**. The end result will be an attractive What's New Page.

WebIndex

If you have quite a number of documents that reside on your server to which you want browsers to have full text access, you may want to consider WAIS

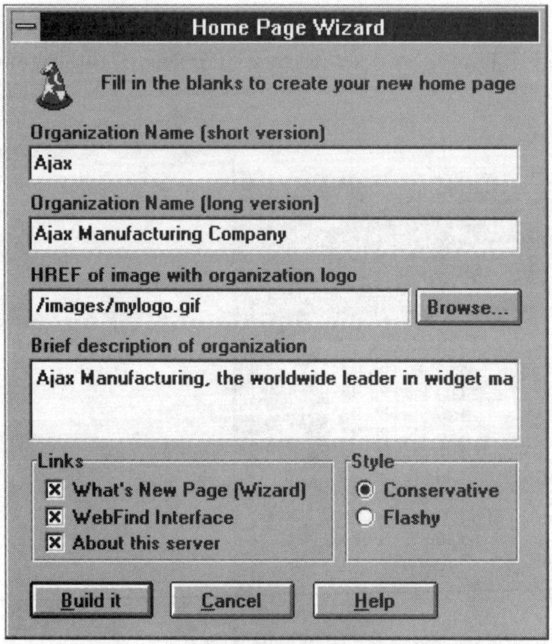

Figure 6.69 Home Page Wizard.

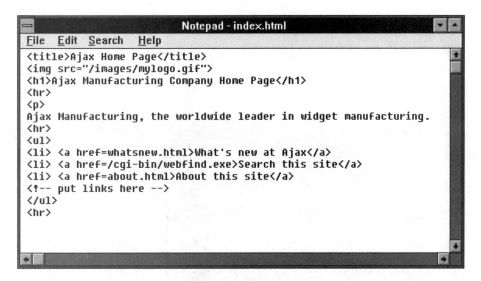

```
Notepad - index.html
File  Edit  Search  Help
<title>Ajax Home Page</title>
<img src="/images/mylogo.gif">
<h1>Ajax Manufacturing Company Home Page</h1>
<hr>
<p>
Ajax Manufacturing, the worldwide leader in widget manufacturing.
<hr>
<ul>
<li> <a href=whatsnew.html>What's new at Ajax</a>
<li> <a href=/cgi-bin/webfind.exe>Search this site</a>
<li> <a href=about.html>About this site</a>
<!-- put links here -->
</ul>
<hr>
```

Figure 6.70 Home Page Wizard output.

(Wide Area Information Server). Then again, if you are using WebSite you'll probably want to try WebIndex, which will allow you to search full-text documents on your server by keyword. WebIndex provides:

- The WebIndex application, which lets you select directories for inclusion in the indexing process. This application allows you to click on directories you wish to add to the index, and then generate the index.

- A WebFind CGI program, which will prompt the user for a keyword, through an HTML form, search the index created by WebIndex, and return the results to the browser.

  Included in the Website directory on the CD are a few files you can use to test the WebIndex and WebFind programs.

Follow these steps to set up a sample search:

1. Create a subdirectory beneath the Website document root directory (HTDOCS). Name the directory C:\WEBSITE\HTDOCS\FILES.

2. Copy the FYI (For Your Information) files from the CD directory

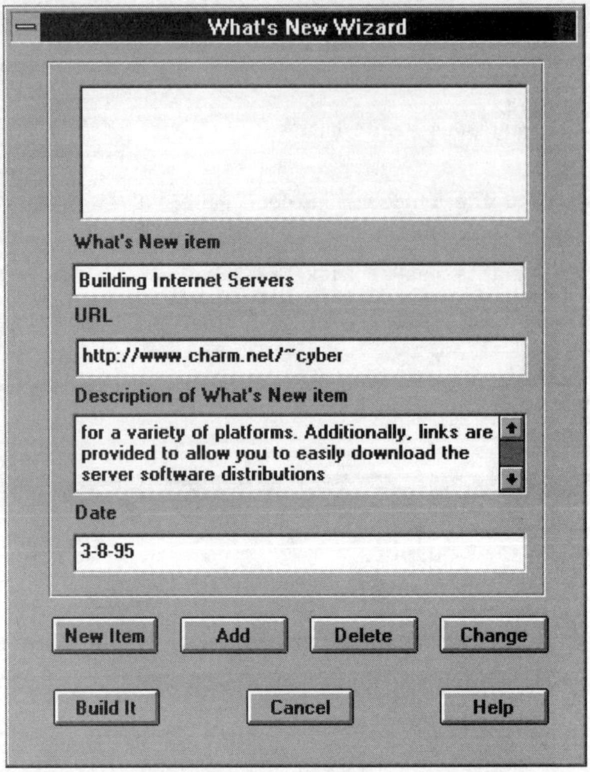

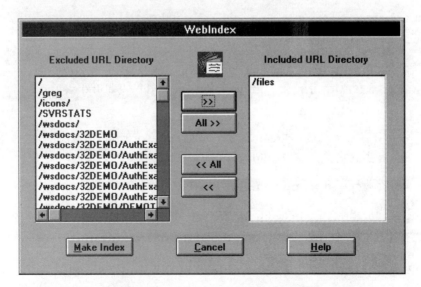

Figure 6.71 What's New Page Wizard.

Figure 6.72 WebIndex.

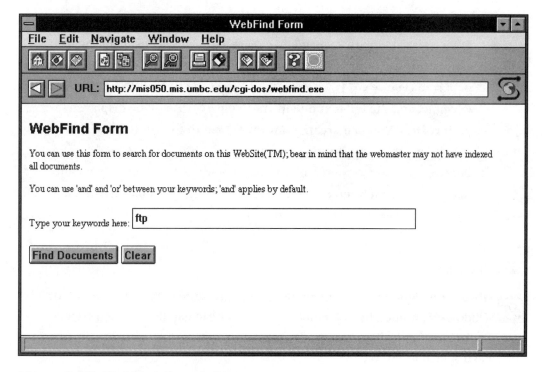

Figure 6.73 WebFind Search form.

\WEBSITE\FILES\ to the FILES directory you created in step 1 above. These files are named FYI10.TXT, and so on.

3. Next, start up the WebIndex application by double-clicking on the WebIndex icon in the Program Manager; a window should appear (Figure 6.72). Click on the directory/files at the left side (titled Excluded URL Directory) and then the > arrow button and /files will be moved to the right-side box (titled Included URL Directory).

4. Click on the **/files** item at the right side and then click on **Make Index**. Your index will be created.

5. Open your favorite browser, such as the Enhanced Mosaic browser included with WebSite, and enter the following URL:

```
http://your.server.name/cgi-doc/webfind.exe
```

and the CGI program, WebFind, will display a form as shown in Figure 6.73. Enter a search term that you might expect to find in the full-text files, such as ftp, and WebFind will return a list of the files where the keyword occurred (Figure 6.74). You can then select the link, FYINDX.TXT, for example, and the full-text document (Figure 6.75) will be displayed for your review. You can create your own form to use with the WebFind search mechanism. Within your form, include the ACTION="/cgi-dos/web-find.exe" statement. You can open the URL: http://your.site. name/cgi-doc/webfind.exe and save the HTML file. Take that file and modify it to create your own search form.

ZBServer

 ZBServer is both a Web and Gopher shareware server for Windows 3.1 or Windows95, written by Bob Bradley. The server can handle up to ten concurrent requests and will queue up to ten more requests (five on port 70 - Gopher, and five on port 80 - HTTP).

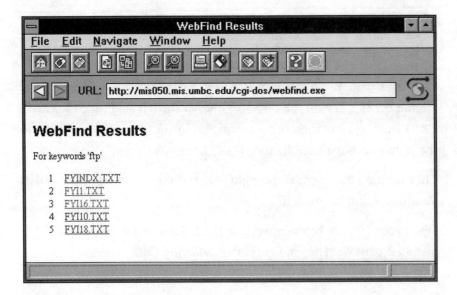

Figure 6.74 WebFind results.

Figure 6.75 WebFind text file.

ZBServer features include:

- Works with Windows 3.1, 3.11, and Win95.

- Places a very small load on your system and can be run in the background.

- Reliable operation, having been tested on servers running with more than 900 connections a day.

- User-definable file type mapping to mime and gopher types based on DOS file extensions.

- Clickable image maps.

- CGI support.

- Works with Willow Glen Graphics PolyForm and TalkBack utilities.

- Directory Aliasing, which allows directories in different locations to appear under one logical tree.

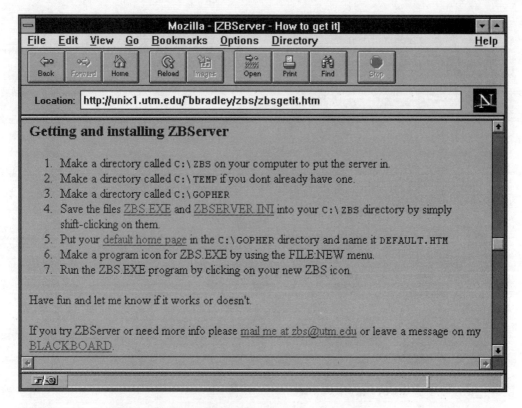

Figure 6.76 ZBServerSetup instructions.

- Directory indexes can include user-created icons and text or html headers.

- Logging with the NCSA/CERN common log format, and compatible with Bob Denny's VBStats.

- Instant Stats, showing quick statistics since last restart.

- A Blackboard capability, allowing users to leave or view messages or links.

- Directory security—by user and group.

Retrieving and Installing ZBServer

By following these seven easy steps, you can be running with ZBServer in minutes. The software author's approach to Web installation, via the Web itself, makes the installation a snap. Essentially, all you have to do is point your browser to:

```
http://unix1.utm.edu/~bbradley/zbs/zbsgetit.htm
```

and follow the instructions shown on the screen (Figure 6.76). The steps instruct you to create three directories, retrieve three files through your browser by clicking on them (including a default home page, as shown in Figure 6.77), and then run the server. It couldn't be simpler. Once you've set up your server, you can modify your configuration and work with some of the more advanced features through the ZBServer Configuration screen (Figure 6.78).

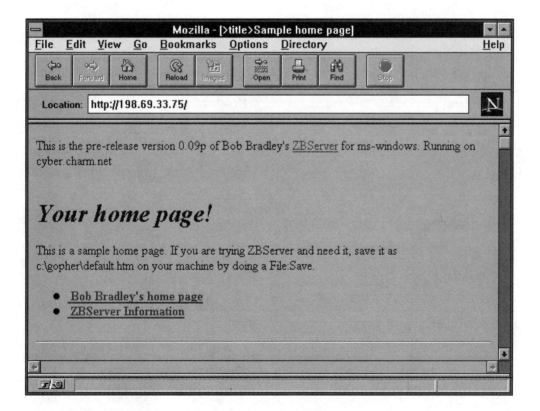

Figure 6.77 ZBServer default home page.

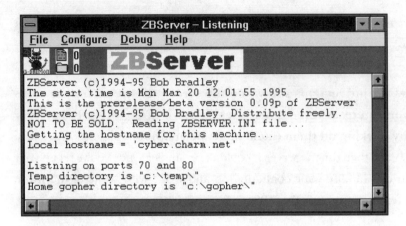

Figure 6.78 ZBServer Main Server screen.

More Web Servers

There are new servers arriving in the Web marketplace everyday. If you want to investigate these new arrivals, follow these links:

Company	Product
Quarterdeck Systems http://www.qdeck.com	Web Server for Win 3.1
Verity, Inc. http://www.verity.com	Windows NT Server
Ameritech Library Services http:netpub.notes.com	NT Server
Quadralay Corp. http://www.quadralay.com	WebWorks for NT
Personal Library Software http://www.pls.com	PLServer / NT
Netscape Communications http://home.mcom.com	Netsite for NT
Great Lakes Area Commercial Internet http://www.glaci.com	GLACI-httpd for Netware

HTML Authoring and Editing

If you are going into the business of setting up a Web server, it won't be long before you decide to author your own Web pages. When you do, you'll have to learn and use the *Hypertext Markup Language* (HTML). As you have already gathered, this will require that you take or make text files and "mark them up" so that they can be published on the Web. Many say that the "real HTML authors" use a simple text editor and mark up their text files by hand. I suppose that it must be a uniquely rewarding experience to do this, but there is a simpler (and possibly more productive) way. There are quite a variety of fully featured HTML editors on the market. They include the following:

- HTML Assistant
- HTML Writer

- HTMLEDIT

- Internet Assistant

A guide that references these and some of the many other available HTML editors can be found at:

http://union.ncsa.uiuc.edu/www/html/editors.html

We will explain a few of these packages to give you an understanding of what they can do and get you off to a quick start in your HTML authoring endeavors. Some of the features of these packages include the following:

- HTML document validation features which enable you to validate your "code" against the HTML standard

- Web Browsing capability, which enables you to "preview" your document as it would be viewed from a remote browser

- Templates, which provide you with a quick start on Home Pages, What's New Pages, and other common documents

- URL management tools, which allow you to maintain a list of your commonly used URLs so that you can quickly and correctly add them to your documents

- Some packages include a WYSIWYG interface, with associated code generating capabilities, so that you can work more with content and aesthetics, and less on the underlying tagging tedium

- Modules that can be added to existing word processing packages, with which you are already familiar and comfortable. HTML authoring then becomes a natural transition or extension of your current word processing activities.

The HTML FAQ

Before we get into these tools, it is worth mentioning that one of the better resources for the HTML author is the *HTML FAQ* (Frequently Asked Questions), created and maintained by Iain O'Cain. It deals with HTML authoring and document conversion. The FAQ has extremely valuable references for anyone working with HTML. Topics deal with available authoring/editing tools, conversion tools (FrameMaker to HTML, for example), and general references about creating HTML documents. The document is available at the following address:

```
http://www.umcc.umich.edu/~ec/www/html_faq.html
```

HTML Assistant

HTML Assistant is a simple text editor with extensions for the creation of HTML hypertext documents. It was developed for the Microsoft Windows environment and written by Howard Harawitz. The software is available from **ftp://ftp.cs.dal.ca/htmlasst**. The files are **HTMLASST.ZIP** and **VBRUN 300.ZIP**. The free version of HTML Assistant includes the following features:

- Context sensitive help

- Integrated testing of documents with WWW browsers, such as Cello, Mosaic, and Netscape

- Access to multiple documents at any one time

- Automatic conversion of Cello bookmark and Mosaic .INI files to text files

- Automatic copying of URLs from Cello bookmark and Mosaic .INI files to text files

- Conversion of HTML Assistant URL files to Cello Bookmark files

- User-defined toolbox.

Additionally, there is a more full-featured version, called HTML Assistant Pro, available for a license fee. This version includes the following:

- An automatic page creator that allows rapid creation of HTML for use with WWW browsers

- Minimal knowledge of HTML is required, and screens can be created in a very short time

- UNIX text files can be converted to DOS text

- DOS text files may be saved as UNIX text

- HTML markings may be removed from text

- The ability to handle files greater than 32k in size

- Future enhancements and upgrades are available.

HTML Assistant Installation

Here we'll install the shareware version of HTML Assistant. The many fine features of the package make it a good choice for getting into the HTML authoring game. The only limitation of the shareware version is its inability to handle file sizes greater than 32k. But if you enjoy the package and want to handle larger files, you can graduate to the "Pro" version.

To install the HTML Assistant you'll need to unzip the software distribution and test the program by completing the steps that follow:

1. Set up a directory, such as **C:\HTMLASST**.

2. Using PKUNZIP, unzip the files into **C:\HTMLASST**. Copy the file **VBRUN300.DLL** to your **C:\WINDOWS** directory.

3. You then can either Run the program **C:\HTML\HTMLASST** from the File menu or set up a program icon.

4. You can test the program by opening the file **PRIMER.HTM**. Figure 7.1 shows access to the file **PRIMER.HTM**. To test the program, click on the Test button and identify Mosaic or Netscape as the browser you want to use. The .GIF files identified in the HTML text will not load (because they don't exist on your machine), so you should get three error messages to that effect.

Using HTML Assistant

HTML Assistant makes it easy for you to create your own Web pages. Once you have identified URLs for your hotlist in Netscape or Mosaic, HTML Assistant allows you to organize them into files, or pages, that meet your requirements.

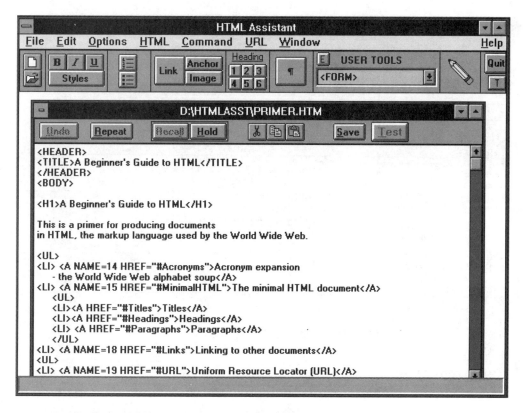

Figure 7.1 HTML Assistant viewing PRIMER.

For example, you can arrange all URLs pertinent to a particular topic within a given page. You can do this in two ways:

To arrange all URLs on a given topic follow these steps:

1. Open a new edit window by selecting New from the File menu. Set up a new file for each topic of interest and copy/paste URLs from your hotlist collection to your new file.

2. Display the URL file edit pop-up window by selecting Edit/Build URL Files from the URL menu. You can then combine URLs from different sources and you can use scrolling lists for editing.

The best way to familiarize yourself with HTML Assistant is to browse through the Windows Help file available from within the program (see Figure 7.2).

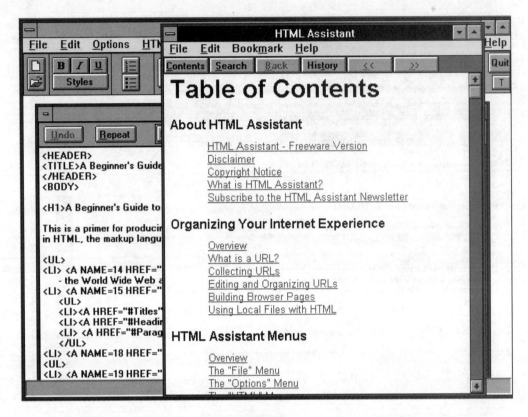

Figure 7.2 HTML Assistant Windows Help.

HTML Writer

HTML Writer, by Kris Nosack, is a freeware (or as the program author says, "donationware") HTML authoring and editing tool for Windows. The features of HTML writer include the following:

- Multiple document interface support that enables you to work on more than one HTML document at a time

- A flexible interface designed to let you work the way you want through a combination of pull-down menus, a pop-up menu, a toolbar, and shortcut keys

- A Test option that enables you to see your document in Mosaic, Cello, or Netscape

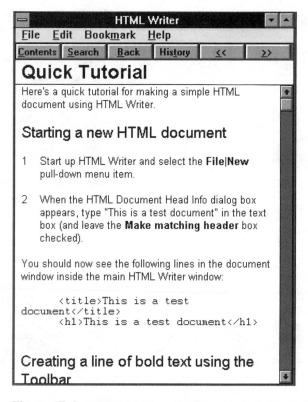

Figure 7.3 HTML Writer HTML quick tutorial.

- A Remove Tags feature that enables you to remove the HTML tags from the entire document or selected blocks of the document

- Templates that make it easy to define and use up to four different "style sheets" with your new documents

- A quick tutorial to get you started in HTML authoring (see Figure 7.3).

HTML Writer Installation

To install HTML Writer you'll need to retrieve the software and copy several files to the \WINDOWS\SYSTEM directory. Once you've copied the files, you can test the program by using the sample template.

To install HTML Writer:

1. Retrieve the HTML Writer (Version 0.9 beta 4a update) zipped files **HW9B4ALL.ZIP** and **VBRUN300.ZIP** from **ftp://ftp.byu.edu/tmp**.

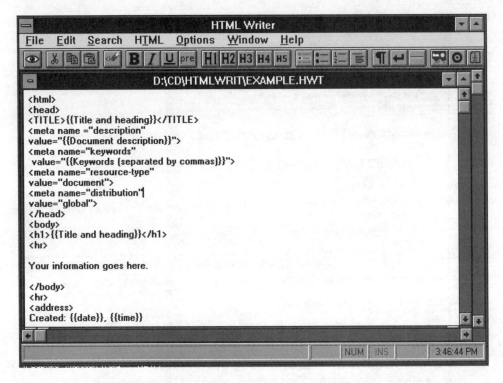

Figure 7.4 HTML Writer template file.

2. Create a directory for the HTML Writer (such as **C:\HTMLWRIT**) and unzip the retrieved files into this directory.

3. The files **CMDIALOG.VBX**, **COMMDLG.DLL**, **TOOLBARS.VBX**, **EMEDIT.VBX**, and **VBRUN300.DLL** must be transferred to your **WINDOWS\SYSTEM** directory if they are not already there. If you have older versions of these files, you should back them up before replacing them.

4. From the Windows Program Manager, Run the program **HTMLWRIT.EXE**.

5. Open the sample template file **EXAMPLE.HWT** to test the program and examine an editor template (see Figure 7.4).

For more information on HTML Writer, you can access the program's home page at the following address:

http://lal.cs.byu.edu/people/nosack/

HTMLed

HTMLed (version 1.0) is an HTML editor for Microsoft Windows 3.1 produced by Peter Crawshaw of I-Net Training & Consulting Ltd. of Canada. HTMLed is distributed under the "shareware" concept. Therefore, as with other shareware, you may use this software for 30 days for evaluation purposes, after which you should either register the software or discontinue its use. If you register, you get the "registered" version of the software in which the "about" box will not pop up every time you start the program. You also get free updates and a floppy disk that contains the software.

The program contains numerous helpful authoring and editing features, including the following:

- Reads and writes UNIX files

- Provides foreign character tags support

- Implements the full set of HTML markup tags

- Contains floating toolbars

- Allows a customizable floating toolbar

- Has a Multiple Document Interface

- Provides "Intelligent" insertion of HTML tags on a line-by-line basis

- Converts the URLs in a MOSAIC.INI file to an HTML document while retaining the original menu structure

- Has a Test button to launch an HTML browser to test your HTML documents

- Saves files without HTML tags.

HTMLed Installation

HTMLed installation is simple and straightforward. You'll just need to unzip the software distribution and then run the program. Once the program is installed you can go into the program's Options menu item and configure the editor's options. By using the Setup dialog box you can identify the path or location of the browser you wish to use for testing of your HTML documents.

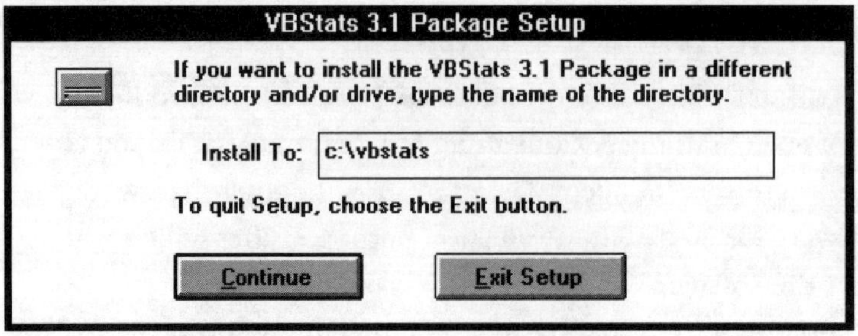

```
┌─────────────────────────────────────────────────────────────┐
│                  VBStats 3.1 Package Setup                    │
├─────────────────────────────────────────────────────────────┤
│  ┌───┐   If you want to install the VBStats 3.1 Package in a  │
│  │   │   different directory and/or drive, type the name of   │
│  └───┘   the directory.                                       │
│                                                               │
│       Install To:  ┌─────────────────────────────────────┐   │
│                    │ c:\vbstats                          │   │
│                    └─────────────────────────────────────┘   │
│                                                               │
│       To quit Setup, choose the Exit button.                  │
│                                                               │
│        ┌───────────────┐         ┌───────────────┐           │
│        │   Continue     │         │   Exit Setup   │           │
│        └───────────────┘         └───────────────┘           │
└─────────────────────────────────────────────────────────────┘
```

Figure 7.5 HTMLed.

To install HTMLed follow these steps:

1. Unzip **HTMLED.ZIP** into a directory, such as **C:\HTMLED**. You can create an icon for HTMLed in Program Manager or just Run it from File Manager by double-clicking on HTMLED.EXE. HTMLed does not require any dll's or any other supporting files. The program will create the file **HTMLED.INI** in the Windows directory to store your configuration options such as the path to your Web browser.

2. Run **HTMLED.EXE** from the Program Manager or by clicking on a Program item on the Windows desktop, if you have one set up. Figure 7.5 shows the HTMLed window.

Internet Assistant

Internet Assistant is an add-on module to Microsoft Word for Windows (6.0a or later), produced by Microsoft, that gives you the both the capability to create and edit Web pages, as well as browse pages on local and remote Web servers. Because there is such an installed base of the Microsoft Word product in the marketplace, Internet Assistant should quickly become an attractive HTML authoring alternative.

Installing Internet Assistant

Internet Assistant is available at Microsoft's anonymous FTP server as a self-extracting file named WORDIA.EXE. Retrieve the file by using your Web browser or favorite FTP program.

You can retrieve Internet Assistant from the following address:

ftp://ftp.microsoft.com/deskapps/word/winword-public/ia/wordia.exe

Figure 7.6 Internet Assistant setup.

To install Internet Assistant:

1. Move the retrieved file, **WORDIA.EXE**, to a temporary directory, such as **C:\TEMP**.

2. From the Program Manager, Run **WORDIA.EXE** to unpack the software.

3. From the Program Manager, Run **SETUP.EXE**. The screen in Figure 7.6 should appear. Click on OK to continue.

4. As the legalese screens appear, read each screen and click on Continue and Agree to move to the next step.

5. The screen in Figure 7.7 prompts you for the directory in which you want to install Internet Assistant. The default directory is **\MSOFFICE\WINWORD\INTERNET**. You can leave the path to the default or you can click on the Change Directory button if you want to change the path. Click on Continue.

6. Next, you are prompted to install the Internet Assistant browser (see Figure 7.8). Click on Yes. Files will now be transferred to the appropriate directories.

Figure 7.7 Internet Assistant installation directory.

7. When the screen in Figure 7.9 appears, click on the Launch Word
   button so that you can try out Internet Assistant's Web browsing capabilities. The Word for Windows screen appears briefly, and then the screen
   in Figure 7.10 will appear, informing you that the installation was
   successful. Click on OK.

Using Internet Assistant

Web Browse and Edit views turn Word into a Web "browser," as well as an HTML
document editor. You accomplish this using templates. In Web Browse view
(see Figure 7.11), you can read Web documents and activate hyperlinks in them
to navigate around the Web. You can't, however, modify documents in Web
Browse view. While you are in Web Browse view, your document is based on the

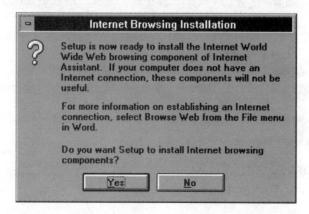

Figure 7.8 Internet Assistant Browser installation.

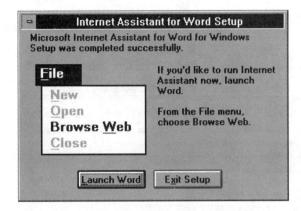

Figure 7.9 Internet Assistant Launch Word.

WEBVIEW template. To switch to Edit view, click on the small icon with the pencil. Then, in Edit view, you can create and modify documents.

When you edit an HTML document, that document will be based on the HTML template. If you are editing a Word document, the Word document will be based on **NORMAL.DOT** or the template on which it was originally based. To switch to Web Browse view, click on the small icon with the eyeglasses. Experiment with Internet Assistant's capabilities by viewing a document through the browser (see Figure 7.12), and then toggle the Html Hidden button ({a}) to view the underlying code (see Figure 7.13).

Creating Documents

When you create a document with Internet Assistant, you use Word's "styles" capability. By converting these styles to HTML after you finish creating a document, you are shielded from the complexity of HTML. You can create or edit

Figure 7.10 Internet Assistant successful installation.

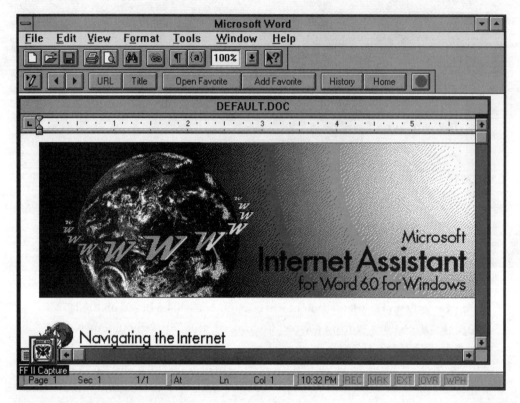

Figure 7.11 Internet Assistant Web Browse.

documents, concentrating on content and aesthetics rather than being concerned with HTML. The documents you generate are fully compliant with level 2.0 HTML.

Viewing HTML Source

When you're browsing your own documents or those of others, you'll want to view the source behind what you're viewing. Internet Assistant provides an easy means to accomplish this through it's Web browsing capabilities.

To view the HTML source follow these steps:

1. While viewing the document through the Web Browse view, choose Save As from the File menu. Make sure that HTML Converter is selected in the Save File As Type box.

2. Type the name you want to give the file in the File Name box and click on OK.

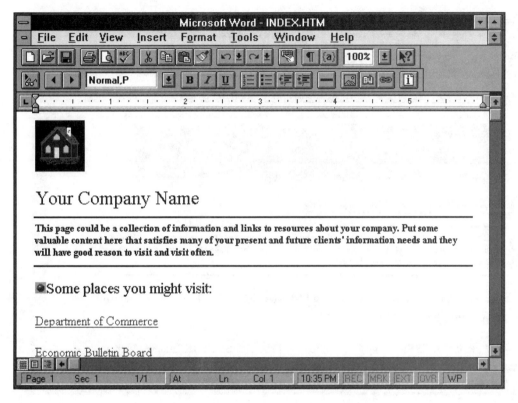

Figure 7.12 Internet Assistant viewing a document.

3. From the File menu, choose Close.

4. From the File menu, choose Open. Select the Confirm Conversions check box.

5. In the Convert File dialog box, choose Text Only and then choose OK.

Mapedit

Mapedit is a WYSIWYG editor for creating and maintaining image maps. The Mapedit program was developed by Thomas Boutell. Commercial users must pay for it to continue using it after 30 days. You do not need to register again when new versions are released. You can retrieve Mapedit from the following address:

http://sunsite.unc.edu/pubpackages/infosystems/WWW/tools/mapedit

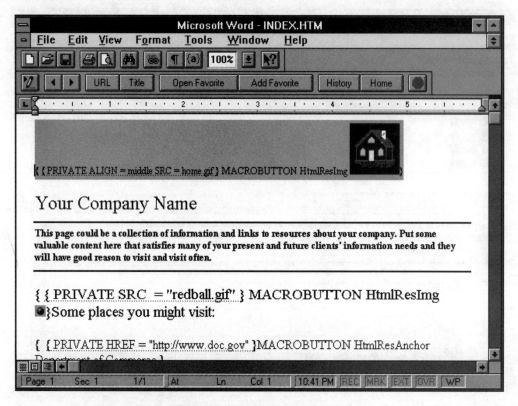

Figure 7.13 Internet Assistant viewing HTML.

Image map files are a feature of both NCSA and CERN httpd servers. They enable you to turn a .GIF image file into a clickable map on your Web page by designating polygons, circles, and rectangles within the .GIF and specifying a URL for each designation, or "hot spot," on the map. Then, when you click on a point on the map, the associated Web page will appear. There are many applications for image mapping; the most common are those that display a map of a geographic region so that you can click on particular points on the map and receive detailed information on your point of interest. In addition to geographic representations, there are many other examples in scientific, technical, and business applications. For example, you might want to display a picture of intricate products, such as assembled components, and allow clients to click on particular parts to receive product and pricing information.

GIF (Graphics Interchange Format) is a picture or image stored in this special format. You usually will find these files named with a .GIF extension. Your most frequent association with .GIF files is the many images you see "inline" within Web documents. The image map file is nothing more than a picture or carto-graphic representation (map) with clickable points defined on it.

Unfortunately, creating good image maps manually is a lot of work because you must locate the points using an editor not explicitly designed for that purpose. Mapedit enables you to load your .GIF image into a scrollable, resizable window, and then draw polygons, circles, and rectangles on top of it, speci-fying a URL for each. It also enables you to go back and edit these "hot spots," set a default URL for clicks outside of the "hot" areas, and so on. In addition, it allows you to associate comments of arbitrary length with each object.

In order to use the files created with Mapedit, you'll need a Web server that has an image map program. The Whttpd server described previously meets this requirement, as do a number of other servers covered in this book. The example files from the CD, explained here, assume that you are using the Whttpd server's image map capabilities.

Mapedit Installation

The installation of the Mapedit program itself will also include several example files that will provide you with a good working example of how imagemap files are constructed. By installing the sample imagemap files from the CD you'll have a model upon which you can fashion your own imagemaps.

To install the Mapedit program:

1. Create a directory to house the Mapedit program and related files (such as **C:\MAPEDIT**).

2. Unzip the **MAPEDIT. ZIP** file's contents into the directory you just created.

3. Install the **MAPEDIT.EXE** file as an icon in a program group or Run the program from the Windows File Manager.

4. If you want to see how an image map was created, retrieve the following files from the CD in the **\MAPEDIT** directory. (The steps taken to create the example are reviewed in a moment.) Copy the following files shown in Table 7.1 from the CD to the directories listed:

Table 7.1 CD Files	
Files on CD	**Destination Directory**
MAP.HTM	C:\HTTPD\HTDOCS\DEMO\
MISSED.HTM	C:\HTTPD\HTDOCS\DEMO\
CNTOWER.HTM	C:\HTTPD\HTDOCS\DEMO\
ARCH.HTM	C:\HTTPD\HTDOCS\DEMO\
METH.HTM	C:\HTTPD\HTDOCS\DEMO\
MONUM.HTM	C:\HTTPD\HTDOCS\DEMO\
MTMC.HTM	C:\HTTPD\HTDOCS\DEMO\
SEARS.HTM	C:\HTTPD\HTDOCS\DEMO\
STATUE.HTM	C:\HTTPD\HTDOCS\DEMO\
TEO.HTM	C:\HTTPD\HTDOCS\DEMO\
TEST.MAP	C:\HTTPD\CONF\MAPS\
NA.GIF	C:\HTTPD\HTDOCS\IMAGES\

The placement of the files in this step and those that follow is critical to making the example listed here work.

5. With Windows Notepad, or your favorite editor, modify the
   C:\HTTPD\CONF\IMAGEMAP.CNF file to include the line: test
   C:\httpd\conf\maps\test.map (see Figure 7.14). Save the file and
   exit Notepad.

6. To test the image map example you just installed, run the program
   HTMLASST (or your favorite HTML editor) and open the file
   C:\HTTPD\HTDOCS\DEMO\MAP.HTM. Change the address of the

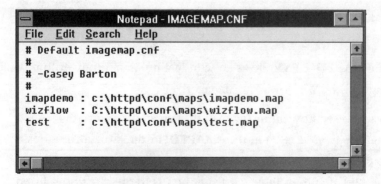

Figure 7.14 Mapedit: Edit IMAGEMAP.CNF.

server listed in the HTML from **198.69.33.75** to your server's IP address (or fully qualified domain name). Save the file.

7. Start up the Windows httpd server and use your favorite browser to access **http://your.server.here/demo/map.htm** (substitute your server's name or IP address for *your.server.here*). The example in Figure 7.16 should be displayed. Click on any of the blue dots to see the particular attraction in that locale.

Image Maps Illustrated

Now, how is all this accomplished?

To understand the example that's provided, review the steps that follow. This example will display a map of North America and allow you to click on a particular point or scenic attraction and display information about that attraction.

1. First of all you need a .GIF image. Use file **C:\HTTPD\IMAGES\NA.GIF**.

2. Select the Mapedit icon from the Windows Program Manager to Run the program.

3. Select the File menu item and Open/Create Map. An Open/Create Map dialog box will appear (see Figure 7.15).

4. Type C:\HTTPD\CONF\MAPS\TEST.MAP for the name of the map you want to edit (Map Filename) and enter the location and name of the image (GIF Filename) you want to work with (such as

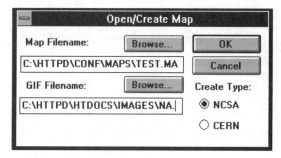

Figure 7.15 Mapedit Create/Open Map.

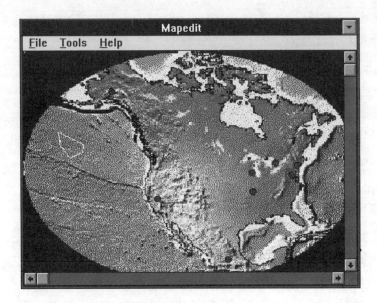

Figure 7.16 Mapedit sample image.

    C:\HTTPD\HTDOCS\IMAGES\NA.GIF). Click on OK. After a minute or so (be patient), a map will appear in a Mapedit window as in Figure 7.16.

5. The "hot spots," or clickable regions, were created by selecting Circle from the Tools menu to define a hot spot on the map. Notice the faint circles around the blue dots. These hot spots were created by clicking the left mouse button on center of the image, and then moving outward to form a larger circle. Once a proper size circle was formed, the right mouse button was clicked. You can press **Esc** at any time to restart the hot spot definition. After the right mouse button was clicked, a window popped up, requesting that a URL be associated with this hot spot. One of the preceding HTML files (such as **ARCH.HTM**) was associated with each hot spot. The name of each attraction (e.g., the Gateway Arch) was also added in the comments section of the Object URL dialog box.

6. A default URL was defined for the many occasions when a click misses the defined hot spots. Select Edit Default URL from the File menu. Here you'll see the default URL that was defined for those times that you missed. Click on Cancel.

7. Select Test/Edit from the Tools menu. Try to click on various points on the image. The URL window should appear, showing the URL associated with the hot spot. The region, as well, should be identified in inverse video. Click on Cancel to go back and view another URL. If you miss one of the hot spots, the default URL will not be displayed during the test/editing procedure. If nothing appears, you missed a hot spot.

8. Once you've completed the preceding steps, select Exit from the File menu. You can modify this example if you want to test the capabilities of Mapedit and image mapping in general.

Mapedit Example Files

You probably want to examine the following files so you can see the interrelationships of the image map files. Each of these files are included to provide a complete imagemap example. For testing purposes, you will simply need to modify the MAP.HTM file to specify the IP address for your own server. You'll then quickly have a working imagemap example.

MAP.HTM

The MAP.HTM file displays the map and provides the link to the **IMAGEMAP.EXE** program that is provided with the Windows httpd distribution. Change the **198.69.33.75** references to the IP address or domain name of your server .

```
<html>
<head>
<title>Mapedit Demonstration </title>
</head>
<body>
Here is a map of North America with blue dots representing some of the continent's
human-made and natural wonders. Click on one of the buttons on the map and informati
on describing the site will be displayed. <P>
><a href=http://198.69.33.75/cgi-win/imagemap.exe/test>
<img src="http://198.69.33.75/images/na.gif" ISMAP></img></a><P>
Facts courtesy Rand McNally Almanac of World Facts.
</body>
</html>
```

TEST.MAP

You create the TEST.MAP file using the Mapedit program. This file contains all the information you entered, first listing the default URL or the URL which will be referenced when you click outside a hot spot area. It also contains the information you entered in comment fields (prepended with a #). Most importantly, it contains the computed coordinates of the hot spots you created.

```
default /demo/missed.htm
#Mt McKinley
circle /demo/mtmc.htm 115,50 99,60
#Methuselah
circle /demo/meth.htm 174,183 188,197
#Teotihuacan
circle /demo/teo.htm 264,259 271,274
#Gateway Arch
circle /demo/arch.htm 297,174 298,183
#Sears Tower
circle /demo/sears.htm 296,151 300,160
#CN Tower
circle /demo/cntower.htm 326,139 324,150
#Statue of Liberty
circle /demo/statue.htm 353,141 355,148
#Washington Monument
circle /demo/monum.htm 346,155 347,162
```

NA.GIF

The NA.GIF is a GIF file of North America.

ARCH.HTM, CNTOWER.HTM, etc.

These files are associated with certain hot spots (the blue dots). They are simply small HTML files that describe the attraction you clicked on, as in the following example:

```
<html>
<head>
<title>Gateway Arch</title>
</head>
<body>
<h1>Gateway Arch, St. Louis, Missouri</h1>
You clicked on the Gateway Arch, a tribute to the settlers who moved westward.<P>
<a href="/demo/map.htm">Back</a> to the Mapedit Demonstration...
</body>
</html>
```

MISSED.HTM

This file is the default URL to be displayed when the client clicks outside of the hot spot areas (misses the mark). When you attempt to click on one of the attractions and you click outside of the "sensitive" area, this file will be displayed.

```
<TITLE>Mapedit Demonstration</TITLE>
<H2>Sorry. You missed the blue dot.</H2>
<HR>
<H2>Try again...</H2>
<A HREF = "/demo/map.htm">Back to the Mapedit Demo...</A>
<HR>
```

Web Utilities

Various *CGI* (Common Gateway Interface) programs have been developed to extend the functionality of Web servers and more are arriving every day. These programs run the gamut of applications (and utilities), from those that can look at the guts of your machine and tell a remote user which programs you are running, to those that can handle feedback forms, provide e-mail responses to queries, act as a pager for the system administrator, or generate charts and graphs from your Web server log. Some of these CGI programs are referenced in other chapters in this book (such as in Chapter 6, "World Wide Web Servers"). A few are covered here to give you an idea of the range of capabilities that you can add to your server.

Web utilities provide the necessary functionality for your server to do a lot more than simply provide text and graphics. The real benefit is that you don't have to do any programming to add extremely advanced features to your Web pages. These, and other utilities, allow your server to take orders on-line through fill-out forms, send e-mail confirmations of transactions, record information in server files, and act as a front-end to databases. The products covered in this chapter give you excellent examples of what you can do with "off-the-shelf" utilities. And, if you're inclined to get into the CGI programming business yourself, an excellent example is provided in Visual Basic source code to help start you on your way with Windows CGI programming.

PolyForm

PolyForm is a configurable CGI forms-handling package that you can use to create forms for customer feedback, provide automatic mail response to customers, and offers a variety of other helpful features that you'll most probably want and need on your server. And, all this is done without programming on your part. The necessary shareware software is provided by Mark Bracewell of Willow Glen Graphics (**http://www.wgg.com**). Without PolyForm, you would be tasked with creating CGI scripts and back-end programs in Visual Basic, Perl, or C++ to manage forms and electronic mail-enabled applications.

PolyForm contains a built-in SMTP mailer that can send mail as part of the CGI back-end execution. If there was ever a reason to invest in shareware, this is it. Not only does PolyForm, and Mark's other utilities, provide tremendous functionality for your server, but the software is continually enhanced. You'll want to get on the distribution list so that you can take advantage of the many enhancements as they are released.

You can retrieve the PolyForm (version 1.2) distribution, POLYFORM.ZIP, from **ftp://ftp.best.com/pub/cbntmkr/polyform.zip**. Use PKUNZIP to unzip the zipped file into a directory (such as **C:\POLYFORM**). PolyForm also requires that **VBRUN300.DLL** be placed in your **WINDOWS\SYSTEM** directory. This file is readily available on the Internet. Refer to the information on HTML Writer and HTML Assistant for two sites that house this DLL.

PolyForm Installation

The PolyForm program requires the Windows httpd or WebSite, the 32-bit WWW Server for Windows 95 and Windows NT by Robert Denny. You will also need VBRUN300.DLL, which is available at a number of sites. (For more information, see the information on HTML Assistant or HTML Writer).

To install PolyForm shareware version 1.2:

1. One of the files from the zipped distribution, **WGGSETUP.EXE**, is a Windows self-extracting Install Program. During installation, you will be given the option to determine locations of the installed files, and to make backups of any updated files. Run **WGGSETUP.EXE** from the Program Manager, or double clicking on it in File Manager. An installation log will be created in the directory containing the PolyForm Documentation. You can delete **WGGSETUP.EXE** after you complete the installation.

   The /M option enables you to run the installation in a "manual" mode. You will be prompted for the locations of your **WINDOWS**, **WINDOWS\SYSTEM**, and **TEMP** directories. You can specify any directories, and if they do not exist, they will be created. Any changes to .INI files will be saved into the Windows directory you specify. With the /M option, you can run the installation without installing any files into your real Windows and System directory. You can then manually copy the files to their proper destination using the install procedure outlined in **POLYFORM.HLP**.

2. A screen appears and advises you that the program will install files and backup previous PolyForm files (see Figure 8.1). It also describes the /M option. Click on OK.

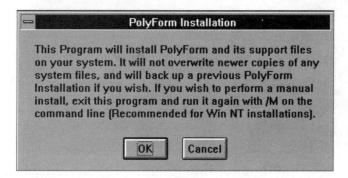

Figure 8.1 PolyForm installation.

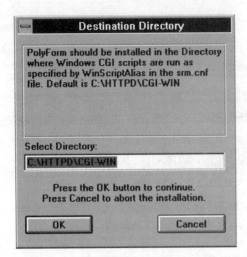

Figure 8.2 PolyForm destination directory.

3. Next, you are informed that PolyForm should be installed with the Windows CGI scripts as specified by the WinScriptAlias in the **SRM.CNF** file (see Figure 8.2). The default is **C:\HTTPD\CGI-WIN**. Click on OK.

4. You are prompted to select a directory for the text files and samples (see Figure 8.3). The default is **C:\HTTPD\HTDOCS\WGG_DOCS**. Click on OK.

5. You are asked if you want to make backups of files replaced during installation (Figure 8.4). Choose Yes to retain any files that the installation will replace.

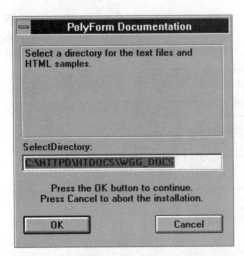

Figure 8.3 PolyForm documentation.

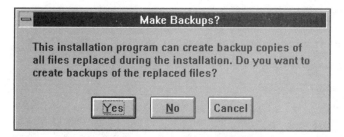

Figure 8.4 PolyForm backups.

6. Files are copied to the appropriate directories and then you are
   prompted to add an icon for PolyForm to the Windows Program
   Manager (see Figure 8.5). Click on Yes.

7. The dialog box shown in Figure 8.6 appears, indicating the default
   Program Group, WHHTPD Utils. Click on OK to continue. An installation
   complete message will appear.

8. The PolyForm Help and a Setup screen appear so that you can configure
   PolyForm (see Figure 8.7). Complete the following fields, and click on
   OK.

   • **E-Mail Return Address**: Insert your e-mail address, which will
     appear in the reply-to field of mail you send.

   • **Server Domain Name**: This is your server's domain name. This is
     used to tell the mail server where the mail is coming from. This
     should be the same name that is used to access your server.

   • **Mail Server Address or Name**: This is the address or IP number of
     your SMTP mail server.

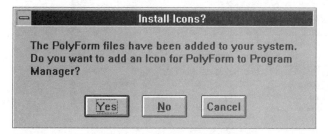

Figure 8.5 PolyForm install icons.

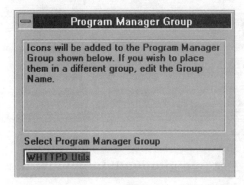

Figure 8.6 PolyForm Program Manager group.

- **Text Editor**: This is the name of your favorite text editor, complete with path, such as **C:\WINDOWS\NOTEPAD.EXE**.

- **HTML Editor**: This is the name of the HTML editor you use.

- **Logs Directory**: This is the directory in which you keep your server log files, such as **C:\HTTPD\LOGS**.

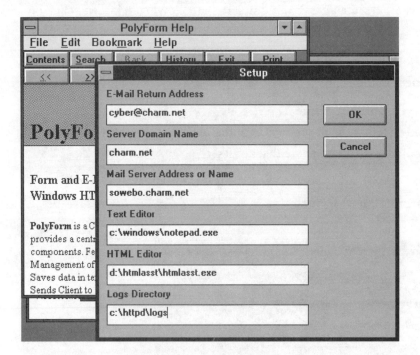

Figure 8.7 PolyForm Setup screen.

After you complete this form (and all fields must be filled) and click on OK, you can change these parameters by running PolyForm and clicking on the Setup button in the lower right part of the configuration screen. Changes will then take effect the next time you start PolyForm.

Running PolyForm

You continue the installation process by filling out the PolyForm configuration screen (see Figure 8.8). In the future, you can click the Polyform icon, in the Program Manager, to run **POLYFORM.EXE**. The following example illustrates the use of the PolyForm program and explains the parameters shown in Figure 8.8. You can configure PolyForm using these parameters and create a useful sample program.

Script Name

Each form created by PolyForm has a *Tag* that indicates which script is to be executed. For purposes of the example, enter the script name **SAMPLE**. In this

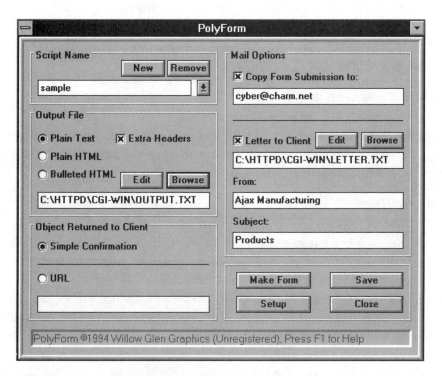

Figure 8.8 PolyForm configuration screen.

section you can create, edit, and delete scripts. Later, by displaying a given script and clicking the Remove button, you will be able to delete a selected script. This will not, however, delete associated forms or files that use the script. Script names can be upper- and/or lowercase and up to 20 characters in length (no spaces).

Output File

The output file is where feedback from your customers is deposited. Data submitted via a feedback form, for example, is stored either in a plain text file, a plain html file, or an html file with the data formatted into a bulleted list. If you are using html output files, the files must exist prior to running the script. If the files don't exist, the script will return a **file not found** error. Minimally, the file must include <!--**footer**--> on a line by itself. You can click the Browse button to select an output file. If the selected file does not exist, you'll be given the option to create it. If you choose to create it, the file written will contain the necessary syntax and some notes, or comments, on its use.

When you initially create the file, if you have chosen html output, you will go to the html editor to fine tune the output file for future writes. At this point, no modifications are necessary to successfully see this example through to completion. Likewise, if you choose plain text, you'll go to your text editor. Click on the Extra Headers box and extra information, such as address and browser type, will be provided in the file.

Object Returned to Client

You can send a simple confirmation to the client browser, which can include a "thank you" and the submitted data, or, you can send the client to a specific URL. Local URLs should be entered relative to the document root. Click on Simple Confirmation for this example.

Mail Options

You can direct information from the form submission to a specific e-mail address. By placing an e-mail address in the Copy Form Submission to: box, any data submitted will be e-mailed to the address listed in the box. You can, for example, include feedback from clients, as well as their e-mail address in a message that will be copied to the webmaster for follow-up. The webmaster will then receive, via e-mail, a message with the configurable "subject," the date and time it was sent, the originating IP address, the all-important comments or feedback, and the e-mail address that was filled in on the feedback form. Fill in your e-mail address in the Copy Form Submission to: box.

- **Letter to Client**: By checking the Letter to Client box, you can send a text file to the client. In order to send these form letters, the form the client completes must have an input or text area field with the key **E-Mail** (such as **<INPUT NAME="E-Mail">**). The text box on the configuration screen must contain the path and file name of the letter to be sent to the client. Browse and Edit buttons are available to enable you to maintain the letter files.

The e-mail message that is sent to the client contains two fields that you'll now need to configure, the From field and the message subject.

- **From**: The From box enables you to put your name or organization in the sender field of the outgoing message.
- **Subject**: The Subject field enables you to specify a subject line. To create your own LETTER.TXT for this example, click on the Letter to Client check box and the Browse button, or use the letter included in the PolyForm directory on the CD (**LETTER.TXT**).

Click on the Save button and a dialog box will be displayed for you to "save the form template as" **SAMPLE.HTM**. Click on OK.

Making a Form

Once you complete the configuration of a script, you can click the Make Form button. Clicking this button creates and saves a form template for use with your script. In this example, the form template is called **sample.htm** (see Figure 8.9). Included with the script is the correct **<FORM...** syntax, an E-Mail input box (if you selected **Letter to Client**), and a standard html outline. The template is then loaded into your html editor so you can add the finishing touches to your form.

Testing the PolyForm Script Example

With the Windows httpd server running, open the **sample.htm** file through your browser (such as Netscape). The URL will be, for example, **http://-198.69.33.75/sample.htm**. This example assumes that you moved the **sample.htm** file to your document root, which in the **out-of-the-box** httpd configuration would be **C:\HTTPD\HTDOCS/**. Next, complete the feedback form (as in Figure 8.10) and click the Submit Comments button. Once you've

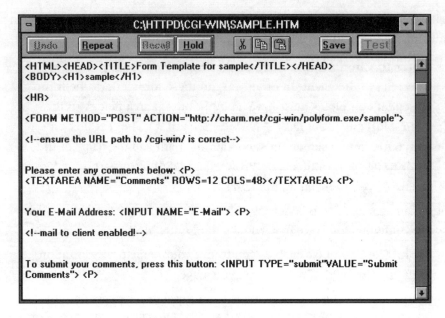

Figure 8.9 PolyForm form template.

done this, mail should be sent to the address designated in the Copy Form Submission to: field, the feedback should be written to the **OUTPUT.HTM** file, and the client should receive, via the e-mail address they entered on the feedback form, the contents of the **LETTER.TXT** file. The client browser will receive a page with a "thank you" confirmation as well.

For additional help with PolyForm, you can press F1 from within the program to access online help.

TalkBack

TalkBack is another handy Web server tool, produced by Mark Bracewell of Willow Glen Graphics, that is designed for Windows httpd and WebSite. Not only does this product add to the effectiveness of your Web server, but it has a bit of entertainment value as well. The TalkBack product is included with the PolyForm software distribution and is only available to registered shareware users.

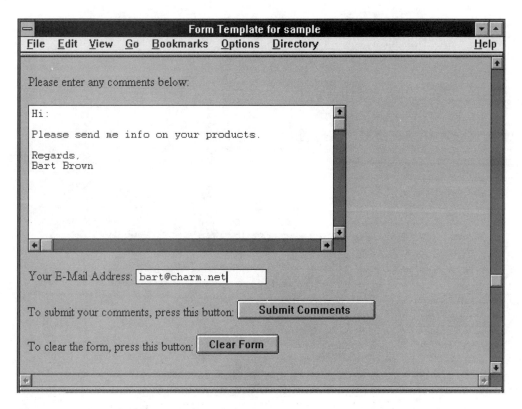

Figure 8.10 PolyForm feedback form.

With TalkBack, you can have a user fill out a browser form (see Figure 8.11) and TalkBack will display a window on your server to show the webmaster the arriving message (see Figure 8.12). The webmaster can then respond to the message and carry on a "chat" session of sorts. And there's more . . . if you're not at the system, TalkBack will record the message and send the client a page you have "prerecorded," informing the client that you're away from your desk, or whatever message you choose to use (see Figure 8.13). It also serves as a Web-based answering machine.

TalkBack Installation

Since the TalkBack program is a Visual Basic executable you'll need to put it into a directory which houses CGI scripts. Once that's done, you'll need to use the Setup procedure to configure TalkBack.

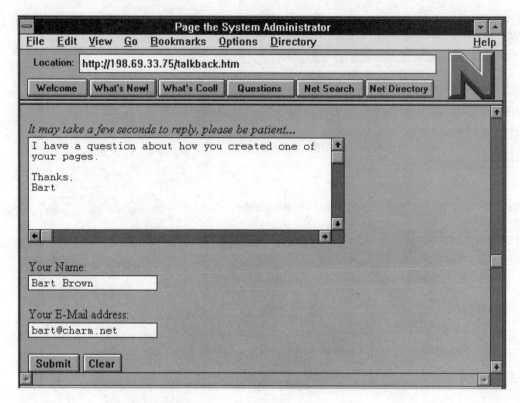

Figure 8.11 TalkBack form.

To install TalkBack:

1. After you unzip the registered PolyForm distribution, move the **TALK-BACK.EXE** file to the **C:\HTTPD\CGI-WIN** directory. Set up an icon in a Program manager group and run the program.

2. Next, you should see the Setup dialog box, as shown in Figure 8.14.

3. The following information describes each field on the TalkBack Setup screen:

   • **Output File**: This file is the output file that contains the information the user entered in the TalkBack form. The Browse and Edit buttons are available for you to view, change, and edit the file(s). You can set up new output files and save the old ones whenever you want.

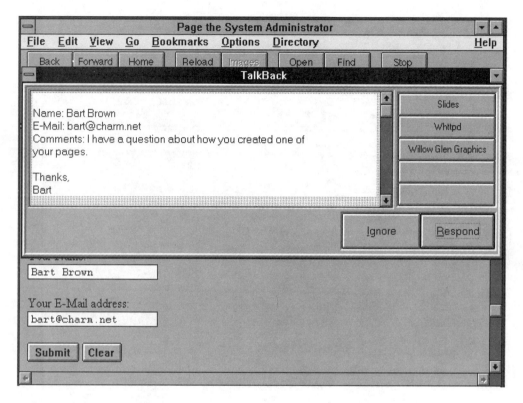

Figure 8.12 TalkBack arriving message.

- **Default URL**: The default URL is where you specify the page to return to the client when you're not available to respond (or if you choose to click the Ignore button). The path specification is relative to the server's document root. For example, with Windows httpd, the path would be **/ABSENT.HTM** when the file is placed in the **C:\HTTPD\HTDOCS** directory.

- **WinScriptAlias**: WinScriptAlias should have the same alias you have entered in **srm.cnf**. The default is **/cgi-win/**.

- **Quick Replies**: When you receive a page from a client, you need to respond fairly quickly because the user is staring at his or her browser wondering what, if anything, is going to happen. In such cases, you may want to create a "quick reply" that will be sent with the click of a button.

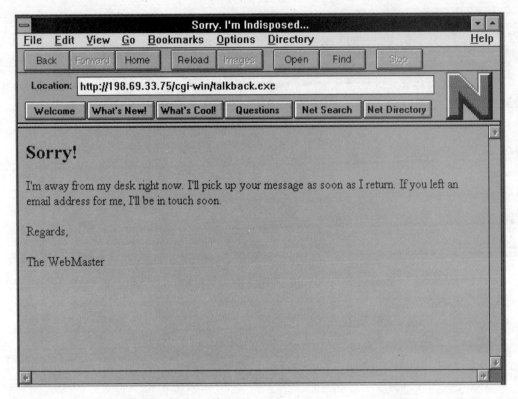

Figure 8.13 TalkBack prerecorded message.

An example might be **Got your message. I'm thinking. Give me just one minute to send you some details.** You may also find that you are repeating the same information to different people. You can put just about anything into quick reply boxes, up to 500 characters each, including HTML markups too, such as **<p>**, and so on. When the paging window appears, there are buttons you can use to add these "quick replies" to your responses (see Figure 8.15). Additional examples might include a signature line, or a link to your home page, or a link that you often find yourself pointing people to. The Button Caption text boxes are those in which you can put a label for the corresponding button. You can indicate hot keys for captions you might have by including an ampersand (&) before the letter you want to designate as the hot key. Note that R, S and I are reserved for Respond, Send & Ignore. You use a hot key by pressing ALT+hotkey.

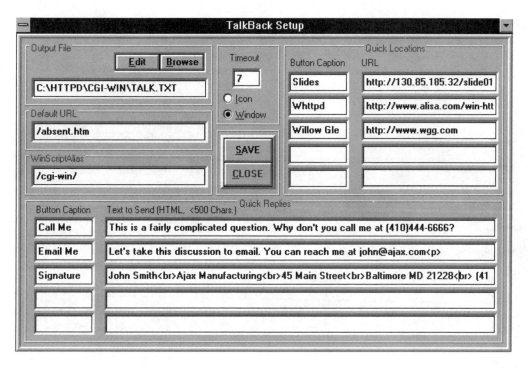

Figure 8.14 TalkBack setup.

- **Timeout**: Timeout specifies the amount of time (in seconds) you
  have to click the Respond button before the Default URL is sent.
  You can click Ignore to send it right away when the TalkBack
  Window is open. If you set Timeout to zero, the TalkBack Window
  will not appear on your desktop, and the default URL is sent.

- **Quick Locations**: Quick Locations will send the caller directly to
  the URL you have specified here. URLs can be local or remote.
  Local URLs are relative to document root. As with Quick replies,
  the text boxes are for you to make labels for the buttons. If
  someone asks where to find a resource that you're often referring
  people to, with the click of a button you can send that person
  there.

Once you've completed the configuration parameters, clicking on "Save" saves
the configuration and exits the TalkBack program. "Close" exits without saving.

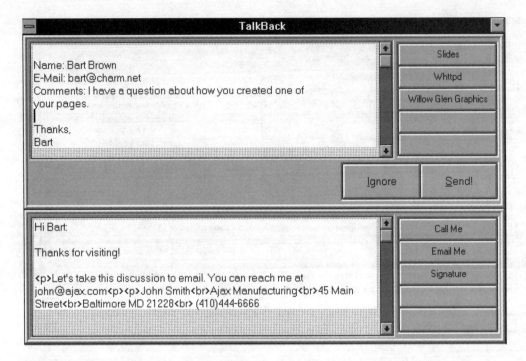

Figure 8.15 TalkBack quick replies.

The example form included with the TalkBack distribution shows the syntax for running TalkBack from a browser. You'll need to change the form tag to point to your server, as in the following example:

```
<FORM METHOD="POST" ACTION="http://your.server.here/cgi-win/talkback.exe">
```

Move the form **TALKBACK.HTM** to the document root directory (**C:\ HTTPD\HTDOCS**, for example), run Netscape or Mosaic, and then open the following URL (be sure your Windows httpd or WebSite server is running):

```
http://your.server.here/talkback.htm
```

Fill in the form with the message for the webmaster and click on the Submit button (see Figure 8.11). When the window appears on the server for the webmaster, click the Respond button (see Figure 8.12). Now is the time to position the window on your desktop where you want it; TalkBack will remember this position and always pop up in the same place. Type in a reply on the form that appears for the webmaster (Figure 8.15), include any quick replies, and click Send. Your message will appear on the browser and also be written to the output file you specified in Setup (see Figures 8.16 and 8.17).

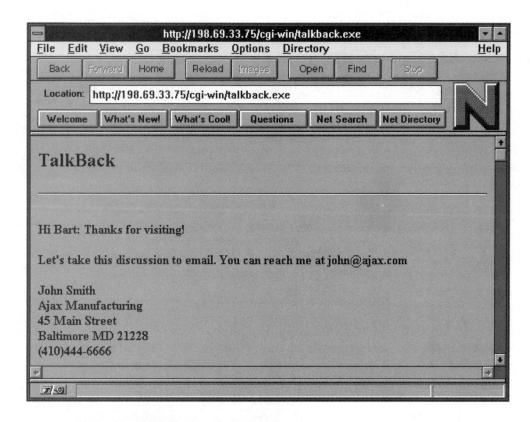

Figure 8.16 TalkBack message at the browser.

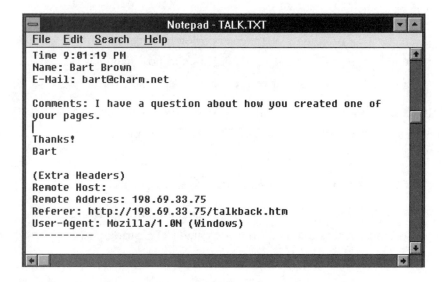

Figure 8.17 TalkBack output file.

VBStats—Windows Web
Server Statistics Reporter

VBStats is a collection of five Visual Basic programs that enable you to analyze Web server log files. It also produces HTML pages for you with usage graphs. The software was written by Bob Denny, author of the Windows httpd server, to provide statistics for your server. It, of course, works with the Windows httpd implementation or any other WWW server implementation that creates log files in the **NCSA/CERN** common log format. A Web server collects statistical information in a log file (such as **ACCESS.LOG** in the **WHTTPD** server), and this system is imported into a Microsoft Access 2.0 database for subsequent reporting by a SQL driven report generator.

You can get the software (**VBSTAT31.ZIP**) from the following address:

```
ftp://ftp.alisa.com/pub/win-httpd/util-support/
```

VBSTATS Installation

To install the software, create a directory, such as **C:\VBSTATS** and use PKUNZIP to unpack the files into the directory you created. Following are the five principal programs that make up the distribution:

- **SETUPWIZ.EXE**: This program enables you to do the initial configuration of the system. Additionally, you will use this program to create your VBSTATS database.

- **LOGTODB.EXE**: This program loads the server log information into the database. It can, as well, translate IP addresses to host names if you have this capability disabled at the server.

- **RESTRICT.EXE**: You use this program to "restrict" the objects reflected in system reports. For example, you may not want access to .GIF files included in your reports.

- **REPORTER.EXE**: This is the actual statistical reporting program.

- **DBMAINT.EXE**: You use this program for the database housekeeping functions, such as clearing old data from the database, clearing past totals, and so on.

There is another very useful program that is included with VBSTATS as a "support" program:

- **WINCRON.EXE**: You can use this program to automate the daily transfers of the log files into the database and to perform periodic reporting.

VBSTATS Installation

After you unzip the files into the proper directory (**C:\VBSTATS**, for example), you are ready to run the setup procedure.

This setup procedure will create the necessary environment for collecting and reporting Web statistics. The necessary program group and related icons will be set up, file names and report locations will be defined, and other parameters will be input to configure the VBSTATS programs.

1. From the Windows Program Manager, via the File menu, Run **C:\VB-STATS\SETUP.EXE**.

   If the program detects that you already have Microsoft Access installed, it will display a Warning message that advises you that the Setup program will upgrade your system to Access 2.0 compatibility.

2. Next, you asked where you want to install the **VBSTATS** programs (see Figure 8.18). The default is **C:\VBSTATS**. Indicate the location and click on Continue.

```
┌─────────────────────────────────────────────────────────┐
│            VBStats 3.1 Package Setup                      │
├─────────────────────────────────────────────────────────┤
│  ┌───┐   If you want to install the VBStats 3.1 Package   │
│  │   │   in a different directory and/or drive, type the  │
│  └───┘   name of the directory.                           │
│                                                           │
│          Install To:  c:\vbstats                          │
│                                                           │
│          To quit Setup, choose the Exit button.           │
│                                                           │
│          ┌──────────────┐    ┌──────────────┐             │
│          │  Continue     │    │  Exit Setup   │            │
│          └──────────────┘    └──────────────┘             │
└─────────────────────────────────────────────────────────┘
```

Figure 8.18 VBSTATS Package Setup.

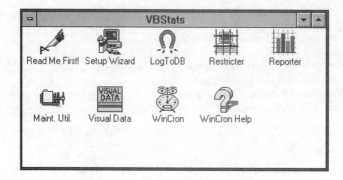

Figure 8.19 VBSTATS program group.

3. Setup now builds a program group and populates it with the program icons for the **VBSTATS** programs listed earlier (see Figure 8.19). Once the program group is complete, you will get a message indicating that Setup completed successfully. You also will see a message informing you that Access 2.0 requires **SHARE.EXE** to run and that it must be configured to **SHARE.EXE /L:500**. Finally, you will be prompted to continue with the Setup Wizard program. Answering Yes causes the welcome screen in Figure 8.20 to appear. Click on the Next button to continue and the screen in Figure 8.21 (Database Setup and Creation) will be displayed.

Figure 8.20 VBSTATS welcome screen.

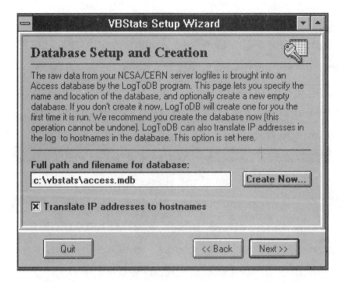

Figure 8.21 VBSTATS Database screen.

4. You now are asked to identify the path and file name for the database. Additionally, you can have the LOGTODB program translate IP addresses to host names in the database by checking the Translate IP addresses to host names box on this screen. After you enter the correct information, click on the Create Now... button and the database will be created. Click on the Next button to continue.

Figure 8.22 VBSTATS File Names and Report Locations.

5. Next, you see a screen that enables you to configure File Names and Report Locations (see Figure 8.22). Here you should identify the Full path and filename of server access log:. This is where the LOGTODB program looks to find the Web server log file. On the Windows httpd server, it normally is found in the **C:\HTTPD\LOGS** directory, which is the default. *Do not specify the name of the current active log file*, which is **ACCESS.LOG**. Leave the default **ACCESS.001** and check Cycle Logs. which causes **LOGTODB** to signal the server to "cycle" the logs and create **ACCESS.001** for you. Indicate the Directory path for report output: by accepting the default, which is **C:\HTTPD\HTDO-CS\SVRSTATS**. The output (reports and graphs) generated by the REPORTER program will be placed in this directory. When you complete this information, click on Next to continue.

6. Report configuration information should be loaded into the Report Generation screen displayed in Figure 8.23. The Site Name will be the report title. Administrator's Name and Administrator's E-mail address should be provided since it will be displayed at the bottom of each

Figure 8.23 VBSTATS Report Generation Setup.

report page. The URL Back Link will take clients to the specified page when they select Back from the report index page. Enter the logical path name for the page to which you want clients to return after viewing the statistics. The example lists **/INDEX.HTM**, which would map to the Windows default home page, **C:\HTTPD\HTDOCS\ INDEX.HTM**. After you complete the necessary information, click on Next to continue.

7. You can configure your preferences for Access Graph Style in the screen displayed in Figure 8.24. You may select from graph type, graph style, and colors. Accept the defaults by clicking on the Finish button.

8. With the Windows httpd server running, run LOGTODB by clicking the icon in Program Manager. This causes the server to cycle the log files and loads the database with the log information. An icon will reflect the program's progress in loading the database.

9. Run the Restriction Editor to eliminate extraneous information from your reports. One example is to eliminate .GIFs from your Top Ten lists. Figure 8.25 shows an example of setting up restrictions. You can restrict objects (such as documents or images), sites (certain hosts), or users

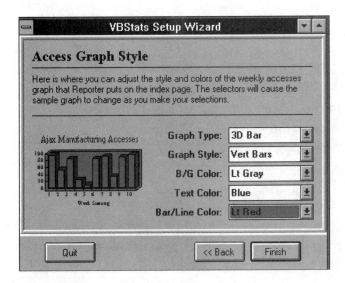

Figure 8.24 VBSTATS Access Graph Style.

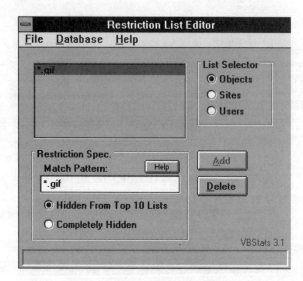

Figure 8.25 VBSTATS Restriction List Editor.

from the reports. You can hide your selections from the Top Ten lists (it will still be reflected in the totals, however), or completely hide them from all reports by selecting the appropriate radio button below the Match Pattern: box. Your restrictions, or "match patterns" should be listed in the Match Pattern: box. Click on the tiny Help box to see wild-card opportunities. Additional help is offered by selecting Help from the menu bar at the top of the screen.

10. Lastly, run the Reporter program and the HMTL statistics files will be created in the **C:\HTTPD\HTDOCS\SVRSTATS** directory. If you run Mosaic or Netscape (with your httpd server running), and access **http://your.domain.name/svrstats/index.htm**, you should now be able to access your server statistics (they should appear as similar to those shown in Figure 8.26).

Database Maintenance (Maint. Util. Icon)

As with any statistical program you'll need to rid your system of older data that you've already analyzed. The DBMAINT.EXE program will allow you to purge old data, clear past totals, and compact the database.

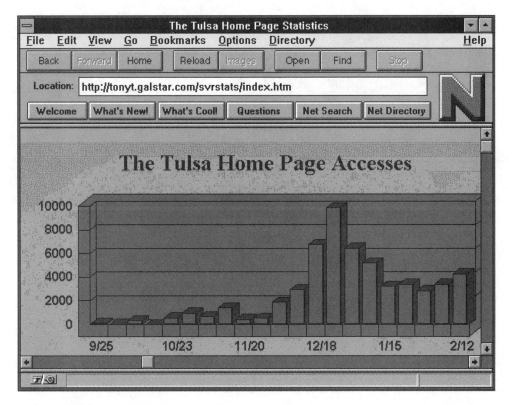

Figure 8.26 VBSTATS server statistics.

- **Purging Old Data**: This program allows you to purge old data from the VBStats database (see Figure 8.27). You simply have to index a date and click the Purge button to delete accesses prior to the indexed date.

- **Clearing PastTotals**: You can clear the PastTotals table so that Reporter will regenerate old reports. If you have purged data in the prior option, Purging Old Data, you cannot regenerate reports for those records.

- **Compact Database**: This option compacts the database so that unused space is removed after purging old data. This also resets report sequence numbers when you select this after clearing PastTotals.

Figure 8.27 VBSTATS database maintenance.

VBStats Source Code

If you want to retrieve the source code to see a sample Visual Basic program
with an interface to a Microsoft Access database, the source is available from
the following address:

```
http://www.CITY.NET/WINHTTPD/LIB/UTIL-SUPPORT/VBSTAT31.ZIP
```

FORM2HTM—A Sample CGI Program

If the many CGI utilities on the market don't seem to do exactly what you want,
perhaps you would like to try your hand at CGI programming. Mark Bracewell,
of Willow Glen Graphics, a true artisan when it comes to developing utilities,
has provided the source code to a sample CGI program on the accompanying
CD. The sample program, FORM2HTM, is written in Visual Basic, and gives you
the necessary modules to help you get started in your own CGI programming.
All the necessary components, with the exception of the Visual Basic programming language, are available on the CD.

What FORM2HTM Does

FORM2HTM, called "Simple Form Support," is a form handling script for Bob
Denny's Winhttpd server. The program prompts the user with a form, and
writes (in html) to a file for storing form data. Each entry is separated with a

horizontal rule tag (**<HR>**). You can specify the file name of the output file, write to a private log file, or you can write to a public file (in the public document root directory, for example), for all to access. The program can also send clients a confirmation of the submission or send them to any URL you specify.

You can create multiple forms to suit varied needs, and each form you create can have its own section in the **CGI_FORM.INI** file so that the "log" file and URL the client is sent to can be tailored to each form. The .INI file also enables you to specify whether to archive extra header information (the remote address of the client, type of browser, and so on) and whether to send the client to a new page or return a confirmation of the submission.

FORM2HTM Installation

There are several files that support the FORM2HTM example and they'll need to be installed in the appropriate directories.

To install FORM2HTM:

1. Create a directory (such as **C:\CGIFORM**) and copy the **CGIFORM2.ZIP** file from the CD (**CGIFORM** directory) to your disk drive.

2. Copy the following files to the appropriate directories:

File	Directory
FORM2HTM.EXE	C:\HTTP\CGI-WIN\
CGI_FORM.INI	C:\WINDOWS\
CGI_F.BAS	C:\CGIFORM\
CGI_FORM.HTM	C:\CGIFORM\
FRM2HTML.BAS	C:\CGIFORM\
FRM2HTML.MAK	C:\CGIFORM\
SAMPLFRM.HTM	C:\HTTPD\HTDOCS\
FORMDATA.HTM	C:\HTTPD\HTDOCS\

Note that the file to which data is written (**FORMDATA.HTM**, labeled as **Archive** in the .INI file) must exist prior to running the script. If it does not exist, it will not be created and the script will return a **file not found** error. Minimally, the file must include **<!--footer-->** on a line by itself.

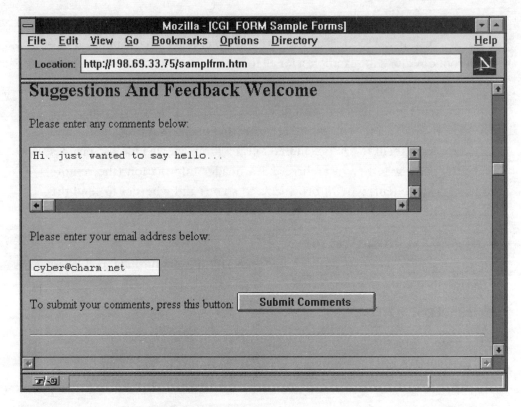

Figure 8.28 FORM2HTM feedback form.

3. With your favorite editor, modify the **SAMPLE.HTM** file to include your server name in the place of **198.69.33.75**.

4. With Netscape or Mosaic, open a URL to the following address:

```
http://your.server.here/sample.htm
```

5 Complete the sample form and check out the results (see Figures 8.28 and 8.29).

Program Logic

The FORM2HTM.EXE program depends on a .INI file for its parameters. The .INI file listed here is commented to explain what each parameter is used for.

Forms access **FORM2HTM.EXE** with the following statement:

```
<FORM METHOD="POST" ACTION= "http://YOUR.DOMAIN/cgiwin/form2htm.exe/SECTION">
```

where **SECTION** is the name of the section in **CGI_FORM.INI** that corresponds to that specific form. The preceding example would look for

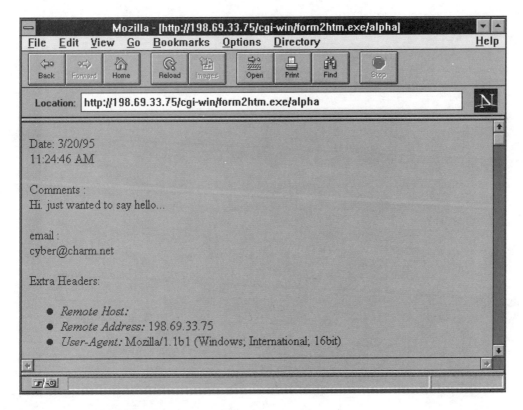

Figure 8.29 FORM2HTM results.

[SECTION] as the configuration file for that form. Following is what the .INI
file looks like:

```
[SECTION]
;the file you want the form data appended to, don't forget the quotes
Archive="c:\temp\formsubm.htm"
;where you want the client to be sent after they submit the form
SendURL=/demo/
;add extra header info to archive file? (what you get depends on the browser)
ExtraHeaders=yes  (or 'Yes', anything else is the same as 'no')
;send only a confirmation of the submission?
Confirm=no  ('no' will send them to SendURL, 'yes' will send only a confirmation)
[AnotherSECTION]
Archive="c:\temp\data.txt"
SendURL=/demo/
ExtraHeaders=no
Confirm=yes
```

Finger Servers

As you begin to advertise your Web or Gopher server, or as people notice your e-mail address, they may try to "finger" you or your server. As you recall from Chapter 3, the finger command can tell you who is logged in on local and remote machines, together with information about each user including the user's real name, when they logged in, etc. If you would like to provide information to Finger clients, you can easily implement a server that will provide information normally provided by UNIX hosts. There are, as well, some rather novel applications supported by Finger servers. Visit by fingering the following sites. For example, at the Unix command prompt type:

```
finger help@dir.su.oz.au
finger help@dir.su.oz.au
finger quake@geophys.washington.edu
finger graph@drink.csh.rit.edu
```

Of course, you may want to simply develop a more traditional "plan" file, such as those at the following addresses:

```
web@charm.net
cnordin@charm.net
rdenny@netcom.com
```

wsfngrd—Winsock Finger Daemon

wsfngrd is a freeware winsock finger daemon, or server, for Microsoft Windows, written by Jim O'Brien of Tidewater Systems. Finger is a service, normally found on UNIX systems, that returns a personal information file (usually a **.plan** file residing in the "fingered" person's directory) to a client that requests it. When a user types in a request from the UNIX prompt such as

```
finger @cyber.charm.net
```

or

```
finger user@cyber.charm.net
```

a "plan" file is returned (see Figure 9.1).

This is a useful feature to let others on the Net know a little bit about you.

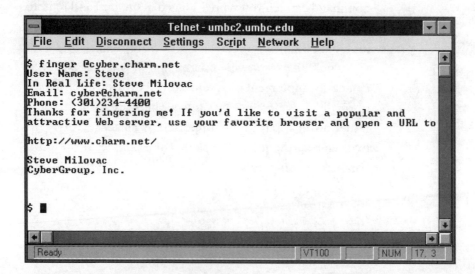

Figure 9.1 A wsfngrd plan file.

```
┌──────────────────────────────────────────────┐
│              Fingerd Setup                     │
├──────────────────────────────────────────────┤
│  Username:   │ Steve                         │ │
│                                                │
│  Full Name:  │ Steve Milovac                 │ │
│                                                │
│  Email:      │ cyber@charm.net               │ │
│                                                │
│  Phone:      │ (301)234-4400                 │ │
│                                                │
│  Plan File:  │ plan.txt                      │ │
│                                                │
│            [   Ok   ] [ Cancel ]               │
└──────────────────────────────────────────────┘
```

Figure 9.2 wsfngrd dialog box.

wsfngrd Installation

To install wsfngrd you'll need to unzip the software distribution and then run the program to set up certain parameters such as your name, email address, and location of your "plan" file. You'll also want to create a plan file using an editor such as Windows Notepad. Follow these steps and you'll be running in no time:

To install wsfngrd:

1. Set up a directory and copy the **WFNGRD10.ZIP** file into it (**C:\WFNGRD**).

2. Unzip the **WFNGRD10.ZIP** file into the directory.

3. Using Program Manager, add a Program Item to a group for **WSFNGRD.EXE**.

4. Select the program icon and run **WSFNGRD.EXE**. An .INI file named **WSFNGRD.INI** will be created in your WINDOWS directory. A dialog box will be displayed (see Figure 9.2) for you to fill in the information to be returned when your machine is fingered. wsfngrd will read and return a **PLAN.TXT** file if one exists. You should define the path to **PLAN.TXT** under the Setup option.

BW—Connect Finger Server

FINGERDW is a daemon program, available through Beame & Whiteside Software, running under the inetd daemon (or program), that allows a remote user to query your PC for certain information (see Figure 9.3). The remote user

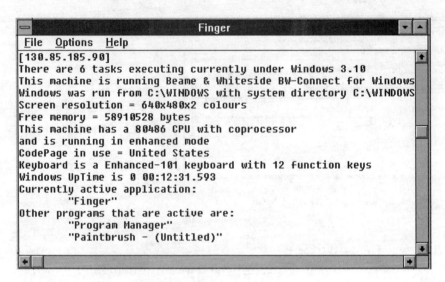

Figure 9.3 Beame & Whiteside Finger Information.

can query the state of your Windows configuration and list which programs are running. If the remote user requests a long listing, the program will additionally pass to the remote user the contents of the **PLAN.BW** and **PROJECT.BW** files in your **BWTCP** directory. The plan file normally contains information such as that normally found in an e-mail signature file (such as address, phone number, and so on), while the project file normally contains information about what you are working on.

The Beame & Whiteside Finger server is part of an entire suite of client and server products available for Windows 3.1. The Finger application runs as a server process under the Beame & Whiteside inetd server. The installation of the Beame & Whiteside client and server product suite, including their TCP/IP implementation, is covered in detail in Chapter 4 and is required reading for installation and support of their Finger server. To start up the Finger server, from the inetd menu, select Setup and then fingerd. Click on the Enable box to start the fingerd daemon. Figure 9.4 shows your options for running the Finger server through inetd.

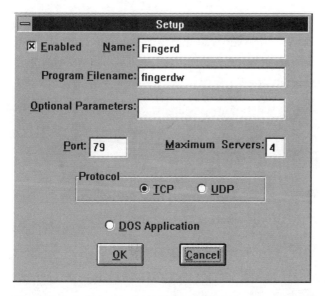

Figure 9.4 Beame & Whiteside Finger server configuration.

Finger for NT

Finger, as it has been explained, enables you retrieve information about users on remote systems.

The freeware Finger server for NT, known as *Fingers*, is an implementation of the Finger protocol as defined in RFC 1288 and is available from EMWAC.

NT Finger Installation

The server software is included on the accompanying CD or may be retrieved from:

```
ftp://emwac.ed.ac.uk/pub/finger
```

You'll want to retrieve the Intel version of Fingers which is distributed in the **WSI386.ZIP** file. This version of the program requires a Windows NT system with a network connection and 16MB of memory to support this server.

To install Fingers:

1. Use PKUNZIP to unzip the software distribution files into the directory you want or a directory you create (such as **D:\FINGERS**). Later, you

will want to plan a directory structure that makes sense for your installation, moving files to be served to the data directory, and the software distribution files to another directory. But for now, for purposes of simplicity, we'll commingle the files in one directory.

Following are the files that will be unzipped:

FINGERS.EXE   Server executable

COPYRITE.TXT   Copyright statement

READ.ME   Version features, installation
                      instructions, etc.

2. Sign onto an administrator's account on the NT system.

3. Copy the file **FINGERS.EXE** to the **\WINNT35\SYSTEM32** directory. Go to the Security/Permissions menu item in the File Manager, and verify that the System user has read permission on **FINGERS.EXE**.

4. From Windows, click on the MS DOS icon to go to the MS DOS command line. Type **fingers -install**. This installs Fingers as a service and also registers it with the Event Logger.

5. Start the NT Control Panel and double-click on the Services icon. The Fingers Server should be shown as a service, as in Figure 9.5. Start the Fingers Server by clicking on the Start button.

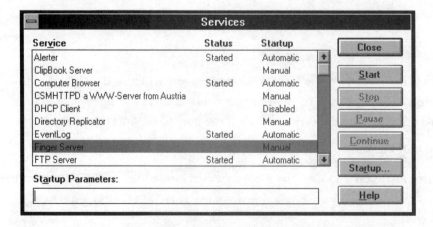

Figure 9.5 Starting the NT Finger service.

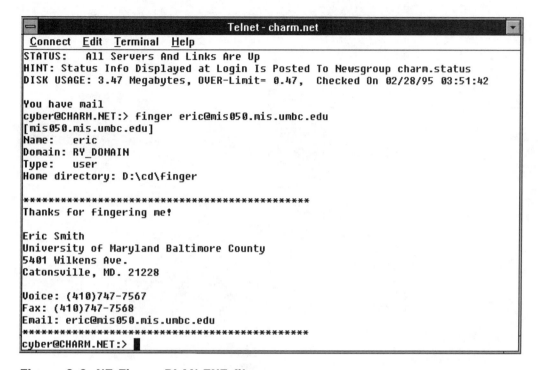

Figure 9.6 NT Finger PLAN.TXT file.

The server will respond to the finger client's command of **finger name@machine** command. The server should respond with the "real name" of the user and the description as configured in the User Manager. If the user has been assigned a home directory, the server will report its locations and return the contents of the **PLAN.TXT** file if it is found in the directory (see Figure 9.6). If the client simply issues a **finger @machine**, the server will return a list of users currently logged on.

Mail Servers

Electronic Mail is probably the most widely used application on the Internet. One of the constraints of maintaining your own Internet connection in a PC environment has been the inability to run your own Internet mail server. If you wanted to receive Internet mail, you had to have an account, or mailbox, for each individual in your organization, with an Internet service provider. Now, with products covered in this chapter, you can maintain mailboxes for yourself and others within your organization. Not only do these servers provide the essential ingredients of SMTP mail and POP3 server capabilities, but features often include advanced capabilities, such as mailing list (Listserv) software.

IMail for Windows 3.1 and Windows NT

Imail is an electronic mail system comprised of a client and server component with SMTP and POP3, the two popular Internet mail protocols. Imail is a reasonably priced commercial product from Ipswitch, Inc. of Wakefield, Massachusetts. The Mail server capabilities function well in either a Windows 3.1 or in a Windows NT environment using the NT 16-bit subsystem.

Although this chapter is particularly concerned with the mail server programs, the package sports a number of other useful features including the following:

- An intuitive graphical user interface with capabilities such as mail filtering, searching, file import and export, and address books

- Full capability available as either client or server through SMTP and POP3 client and server programs

- Mime support to allow you to send and receive binary files as attachments

- Easy and intuitive installation and configuration

- Compatible with Windows 3.1 or Windows NT

Imail Installation

Imail is available for downloading from **http://www.openmarket.com** under the Ipswitch, Inc. pages.

The Imail distribution is a self-extracting file that will "unarchive" the necessary files when you run it. Once that's completed, you'll run an install program that will prompt you through a setup procedure that includes the setup of directory paths, mail server host name, and other mail server parameters.

Once you have acquired the software follow these steps for installation:

1. Create directories for the temporary storage of the archived software product (**C:\IMAILTMP**, for example) and the directory where you will install the program (such as **C:\IMAIL**). Do not use **C:\IMAIL** for the *temporary* directory because Imail will use this as the default installation directory.

Figure 10.1 Imail Setup screen.

2. Move the archive, **IMAILZIP.EXE**, into the temporary directory (**C:\IMAILTMP**).

3. From the Program Manager, select Run from the File menu and select the program **IMAILZIP.EXE** to start the unzipping process.

4 Select Run from the Program Manager File menu and select the INSTALL.EXE program. The Imail Setup screen in Figure 10.1 should appear. Click on Continue to begin the installation.

5. You are prompted for the directory for the Imail executable files (see Figure 10.2). Enter the directory you want to use for Imail (such as **C:\IMAIL**). Click on Continue.

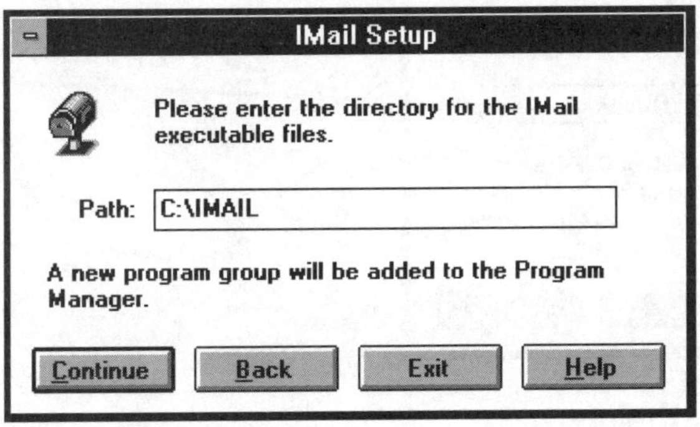

```
 ┌──────────────────────────────────────┐
 │ ▬          IMail Setup               │
 ├──────────────────────────────────────┤
 │  🎥   Please enter the directory for the IMail │
 │       executable files.               │
 │                                       │
 │   Path: │ C:\IMAIL          │         │
 │                                       │
 │  A new program group will be added to the Program │
 │  Manager.                             │
 │  [Continue]  [Back]  [Exit]  [Help]   │
 └──────────────────────────────────────┘
```

Figure 10.2 Imail directory.

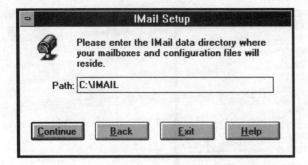

Figure 10.3 Imail directory for mailboxes.

6. The next screen prompts you for the directory in which the mailboxes and configuration files will reside (see Figure 10.3). Enter the directory you want to use (**C:\IMAIL**, for example) and click on Continue.

7. Enter the host name for your PC (see Figure 10.4). This is the domain name that equates to your TCP/IP address. Enter your PC's (the mail server) host name and click on Continue. If you need assistance in determining this parameter or any other parameter, contact your network administrator, your service provider, or try one of the helpful newsgroups.

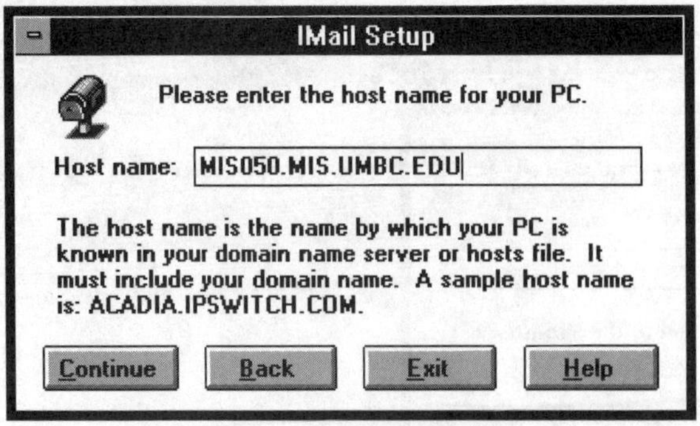

Figure 10.4 Imail PC host name.

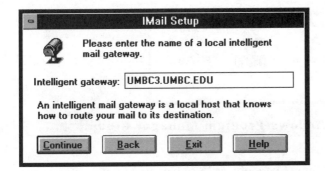

Figure 10.5 Imail mail gateway.

8. You are prompted for the name of a local intelligent mail gateway (see Figure 10.5). Enter the gateway name and click on Continue.

9. And finally, the necessary files will be copied to the appropriate directories and you will receive the **Imail Setup Complete** message. A Windows Program Manager Group will be created, as shown in Figure 10.6.

IMail Configuration

Configuring Imail essentially involves two categories of configuration information. First, each mail user will need to be defined so that they will have a mailbox on your system. Next, you'll need to define parameters that are critical to server operation. This operational information includes gateway definition, host name, time zone, and other mail system parameters.

To configure Imail follow these steps and complete the fields such as Userid, Full Name, and so on for each user you wish to set up:

1. Double-click on the IConfig icon in the Imail program group of the Windows Program Manager

2. Register yourself as a user by selecting Users... from the menu bar. Complete the following fields:

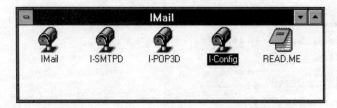

Figure 10.6 Imail Windows Program Manager Group.

- **Userid**: The userid must be eight or less characters and cannot
  contain a space, hyphen. or equal sign.

- **Full Name**: Enter the user's full name in the Full Name field (enter
  it the way you want it to appear to recipients of mail messages).

- **Return Mail Address**: Enter the Return Mail Address; for example,
  john@ajax.com. This is an address that others will use to send
  mail to you. It can be on your system or on another system, but
  must be a fully qualified domain name.

- **Main Mailbox**: Leave the Main Mailbox as (default). If you need to
  place your mailbox in a different directory, you would enter it here
  with the .MBX extension.

- **Inbound POP Password**: Fill in an Inbound POP Password for
  each user you set up. When the user tries to connect to the POP3
  server to read mail, the server will query them for this password.

Once you've entered this information, click on Save to save each user's
configuration. Click on Exit after you set up your users.

3. Under the Alias... menu bar, register any desired aliases. It is a requirement that postmaster exist as an alias and this alias is preconfigured to
   equate to the user root by default. The following fields should be
   completed for each alias:

- **Aliases**: Enter the alias, or nickname, here. The alias may not contain spaces, hyphens, or equal signs.

- **Mail Address**: Enter the mail address that the alias should point to. The example that comes preconfigured is an alias for the post-master. You must have a postmaster alias on your system: the only way to do it is through aliases because userids can only be up to eight characters long.

You can also set up distribution lists through the alias feature. Simply enter the name of a file here that contains a list of mail addresses (with one address per line in the file).

- **Registered Users**: This is a list of all users who have been set up on this machine. You can select the mail address from the list when configuring aliases.

After you enter this information, click on Save to save each user's configuration. After you set up your aliases, click on Exit.

4. Select Options... from the menu bar. Configure each of the following options:

- **Smart Gateway**: You must set a local host name in the Smart Gateway field. This should be a host that is operational at all times and knows how to send mail to any remote networks (BITNET, for example) to which you routinely send mail. Mail headers are not modified when sent through the Smart Gateway.

- **Send Direct**: The Send Direct option should be checked. If this option is not checked, then all mail (except local to the workstation) is sent to the Smart Gateway for delivery.

- **Default host name**: The name that is entered in this field is automatically appended to any recipient userid that is not on the local workstation if no host is specified. This enables you to send mail to a local mail hub that knows how to redirect mail to specific mail systems based on a userid. If you do not have a common host at your site, then this should either be set to the string **LOCALHOST** or left blank. Leave this blank for testing.

• **Queue Timer**: The Queue Timer is used to determine how often the Imail SMTP server (**ISMTPD.EXE**) will retry sending messages that are not deliverable due to a remote system being inaccessible. If you do not want to run the Imail SMTP server, you can run a third party application that can activate the alternate server program **ISMTPD1.EXE** on a regular basis, or you can run **ISMTPD1.EXE** when you want to attempt to clear any outbound mail. Leave this at the default of 30 minutes.

• **Auto start**: If this box is checked, the Imail SMTP server will automatically start when you execute imail. For purposes of testing, check this box.

• **Auto stop**: If this is checked, the Imail SMTP server will automatically stop when you exit the Imail program. Leave this unchecked for testing so that your server runs after you sign the client off by exiting the Imail program.

• **Gateway mail for remote hosts and clients**: If this is checked, the Imail SMTP server will accept mail addressed to any host, not just hosts that it knows the IP address of. This is only useful if you are running a "hub" system and you have client workstations that you want to point to a single host system (this host) and if you have the Smart Gateway defined. This can increase the load on your system! The primary reason for this option is to be able to handle mail from POP3 clients that want to send their mail to the same place in which they retrieve mail. Leave this unchecked for testing.

- **Allow remote access to local lists**: If you check this option, remote users can send mail to distribution lists that you have defined. The default for this option is on. You may, however, want to turn it off to keep others from being able to send mail to a list, thereby tying up your system.

- **Official Host Name**: This is the full domain name for your work-station. It must be a name that is registered with the Domain Name Server for your domain or a name that exists in the local hosts file in your organization. This name will be ignored if it is set to a name that doesn't resolve to your current system.

- **Time zone**: Enter up to ten characters of time zone information. This can be EST, EST5EDT, -500, or whatever your network adminis-trator recommends.

Logging onto IMail

Because Imail allows multiple mail users on the same computer system, you have to "logon" to the mail system. When you run IMail, you logon by selecting the userid (Figure 10.7).

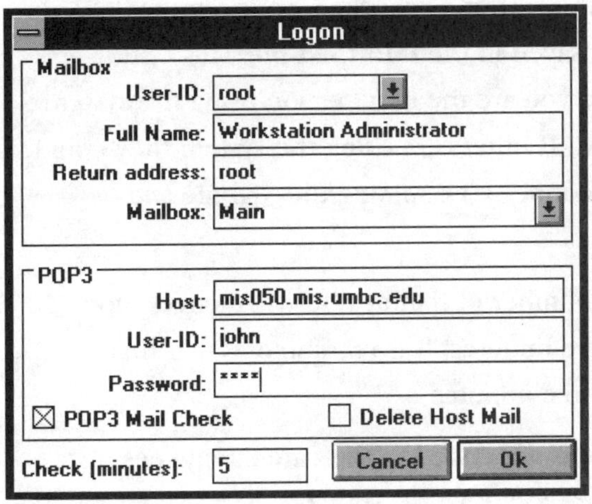

Figure 10.7 Imail Logon.

In the lower half of the screen, in the area marked POP3, you can identify the system from which you want to get your mail. This can be any system running the Post Office Protocol (POP3) protocol, including a UNIX host system where you have an account or another IMail system. Enter the host name, your userid, and your password.

Leave the Delete Host Mail option unchecked so that your non-deleted mail remains on the remote system. Also check the POP3 Mail Check option.

To transfer mail from the remote POP3 server, check both the POP3 Mail Check and Delete Host Mail options. The "Check (minutes)" box at the bottom of the screen determines how often IMail will connect to the server to check for new mail. IMail will transfer the mail from the server to your mailbox, displaying the contents of your mailbox.

Imail Options

There are a number of configuration options that are available to both the individual user as well as the mail system administrator. These options range from how often you want to check the server for new mail to such items as whether you want to append a signature file to your mail messages. Each option is explained below.

Imail contains a number of configurable options and they can be accessed through the Options menu item in the Imail program. These options include:

- **Save POP password**: If this option is checked, your remote POP password is automatically saved in the **IMail.INI** file. This option should only be used when you are the only person using the system because the .INI file is text. If others are using the system they could compromise your mail account by examining the .INI file and reading your password.

- **Check delay**: This is the number of minutes between checks for new mail. The default is five minutes. It is recommend that this option be set to at least three minutes.

- **Timezone**: The time zone is appended to the date in any messages that you send. Examples are EST, CST, or -500, -600, and so on.

- **Queue Timer**: Once you've tested the ISMTPD program, you should put the program in your Startup group. The value that is specified here is how often the program will attempt to deliver any messages that may be in the outbound queue. The default is 30 minutes and it is recommend that you set this between 20 and 60 minutes.

- **Auto Start**: With this option set, the SMTP server will be start automatically when you start IMail.

- **Auto Stop**: When this option is set, ISMTPD will be stop automatically when you exit Imail. Leave this unchecked to keep the server running.

- **Word Wrap**: When mail is created by some mailers, lines are not automatically wrapped. If this option is turned on, IMail will wrap the text to fit in the current window.

- **View MIME Raw**: You can enable this option for troubleshooting. Normally, Imail will format and decode MIME messages without displaying content headers. If you check this option, you will see the headers.

- **Auto save attachments**: If you enable this option, when you receive mail with a MIME attachment, the attachment will be saved to a directory called **ATTACHED** beneath your user directory. If you don't enable this option, you will be prompted for the name of the file to save it to.

- **Allow tabs in msg text**: When you enable this option, you will be able to use the Tab key when creating mail messages. If it is not enabled, the Tab key will move you from the message window to the send button.

- **Include signature file**: When you enable this option, your signature file will be appended to your mail messages. You can edit your signature file from the Create Message Window options choice.

- **SMTP send direct**: When this option is enabled, mail will be delivered directly to the recipient's machine. If not enabled, the message will be sent to a gateway for delivery.

- **Auto wrap at**: This option enables word wrap for your message creation.

- **Encode attached text**: When you enable this option, your messages will be encoded before transmission, ensuring some degree of security when traveling the Net. The recipient must have a MIME-compliant mailer to handle the decoding.

- **Verbose (debug) messages**: This option is used for troubleshooting and generates messages to the **SYSLOG** file.

- **Message Font**: This option enables you to select your choice of fonts for the creation and display of messages.

Imail Programs

There are several programs that comprise the Imail system. These programs provide SMTP and POP3 client and server functionality. On the client side, the system has extensive capabilities such as mail filtering and searching, as well as the more common client features such as address books and file import/export.

The following programs are included in the Imail package:

- **IMAIL.EXE**: The primary function of the Imail program is to retrieve mail from a POP3 server and display it for a user.

- **IMAIL1.EXE**: Imail1 serves as the primary user interface for creating mail messages and also handles the delivery of mail to a local mailbox or to remote hosts via SMTP.

- **ISMTPD.EXE**: This program is the SMTP server that allows the system to receive mail from remote systems.

- **ISMTPD1.EXE**: ISMTPD performs the same functions as IMAIL1, but without any user interface. ISMTPD processes messages in the

SPOOL directory and attempts to deliver mail to local addresses and remote addresses via SMTP.

IPOP3.EXE: This program serves as the system's POP3 server. Remote clients, running either a POP3 compatible client or an Imail client, can retrieve mail from this server. The server can handle up to 20 concurrent connections from remote hosts.

Note for NT users: When using Imail with Windows NT, you must ensure that you have gone into the Control Panel of the system application and set pre-emptive multitasking to 50/50.

NT Mail

The NT Mail system was developed and is distributed by Internet Shopper Ltd. The system includes an SMTP and POP mail server, as well as Listserv capabilities. Internet Shopper Ltd's Web server can be reached at the following address:

```
http/www.net-shopper.co.uk/
```

Internet Shopper also provides all documentation on line via the Web, so that you can access all current documentation at the following address:

```
http/www.net-shopper.co.uk/software/ntmail/index.htm
```

NT Mail has quite an extensive set of features that include the following:

- The SMTP server is RFC821 compliant.

- The POP server is RFC1725 compliant.

- All servers operate as services under Windows NT 3.5 and code was written to take advantage of the features of NT.

- Services can use a password in the registry or NT User Database. The password in the registry may be either plain text or encrypted.

- A list server will allow multiple lists and list managers to be set up with access restricted or open.

- All parameters are configurable in the NT registry.

- Multi-threaded—Any number of threads may be used in each server.

- Dial-up facilities are available.

- Full logging is provided at several levels to allow any network problems to be located.

NT Mail Installation

Since NT Mail is a commercial product you'll need to retrieve a product key from the Web server at Internet Shopper Ltd. Once you've retrieved the zipped file and the associated key, you can set up the necessary parameters, add a few users, and then begin sending and receiving mail.

To install, configure, and test run the NT Mail program follow these steps:

1. Retrieve the NT Mail zipped file from the following address:

   `http://www.net-shopper.co.uk/software/ntmail/ntmail05.zip`

2. In order to install and test the software, you will need to get a "key" for the installation process. The key can be retrieved from the following address:

   `http://www.net-shopper.co.uk/software/ntmail/mailkey.htm`

   The key is used to allow execution of the program and sets the maximum number of users of the mail server. To continue using the software after the key expires, contact Internet Shopper for the purchase of an unlimited key.

3. In addition to the product key, you will also need the following information for mail configuration:

   - Your domain name (such as **fido.ajax.com**).

   - The name of an intelligent gateway to send outbound mail to. This will be either a mail gateway at your site or the mail gateway at your Internet service provider.

   - The names of all the users who will be using the mail system (if you are not using the NT User Database).

4. Create a directory for the mail servers, mail message temporary storage, and log files, such as **C:\NTMAIL**.

5. Use PKUNZIP and unzip the distribution into the **NTMAIL** directory.

6. From the DOS prompt, change to the **NTMAIL** directory with the **CD** command and enter the following three commands to install each of the mail services:

   SMTP-i-k shareware_key (Replace **shareware_key** with the cryptic number (the shareware key) you retrieved from the Web server at Internet Shopper, Ltd.)

   ```
   POP-i
   POST -i
   ```

7. Add users with the LOADMAIL program. From the DOS prompt (in the **NTMAIL** directory), you will run this program to assign users to the NT registry. First create a script file (**LOADMAIL.TXT**, for example) with Notepad or your favorite editor that looks something like the following:

   ```
   MB0000 greg password greg hostmaster
   MB0001 ryan password ryan rdobb
   ```

   Following are the preceding parameters :

   ```
   mailbox name user name password alias (if any)
   ```

   There will always be at least one alias otherwise the user will never get any mail.

   Run the LOADMAIL program using the following syntax:

   ```
   C:\NTMAIL> LOADMAIL LOADMAIL.TXT
   ```

   The entries you listed in the text file will be copied to the NT registry. If any error is found, that line in the script will be skipped and no entry made for it. Refer to the online documentation should you encounter any error messages. If the "password" field is replaced by a dash, the POP server will check the password in the NT User Database.

8. To set up the intelligent gateway in the registry, Run **\WINNT35\SYSTEM32\REGEDT32** from the Program or File Manager and select **HKEY_LOCAL_MACHINE**. Then select Software, InternetShopper and Mail (see Figure 10.8).

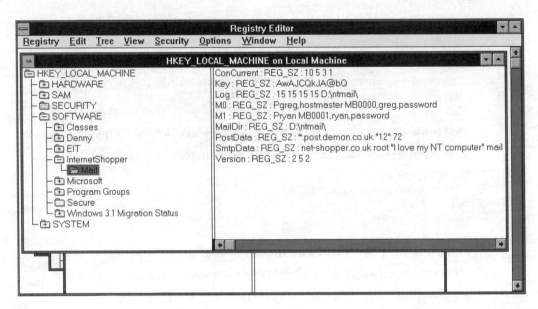

Figure 10.8 NT Mail REGEDT32.

9. Double-click on the entry called PostData and edit the first parameter
and place your gateway name after the first colon (see Figure 10.9).

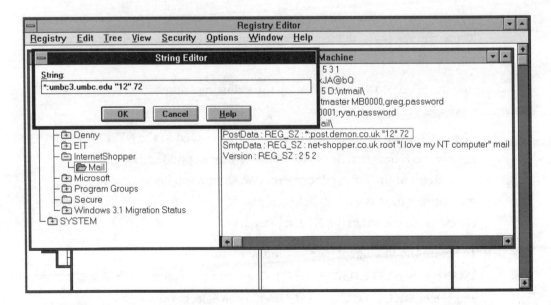

Figure 10.9 NT Mail edit gateway name.

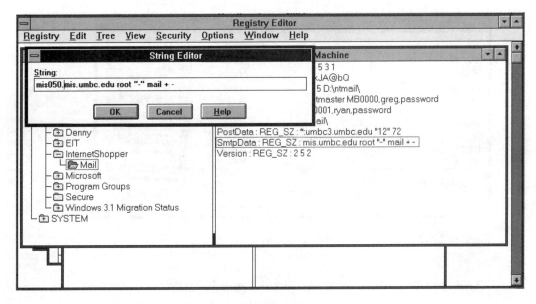

Figure 10.10 NT Mail edit domain name.

The default is *:post.demon.co.uk. You must replace this address with a valid address for your site.10. Double-click on the entry called SmtpData and change the first parameter from **net-shopper.co.uk** to your domain name, such as **mis050.mis.umbc.edu** (see Figure 10.10). You should also change the message that is added to all your outgoing mail. Find the string **I love my NT computer** and change the portion in quotes to your message (sixty characters maximum). If you don't want a message, replace the message with a dash and none will be added.

11. Once you have finished these configuration steps, you can start the services by going to the Control Panel and selecting Services (see Figure 10.11). Start each of the mail services SMTP Server, POP Server, and POST Server. Note that if you change any values once a service is running, you must remember to stop the service and restart it. You can also configure each server to automatically start on boot up.

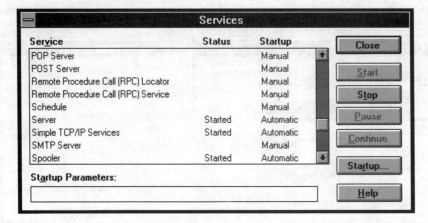

Figure 10.11 NT Mail start services.

12. Go to a POP3 Mail client and identify your NT server name as you did previously for domain name and log in. Your user name and password should be one of those you set up through **LOADMAIL**. Now you're ready to send and receive mail. If you set up a user "Dan," your mail address will be **dan@your.server.name**.

Wide Area Information Servers (WAIS)

The WAIS implementation covered in this chapter enables you to provide full text databases from your NT system. You might want to implement the WAIS server as a complement to your Gopher or Web server. You can then use either the Gopher or Web model to display information, yet have the power of full-text searching available through the client browser. If you're interested in full-text searching, you may also want to look at the searching capabilities included in the WebSite WWW server implementation. The WebSite modules WebIndex and WebFind give you the power of WAIS-like full text indexing server in an integrated Web server package.

NT WAIS

You can retrieve the server software included on the accompanying CD from the following address:

`ftp://emwac.ed.ac.uk/pub/wais`

There are three zipped files; one for Intel based hardware, one for DEC Alpha, and one for MIPS. The Intel version is distributed in the WSI386.ZIP file. If you are implementing the server on the Intel platform, a Windows NT system with a network connection and 16MB of memory should suffice. You'll want to complete the installation of NT WAIS as well as the NT WAIS Toolkit so that you'll have a few sample files to test the WAIS server capabilities. The NT WAIS Toolkit is explained later in this chapter.

NT WAIS Installation

The installation of NT WAIS includes copying the WAIS executable to the WINNT35\SYSTEM32 directory and setting up and configuring the WAIS Control Panel applet. By following the installation instructions here, WAIS will be installed as an NT system service.

To install NT WAIS:

1. Use PKUNZIP to unzip the software distribution files into a directory you create (D:\WAIS, for example). Later, you will want to plan a directory structure that makes sense for your installation, moving files to be served to the data directory, and the software distribution files to another directory. For now, however, for purposes of simplicity, commingle the files in one directory.

   The files that will be unzipped include the following:

WAIS.EXE	Server executable
WAIS.CPL	Control Panel applet
WAIS.PS	WAIS Manual - Postscript
WAIS.DOC	WAIS Manual - MS Word
WAIS.WRI	WAIS Manual - Windows Write
COPYRITE.TXT	Copyright statement
READ.ME	Version features, installation instructions, and so on.

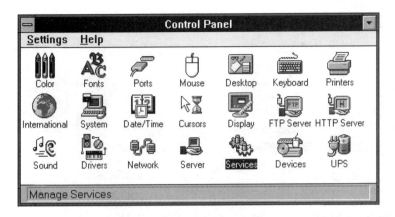

Figure 11.1 NT Control Panel services.

2. Sign on to an administrator's account on the NT system.

3. Copy the file **WAISS.EXE** to the **\WINNT35\SYSTEM32** directory. Go to the Security/Permissions menu item in the File Manager, and verify that the System user has read permission on **WAISS.EXE**.

4. Copy the **WAIS.CPL** file to the **WINNT35\SYSTEM32** directory. Select the Control Panel from the Program Manager to verify that the WAIS Server icon is in the Control Panel.

5. Set up a subdirectory from the main Gopher directory (**D:\GOPHER\ALIAS.GFR**, for example). Copy the file **ABOUT.TXT** from the **\EMGOPHER\ALIAS.GFR** directory on the CD. This is the alias information file and should not be confused with the other **ABOUT.TXT** file, which contains the welcome message for your server. Copy the files **ABOUT.TXT** and **GOPHER.GFR** from the CD to the main Gopher directory (**D:\GOPHER**, for example).

6. From Windows, click on the MS-DOS icon to go to the MS-DOS command line. Type waiss -install. This installs WAIS as a service and also registers it with the Event Logger.

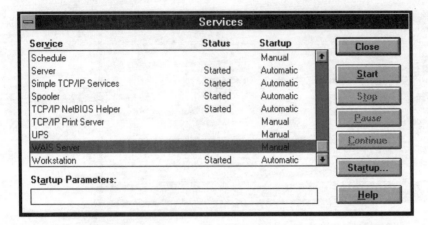

Figure 11.2 NT WAIS service.

7. Start the NT Control Panel and double-click on the Services icon (see Figure 11.1). The WAIS Server should be shown as a service as in Figure 11.2.

8. Select the Control Panel and click on the WAIS Server applet (see Figure 11.3). The Configuration window appears, as in Figure 11.4.

9. Set the Data Directory for the server. This is the directory in which the WAIS files you want to make available will be stored. The default is **D:\WAIS**. You can put this directory on a file server if you want, but there are some considerations.

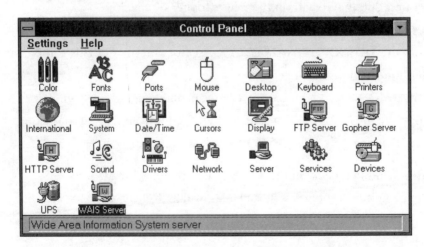

Figure 11.3 NT Control Panel WAIS Server applet.

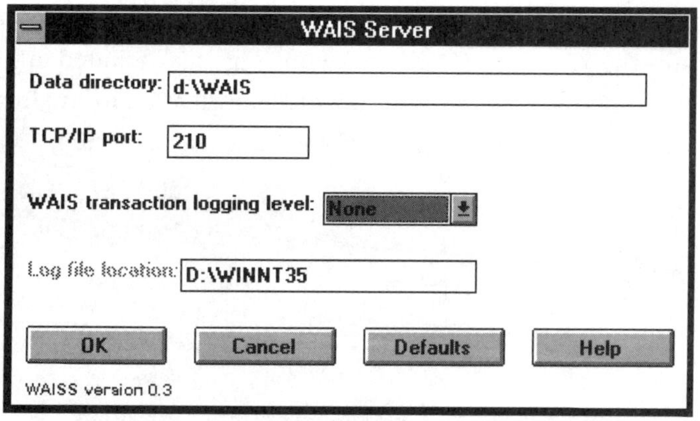

Figure 11.4 NT WAIS Configuration window.

For purposes of testing, leave the directory set to the default. One consideration you should understand is establishing directories on a file server versus a local computer. On a local system, directories are mapped to individual users, and when the user logs off, the mappings go away. So, if your WAIS server starts up when the operating system loads, you should specify the Data Directory using a UNC form of directory name. For example, on the server GUMBY with the data directory (or sharename) of **DOCS**, your Data Directory specification would be the following:

```
\\GUMBY\DOCS
```

10. Indicate the TCP/IP port from which the server will listen for connections. The default is 210.

11. If you select anything other than None for the field marked WAIS transaction logging level, then for every request, the server will write a record to the log file specified in Log file location. A new log file is created daily. The filename format is **WSyymmdd.LOG**.

12. After you complete the configuration options, click on OK.

13. Go to the Control Panel and click on the Services applet. Start the WAIS Server by clicking on the Start button (refer to Figure 11.2).

When a connection from a WAIS client is received by the WAIS Server program, **WAISS.EXE** executes the **WAISSERV.EXE** program, which is included in the WAIS Toolkit. The WAISSERV program reads and writes information to and from the connection and handles the Z39.50 protocol and database searching.

For more information on creating WAIS databases, read the next section, "WAIS Toolkit."

WAIS Toolkit

In order to both prepare and search full text databases under Windows NT, you will need EMWAC's WAIS Toolkit. Whether you plan to search these databases through Gopher, the Web Server, or via the WAIS Server for NT, the tools described here will add a new dimension to your server. Following are the tools included with the kit:

- **WAISINDEX**: This program creates a WAIS index of all words in a set of files you define.

- **WAISLOOK**: The WAISLOOK program takes one or more words and displays the names of those files in the index that contains those words, ranking them according to occurrence.

- **WAISSERV**: This program accepts Z39.50 requests and sends back responses. It is used with the WAIS server described previously.

NT WAIS Toolkit Installation

The WAIS Toolkit includes the necessary software to create indexes for your full text databases. In addition to the Toolkit, test files are included on the CD to give you a test system for your initial WAIS efforts.

You can retrieve the server software included on the accompanying CD from the following address:

ftp://emwac.ed.ac.uk/pub/wais

There are three zipped files; one for Intel based hardware, one for DEC Alpha, and one for MIPS. The Intel version is distributed in the **WTI386.ZIP** file.

If you are implementing the server on the Intel platform, a Windows NT system with a network connection and 16MB of memory should suffice.

To install NT WAIS Toolkit:

The installation procedure simply involves restoring the files to your system. The executable files will be used for indexing and testing your full text databases.

1. Use PKUNZIP to unzip the software distribution files into a directory you create (**D:\WAISTOOL**, for example). Add this directory to your path so that the tools can be easily located and executed. Later, you will want to plan a directory structure that makes sense for your installation, moving files to be served to the data directory, and the software distribution files to another directory. For now, however, for purposes of simplicity, co-mingle the files in one directory.

    The files that will be unzipped include the following:

WAISINDX.EXE	WAISINDEX program
WAISLOOK.EXE	The search program
WAISSERV.EXE	The Z39.50 searching program
WAISTOOL.PS	Manual in Postscript
WAISTOOL.DOC	Manual in Microsoft Word
WAISTOOL.WRI	Manual in Windows Write
READ.ME	Version features, installation instructions, and so on.

2. Sign onto an administrator's account on the NT system.

3. Copy the .EXE files to the **WINNT35\SYSTEM32** directory. If you are using NTFS on the volume in which the tools are stored, you should rename the **WAISINDX.EXE** program to **WAISINDEX.EXE**.

Creating and Searching WAIS Databases

The following steps will give you a basic understanding of how to create and search a simple database. The files have already been created and placed on the CD for the sample WAIS database that is used in the EMWAC HTTP Server / WAIS searching example. You can take any text files that could benefit from a keyword search front-end and create WAIS databases of your own. By using WAIS with Gopher or the Web, you'll be able to allow your client browsers to search your full text databases.

To create a sample database that could be accessed via the EMWACS Web server, follow these steps:

1. Create a directory to house the sample database and index files (**C:\TEST**, for example). Create a subdirectory within that directory to store the indexes we will create. Name the subdirectory **\FILES** (**C:\TEST\FILES**, for example). Copy the **FYI*.*** files from the **\EMHTTPS\FILES** directory on the CD to the **\TEST\FILES** directory on your machine. These are simply a group of text files from the FYI (For Your Information) collection.

2. To create an index, make the **\TEST** directory the current directory. Use the following command to run WAISINDEX:

   ```
   WAISINDEX -d myindex files\*
   ```

   The program should create seven index files, all starting with **myindex**. You may receive one warning (which you can ignore) about synonym files (.SYN).

3. Use the following command to test the searching capabilities and the database, enter a word that you would like to search the database for. In this next example, we'll use the word "ftp":

   ```
   WAISLOOK -d myindex ftp
   ```

   This search peruses the index looking for occurrences of the search word **ftp**. WAISLOOK returns the names of the files that contain the word you selected.

   For more information on WAIS searching capabilities and the integration of WAIS with Gopher and HTTP, refer to the documentation included in the zipped files on the CD for each of these servers.

Appendix

FYIs and RFCs

Quite a few Internet books are on the bookstore shelf and more and more being added every day. You can, however, find some very helpful, and in many cases more relevant information in text files and Web pages on the Internet. Perhaps the best collection of in-depth information on subjects related to this book can be found in the RFCs (Request For Comments) and The FYIs (For Your Information). These documents can be retrieved from a number of locations on the Internet, including:

```
ftp://naic.nasa.gov/files/rfc
ftp://ncnoc.concert.net in the /netinfo
```

Listed below are some of the RFCs and FYIs that will provide you with detailed information about the protocols, security matters, connection methods, and other issues addressed in this book. Additionally, the RFCs and FYIs that are especially appropriate to the topics covered in this book are included on the enclosed CD.

Because you will have to deal with many of the issues covered in these documents, they are offered as good background reading. These are only a few of the many good treatises found in the RFCs and FYIs on just about every topic imaginable related to the Internet. If you need a refresher or a good tutorial or you are just eternally curious, refer to these documents. Do a Veronica search on RFC or FYI and you should come up with indexes listing them all by title, subject, or author.

FYIs—For Your Information

- **FYI-5**. Choosing a name for your computer

- **FYI-7**. FYI on Questions and Answers: Answers to commonly asked "experienced Internet user" questions

- **FYI-8**. Site Security Handbook

- **FYI-16**. Connecting to the Internet—What Connecting Institutions Should Anticipate

- **FYI-19**. FYI on Introducing the Internet— A Short Bibliography of Introductory Internetworking Readings

RFCs—Request for Comment

- **RFC-791**. Internet Protocol (IP)

- **RFC-793**. Transmission Control Protocol (TCP)

- **RFC-821**. Simple Mail Transfer Protocol (SMTP)

- **RFC-959**. File Transfer Protocol (FTP)

- **RFC-1034**. Domain Names—Concepts and Facilities (DNS)

- **RFC-1035**. Domain Names—Implementation and Specification (DNS)

- **RFC-1055**. Serial Line Internet Protocol (SLIP)

- **RFC-1134**. Point to Point Protocol (PPP)

- **RFC-1180**. A TCP/IP Tutorial

- **RFC-1288**. Finger

- **RFC-1310**. The Internet Standards Process
- **RFC-1400**. Transition and Modernization of the Internet Registration Service
- **RFC-1436**. The Internet Gopher Protocol (a distributed document search and retrieval protocol)
- **RFC- 1460**. Post Office Protocol Version 3 (POP3)
- **RFC-1521**. Multipurpose Internet Mail Extensions (MIME)
- **RFC-1591**. Domain Name System Structure and Delegation (DNS)
- **RFC-1580**. Guide to Network Resource Tools
- **RFC-1548**. The Point-to-Point Protocol (PPP)

Other Resources

Choosing a Service Provider

- **The PDIAL List**.

You can retrieve a listing of Internet service providers from the Internet. To do so, send an email message to:

Info-deli-server@netcom.com

In the body of the message put: Send PDIAL

If you want to receive updated lists, send the following message to the same address: Subscribe PDIAL

You can also retrieve the PDIAL list from:

ftp://ftp.netcom.com/pub/info-deli/public-access/pdial

- **Service Providers**.

http://www.eit.com/web/www.servers/networkservice.html

World Wide Web, HTML, etc.

- Tutorial introduction to HTML:

http://www.ncsa.uiuc.edu/General/Internet/WWW/HTMLPrimer.html

- Developer tutorials:

http://hoohoo.ncsa.uiuc.edu/doc/tutorials

- One-stop shop for your advanced HTML and CGI developer's needs

  `http://www.stars.com`

- WWW & HTML Developer's Jumpstation

  `http://oneworld.wa.com/htmldev/devpage/dev-page.html`

- Web Weavers

  `http://www.nas.nasa.gov/RNR/Education/weavers.html`

- HTML reference information:

  `http://info.cern.ch/hypertext/WWW/MarkUp/MarkUp.html`

- Information on writing gateways and servers:

  `http://info.cern.ch/hypertext/WWW/Daemon/Overview.html`

- The Web FAQ:

  `http://sunsite.unc.edu/boutell/faq/www_faq.html`

- The HTML FAQ:

  `http://www.umcc.umich.edu/~ec/www/html_faq.html`

- Getting started with the Web:

  `http://info.cern.ch/hypertext/WWW/FAQ/Bootstrap.html`

- An Information Provider's Guide to HTML:

  `http://www.vuw.ac.nz:80/non-local/gnat/www-html.html`

- What's new on the Web

  `http://akebono.stanford.edu/yahoo/new.html`

- Guide to the Web

  `http://www.eit.com/web/www-guide`

- HTML editors

  `http://union.ncsa.uiuc.edu/www/html/editors.html`

- URL primer

  `http://www.ncsa.uiuc.edu/demoweb/url-primer.html`

- Information on HTTP

  `http://info.cern.ch/hypertext/WWW/Protocols/HTTP/HTTP2.html`

- A listing of HTML conversion tools:

  `http://info.cern.ch/hypertext/WWW/Tools/Filters.html`

- WWW talk by Dan Wallach

  http://www.cs.princeton.edu/grad/Dan_Wallach/www-talk/talk0.html

- Alphabetical list of Web services

  http://info.cern.ch/hypertext/DataSources/WWW/Servers.html

- Archive of information about the Web

  ftp://info.cern.ch/pub/www/doc/

Gopher

- GOPHERJEWELS (moderated)

  A list for posting interesting finds in gopherspace

  Send a subscribe message to:

  listproc@einet.net

  SUBSCRIBE GOPHERJEWELS firstname lastname

- Gopher Jewels Web

  http://galaxy.einet.net/GJ/index.html

- GOPHER-ANNOUNCE (moderated)

  Announcements of releases of Gopher software

  Send a subscribe message to:

  gopher-announce-request@boombox.micro.umn.edu

- GO4LIB-L (unmoderated)

  Discussion list on Gopher topics for Librarians

  Send a subscribe message to:

  LISTSERV@UCSBVM

  SUBSCRIBE GO4LIB-L firstname lastname

- gopher-news (unmoderated)

  Gopher discussions

  Send a subscribe message to:

  gopher-news-request@boombox.micro.umn.edu

- comp.infosystems.gopher

Largest Usenet group for Gopher

- Gopher FAQ

  Link is:

  Name=Gopher.FAQ

  Type=0

  Port=70

  Path=0/Gopher.FAQ

  Host=mudhoney.micro.umn.edu

- Gopher Archive

  Link is:

  Name=gopher-archive

  Type=1

  Port=70

  Path=m/Mailstuff/gopher-archive

  Host=mudhoney.micro.umn.edu

- The Gopher link for Gopher protocol information

  Name=Gopher Protocol Information

  Type=1

  Port=70

  Path=1/gopher/gopher_protocol

  Host=boombox.micro.umn.edu

WAIS

- WAISGATE: WAIS to WWW Gateway

  `http://server.wais.com/directory-of-servers.html`

- WAIS Servers

  `wais:/cnidr.org:210/directory-of-servers?`

- WAIS Sources

  `gopher://liberty.uc.wlu.edu/11/internet/indexsearches/inetsearches`

FTP

- FTP Sites

  `http://hoohoo.ncsa.uiuc.edu/ftp-interface.html`

Example of Anonymous FTP

Throughout this book reference is made to retrieving files via Anonymous FTP. Listed below is a sample session on a UNIX host that retrieves Mosaic for Windows.

Type the following commands at the Unix prompt:

```
> ftp ftp.ncsa.uiuc.edu
```

At the login prompt, enter anonymous

At the password prompt, enter your email address
(e.g., herb@clark.net)

```
> cd PC/Mosaic
```

```
> ls               (To list the available files and directories)
```

```
> bin              (To change to binary mode for the file transfer)
```

```
> get wmos20a1.zip      (To retrieve the file)
```

```
> quit
```

TCP/IP Parameter Form

You should use this form to collect the necessary information for your communications software, as well as other software, such as the mail servers, covered in this book. Your network administrator, or Internet service provider, should be very familiar with the parameters on the form. Send this form to the appropriate individual explaining that you're attempting to configure your PC for an Internet connection and they should be able to complete the form and return it to you with the proper information. Then, as you attempt to install your TCP/IP connection software (e.g., Trumpet) or application (e.g., Imail), you will be well prepared and organized for the configuration exercise (Figure A.1).

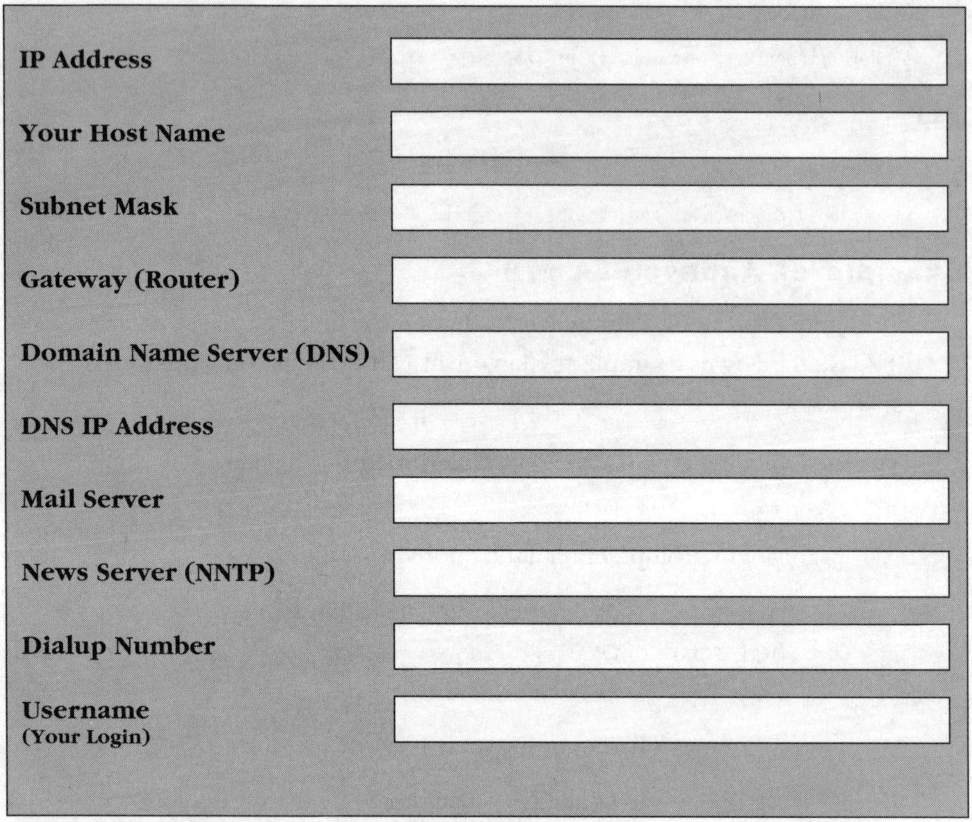

Appendix

IP Address	
Your Host Name	
Subnet Mask	
Gateway (Router)	
Domain Name Server (DNS)	
DNS IP Address	
Mail Server	
News Server (NNTP)	
Dialup Number	
Username (Your Login)	

Figure A.1 TCP/IP Parameters form.

Glossary

10BaseT A type of ethernet that allows machines to be attached via twisted pair cable.

Address class Defined groups of Internet addresses, with each class identifying networks of a certain size. The range of numbers that can be assigned for the first octet in the IP address is based on the address class. Class A networks (values 1-126) are the largest, with over 16 million hosts per network. Class B networks (128-191) have up to 65,534 hosts per network, and Class C networks (192-223) can have up to 254 hosts per network.

Anonymous FTP Allows a user to retrieve files from a Internet FTP server without having to establish a userid and password. By using the special userid of "anonymous," the network user will bypass local security checks and will have access to publicly accessible files on a remote system.

Application A program that performs a function directly for a user. Telnet, FTP, Gopher, and Mosaic clients are examples of network applications.

Archie A system to automatically gather, index, and serve information on the Internet. If you know the name of a particular file, but don't know where to find it, Archie will find it for you.

Bootstrap Protocol (BOOTP) An internetworking protocol used to configure systems across internetworks.

Campus Wide Information System (CWIS) Makes information available on campus via products, such as Gopher and the World Wide Web. Services usually include news, calendars, bulletin boards, and databases.

Client A program or computer that requests information from a server program or computer.

Connection-oriented The data communication method in which communication proceeds through three phases: connection establishment, data transfer, connection release. TCP is a connection-oriented protocol.

Connection-less The data communication method in which communication occurs between hosts with no previous setup or logon. Packets between two hosts may take different routes, as each is independent of the other. UDP is a connectionless protocol.

Daemon Programs that provide network services to users. This term comes from the UNIX world in which daemons often refer to services or servers that handle incoming requests from clients.

Dialup connection A temporary, rather than dedicated, connection between two machines established over a standard phone line.

Domain Name System (DNS) A distributed, replicated, data-query service. The principal use is the look-up of host IP addresses based on host names. The style of host names now used in the Internet is called "domain name" because they are the style of names used to look up anything in the DNS. It is defined in STD 13, and RFCs 1034 and 1035.

Dotted decimal notation Refers to the common notation for IP addresses of the form A.B.C.D; where each letter represents, in decimal, one byte of a four byte IP address.

FAQ (Frequently Asked Question) Collections of documents that all address a common topic (such as the WWW FAQ).

File Transfer Protocol (FTP) A protocol that allows a user on one host to access and transfer files to and from another host over a network. Also, FTP is usually the name of the program the user invokes to execute the protocol. FTP is defined in RFC 959.

Finger A program that is used to find out information about other users, either on local or remote hosts.

Fully Qualified Domain Name (FQDN) The concatenation of host names and their associated domain names. For example, a host with host name **gumby** and domain name **ajax.com** has an FQDN of **gumby.ajax.com**.

FYI (For Your Information) FYIs provide coverage of topics of general interest about the Internet.

Gateway A device connected to multiple physical TCP/IP networks, capable of routing or delivering IP packets between them.

Gopher A distributed information service that makes information available across the Internet in a hierarchical menu paradigm. Gopher uses a simple protocol that allows a single Gopher client to access information from any accessible Gopher server.

HTML (HyperText Markup Language) Used to mark up text documents for presentation through World Wide Web servers.

HTTP (HyperText Transport Protocol) The protocol used by the World Wide Web.

Integrated Services Digital Network (ISDN) A technology that is offered by various telephone carriers. ISDN combines voice and digital network services in a single medium, making it possible to offer customers digital data services as well as voice connections through a single wire.

Internet address An IP address that uniquely identifies a node on the Internet.

Internet Protocol (IP) The network layer for the TCP/IP Protocol Suite. It is a connectionless, best-effort packet switching protocol. See *RFC 791*.

Internet Society (ISOC) A non-profit, professional membership organization that facilitates and supports the technical evolution of the Internet; stimulates interest in and educates the scientific and academic communities, industry, and the public about the technology, uses, and applications of the Internet; and promotes the development of new applications for the system. The Society provides a forum for discussion and collaboration in the operation and use of the global Internet infrastructure.

JPEG (Joint Photographic Experts Group) A file compression scheme used for storage of images.

Listserv An automated mailing list distribution system originally designed for the Bitnet network.

Mosaic A hypermedia browser for the World Wide Web provided by the National Center for Supercomputing Applications (NCSA).

Multipurpose Internet Mail Extensions (MIME) An extension to Internet e-mail that provides the capability to transfer non-textual data, such as graphics, audio, and fax. See *RFC 1341*.

Network News Transfer Protocol (NNTP) A protocol for the distribution, inquiry, retrieval, and posting of news articles. See *RFC 977*.

Packet A transmission unit of fixed maximum size that consists of binary information representing both data and a header containing an ID number, source and destination addresses, and error-control data.

Ping A diagnostic command that verifies connections to remote hosts.

Point Of Presence (POP) A site where there exists a collection of communications equipment, usually digital leased lines and multi-protocol routers.

Point-to-Point Protocol (PPP) Provides a method for transmitting packets over serial point-to-point links. See *RFC 1171*.

Post Office Protocol (POP) A protocol designed to allow single user hosts to read mail from a server. There are three versions: POP, POP2, and POP3.

Protocol A formal description of message formats and the rules two computers must follow to exchange those messages. Protocols can describe low-level details of machine-to-machine interfaces (such as the order in which bits and bytes are sent across a wire) or high-level exchanges between allocation programs (such as the way in which two programs transfer a file across the Internet).

Request For Comments (RFC) The document series, begun in 1969, that describes the Internet suite of protocols and related experiments. Not all (in fact very few) RFCs describe Internet standards, but all Internet standards are written up as RFCs. The RFC series of documents is unusual in that the proposed protocols are forwarded by the Internet research and development community, acting on their own behalf, as opposed to the formally reviewed and standardized protocols that are promoted by organizations such as CCITT and ANSI.

Routing The process of forwarding packets to other gateways in which the packet is delivered to a gateway connected to the intended destination.

Serial Line IP (SLIP) A protocol used to run IP over serial lines, such as telephone circuits or RS-232 cables, interconnecting two systems. See *RFC 1055*.

Server A machine that makes application services (such as WWW) available over the Internet or the application service itself. The term *server* can apply to the hardware that is running a Web application such as Website. Here, one might say, "the power is out, and the server is down." Correspondingly (and confusingly), we also refer to the *software* as the server as in, "I'm trying to decide which Web *server* to implement: WebSite or Purveyor."

Simple Mail Transfer Protocol (SMTP) A protocol, defined in RFC 821, used to transfer electronic mail between computers.

Simple Network Management Protocol (SNMP) The Internet standard protocol developed to manage nodes on an IP network. See *RFC 1157*.

Socket A bidirectional pipe for incoming and outgoing data between networked computers. The Windows Sockets API is a networking API for creating TCP/IP-based sockets applications.

Subnet A portion of a network, which may be a physically independent network segment, that shares a network address with other portions of the network and is distinguished by a subnet number.

Subnet mask A 32-bit value that allows devices receiving IP packets to discern the network ID portion of the IP address from the host ID.

T1 A term for a digital carrier facility used to transmit a DS-1 formatted digital signal at 1.544 megabits per second.

T3 A term for a digital carrier facility used to transmit a DS-3 formatted digital signal at 44.746 megabits per second.

TCP/IP Protocol Suite (Transmission Control Protocol over Internet Protocol) Common shorthand which refers to the suite of transport and application protocols that runs over IP.

Telnet The Internet standard protocol for remote terminal connection service. It is defined in RFC 854.

TN3270 A variant of the telnet program that allows one to attach to IBM mainframes and use the mainframe as if you had a 3270 or similar terminal.

Transmission Control Protocol (TCP) An Internet Standard transport layer protocol It is connection-oriented and stream-oriented, as opposed to UDP. See *RFC 793*.

UNIX-to-UNIX CoPy (UUCP) This initially was a program run under the UNIX operating system that allowed one UNIX system to send files to another UNIX system via dial-up phone lines. Today, the term is more commonly used to describe the large international network, which uses the UUCP protocol to pass news and electronic mail.

Usenet A collection of thousands of newsgroups, the computers which run the protocols, and the people who read and post to Usenet news. Not all Internet hosts subscribe to Usenet and not all Usenet hosts are on the Internet.

User Datagram Protocol (UDP) An Internet Standard transport layer protocol defined in RFC 768. It is a connectionless protocol that adds a level of reliability and multiplexing to IP.

Veronica (Very Easy Rodent Oriented Netwide Index to Computerized Archives) A search tool that searches indexes of Gopher menus.

Wide Area Information Servers (WAIS) A distributed information service that offers simple natural language input, indexed searching for fast retrieval, and a "relevance feedback" mechanism that allows the results of initial searches to influence future searches.

Winsock An abbreviation for Windows Socket. Windows Sockets is an application programming interface (API) designed to allow Windows applications to run over TCP/IP.

World Wide Web (WWW or W3) A hypertext-based, distributed information system created by researchers at CERN in Switzerland. Users may create, edit, or browse hypertext documents. The clients and server software is freely available.

X: The name for TCP/IP based network-oriented window systems. Network window systems allow a program to use a display on a different computer. The most widely-implemented window system is X11, which is a component of MIT's Project Athena.

Index

CATCH THE
Technology Wave
WITH WILEY COMPUTER BOOKS

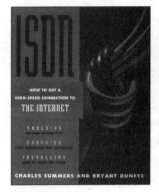

ISDN
How to Get A High-Speed Connection to the Internet

CHARLES SUMMERS AND BRYANT DUNETZ

This book explains in non-technical terms exactly what ISDN is and what it can do. *ISDN: How to Get a High-Speed Connection to the Internet* helps you select the best type of ISDN connection, and then guides you through the process of ordering and installing ISDN on your computer.

ISBN# 0-471-13326-4
Price $22.95/$32.50 CAN
paper 256 pp. 1995

World Wide Web Marketing

JIM STERNE

If you're a marketing pro eager to tap into the commercial potential of the Internet but you are drowning in techno-babble, this book is for you. Written by the expert on Internet marketing, this non-technical guide to Web marketing strategy offers tested tips on everything from managing your company's image to finding customers and selling products to monitoring your success online. And you'll learn from the experiences of marketing managers in a range of industries.

ISBN# 0-471-12843-0
Price $24.95 US/$32.50 CAN
paper 336 pp. 1995

The Web-Page Design Cookbook

WILLIAM HORTON, NANCY HOFT, AND LEE TAYLOR

If you build it on the Web, they won't necessarily come. From online design guru Bill Horton comes a book filled with the do's and don'ts of good Web-page design. With all the ingredients you need to design five-star Web pages, this book offers hundreds of ready-to-use templates that you can use to create instant Web pages. And because the World Wide Web is truly global, it contains tips on how international and cultural issues can be handled.

ISBN# 0-471-13039-7
Price $29.95 US/$41.95 CAN
book/CD-ROM set
624 pp. 1995

Online Resources for Business

ALFRED GLOSSBRENNER & JOHN ROSENBERG

Whether you're doing market research or sizing up the competition, you won't want to venture online without this resource. This guide helps you find the information your company needs to stay competitive.

Online experts Glossbrenner and Rosenberg give you the bottom line on the business services - DIALOG, Lexis/Nexis, Dow Jones, and NewsNet; the consumer services - Compuserve, America Online, and Prodigy; and the Internet. They tell you what type of information is available from each service, how much it costs and discuss sophisticated search strategies, tools and techniques.

ISBN# 0-471-11354-9
Price $24.95 US/$34.95 CAN
paper 384 pp. 1995

WILEY *Publishers Since 1807*

Available at Bookstores Everywhere • Prices subject to change
For more information **e-mail** - compbks@jwiley.com
or **Visit the Wiley Computer Book Web site at** http://www.wiley.com/CompBooks/CompBooks.html